Short Escapes Near Boston

Previously published as

Fodor's Short Escapes in
New England

Fodor's Travel Publications, Inc.
New York * Toronto * London * Sydney * Auckland

▼

SHORT ESCAPES NEAR BOSTON

Publishers/Editors: Bruce Bolger, Gary Stoller
Designer: Nancy Koch
Map Design: John Grimwade
Maps By: Alex Reardon, John Tomanio
Copy Editors: Lauren Bernstein, Michael White, Nicola Coddington
Research Editors: Terry Stoller, Betty Villaume, Shirley Moore, Dan Zanier, Laura Sparks, Paul Rogers
Cover Design: Guido Caroti
Cover Illustration: Edward Parker

Copyright © 1999
by Bruce Bolger and Gary Stoller

Also available:
Short Escapes Near New York City
Short Escapes in Britain
Short Escapes in France

While every care has been taken to ensure the accuracy of the information in this guide, time brings change, and consequently, the publisher cannot accept responsibility for errors that may occur. Prudent travelers will therefore want to call ahead to verify prices and other "perishable" information.

Please address all comments and corrections to Bruce Bolger at 914-591-7600, ext. 230, or Gary Stoller at 203-270-6971.

ISBN 0-679-00309-6

Second Edition

PRINTED IN THE UNITED STATES OF AMERICA
10 9 8 7 6 5 4 3 2 1

▼

ABOUT THE AUTHOR

Bruce Scofield is the author of five hiking guides
that cover many of the mountainous, natural, and
historic areas found in the Northeast. An interest in
nature and the outdoors got him involved in volun-
teer trail building and trail-maintenance for hiking
clubs, as well as public land preservation campaigns
and nature photography. He holds a masters degree
in history and has special interest in ancient history
and Mexican archaeology. He lives in western
Massachusetts, where he is an astrological consultant
and writer on astrology.

ACKNOWLEDGEMENTS

*I wish to thank all who assisted and supported me
during the research and writing of this book. The
many friendly and helpful people I met along the
way, the beautiful places, and the wealth of history
uncovered helped make this writing experience a personal rediscovery of New England.*

*Thanks to all of the bed-and-breakfast owners,
especially Lois Danseraeu and Sue Hamar, who
offered valuable suggestions or provided information
on local history. Thanks also to the park rangers and
forest supervisors, especially John Wiggin and
Marshall Webb, who helped in the planning of walking tours. Anne G. Ball, of the Freeport Historical
Society, and librarian Valerie Vaughn are two I wish
to thank for help in gathering information for the historical and cultural narratives that begin each chapter. In some cases, inside information about local
areas was of great benefit, and, in this regard, I want
to thank Kathy Salzman, Gary Christen, Mark Feller,
Betsy Scofield, Jim Valliere, and Meredith Smith.
Finally, I wish to thank my parents, Larry and Lucy
Scofield, whose generosity made the transportation
requirements of the assignment no problem at all.*

Contents

▼

▼

Introduction

When you come to New England's cities and towns in search of history, you can find monuments to the past everywhere. But not even in the most silent corner of a town can you escape the sounds of modern life—trucks, cars, and machines—that forever encroach upon your effort to experience the past.

This guide is for everyone who would like to escape to the peace of the New England countryside and soak up a more complete sense of the way life once was, and is today. It will take you away from the tourist crowds to unique places with spectacular vistas and remarkable histories. You can stroll alone through an ancient forest, walk along the towpath of a old canal, take in sweeping seascapes, or picnic without neighbors on the grassy banks of a peaceful pond. You can continue the mood at a recommended restaurant in a picturesque setting and then complete the experience at a charming country inn or bed-and-breakfast.

Short Escapes brings you to special places little known even to New Englanders. According to your tastes, you can tramp around historic landmarks, plunge deep into farmland and forest, or just sit undisturbed for hours looking down at gentle waves lapping against a shore. Through the quiet, you will be able to feel what it might have been like when Native Americans ruled the land, when the first European settlers founded their colonies, and when the great Hudson River School painters set up their easels in the 19th-century countryside. Many of the book's suggested walking tours cover country roads and footpaths in use for hundreds or even thousands of years.

The 25 experiences in this guide are scattered around the six states of New England—each tour with its own distinctive

▼

character, flavor, and points of historical, cultural, or natural interest. All are within a short journey of New England's major tourist spots, and a few are accessible by train. Each experience is centered around a walking tour, which can be anything from a short stroll to a five-hour walk.

These experiences cost less than other forms of travel. Nobody charges admission to villages and the countryside, and rural hotels and restaurants match and even surpass their urban counterparts in comfort and luxury at much lower prices.

Short Escapes is more than a travel guide: It's designed to awaken the traveler's senses to the moods and flavors of a place and its people, and to help evoke a real sense of the past and present. We hope that the 25 experiences will have the same uplifting effect on you as they have had on us. We have thrust ourselves into the soul of the countryside and have learned about the land in a way you can't by simply reading about it in a book or observing artifacts in a museum.

In fact, we feel we have stumbled upon a new form of travel—one which combines the cultural and sensual enrichment of traditional travel with the spiritual pleasures of walking. We ended each day with a great sense of accomplishment and, like a local resident, felt we had participated in the place.

The rewards of exploring the countryside are great: You return home having experienced the essence of New England, knowing that you have felt its history, escaped from the hubbub of its cities and tourist attractions, and savored the beauty of the land and its people.

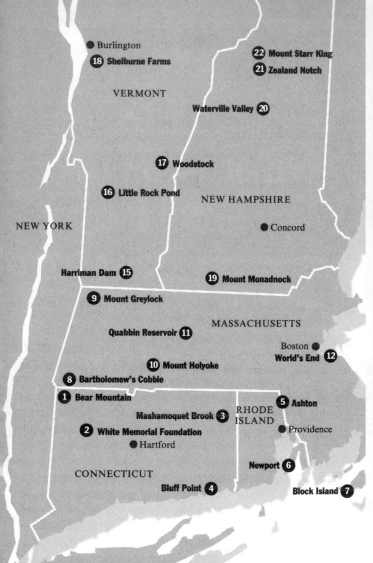

Burlington

18 Shelburne Farms

VERMONT

22 Mount Starr King

21 Zealand Notch

Waterville Valley **20**

17 Woodstock

16 Little Rock Pond

NEW HAMPSHIRE

NEW YORK

Concord

Harriman Dam **15**

19 Mount Monadnock

9 Mount Greylock

MASSACHUSETTS

Quabbin Reservoir **11**

Boston

World's End **12**

10 Mount Holyoke

8 Bartholomew's Cobble

1 Bear Mountain

5 Ashton

Mashamoquet Brook **3**

RHODE ISLAND

2 White Memorial Foundation

Providence

Hartford

Newport **6**

CONNECTICUT

Bluff Point **4**

Block Island **7**

New York City

MAINE

25 Acadia National Park

Mount Battie **24**

23 Wolf Neck Woods
● Portland

WHERE TO FIND
EACH EXPERIENCE

14 Great Island

13 Punkhorn Parklands

40 MILES

How to Use *Short Escapes*

T he 25 experiences in *Short Escapes Near Boston* were selected for their historic, cultural, or natural interest and for their
general proximity to areas popular with travelers. At each
location, walking tours permit visitors to get out of their cars
and experience interesting and special places up close. All include
private, easily accessible spots to picnic or to enjoy memorable
views. When possible, itineraries provide options to either shorten
the walk for strollers, or extend it for serious walkers.

Itineraries are organized by state and are chosen so that
travelers visiting in one of the selected areas can easily enjoy
multiple experiences during their stay. We have followed every
itinerary mentioned in this book and have purposely omitted
areas that might present problems for walkers.

To bring your visit to life, each experience comes with a
narrative on historical, cultural, literary, or natural points of interest. Other unique places to explore nearby are also suggested, so
you don't have to be a walker to enjoy this book.

FINDING YOUR WAY

The book was designed to make it as easy as possible to
follow the directions. For your convenience, each walking tour
begins with basic information on duration, length, and level of
difficulty. Walks marked "easy" have few ups and downs, no
areas of tricky footing, and no navigational challenges and are
appropriate for anyone capable of walking. Tours labeled "moderate" require a little more physical commitment and might have

▼

an area of tricky footing, but they require no particular navigational abilities. The few itineraries marked "difficult" are appropriate to regular walkers who feel comfortable walking in a few tricky areas and up steep inclines. The text fully details whatever difficulties the traveler might encounter along the way. Serious walkers will probably find even "difficult" trails relatively easy. And even the least experienced walkers can safely follow almost all "difficult" and "moderate" itineraries just a short way to a scenic view or historic site, and then retrace their steps.

Walking time is based on a very leisurely 2 mph, except in itineraries with exceptional ups and downs. The numbered text directions enable you to complete a walking tour without using the map, but some may find it easier to simply follow the map and refer to the text when necessary. We strongly recommend that you use both the text and the maps, which provide navigational aids. At each numbered point on the map, the same number in the text gives the information you'll need to find your way from that location on the map, as well as additional observations about the terrain.

For the few difficult itineraries, experienced walkers may wish to use a compass in conjunction with a more detailed trail or topographic map. These may be purchased at various stores throughout the region or by mail. (*See* For Serious Walkers section below.)

Most of the itineraries follow footpaths or wooded lanes for at least a portion of the route. Most of the routes are designated by some sort of marker or blaze (a term retained from the days when trails were marked with an axe cut). These are usually painted rectangles or metal or plastic tags on trees. A word of caution: Trail markings can mysteriously disappear (due to vandalism, logging, or storm damage) and footpath conditions often change (bridges go out, paths get rerouted, etc.). While every effort has been made to select well-established itineraries and every single one has been walked, there is no guarantee that the character of an itinerary has not been altered or deformed. If you

▼

encounter a dramatic change, the author and the publisher would like to hear from you. Contact us at the address provided on the copyright page.

THE REGIONAL FOOTPATH SYSTEM

Before you head off on a walking tour, familiarize yourself with the trail system. In many areas, trails are marked with different colors and shapes, which are often found on a tree, a post, or a rock. Occasionally, trails are marked with stone piles called cairns or with signs. Generally, three markers placed together in a triangle indicates the beginning or the end of a trail. One marker placed atop another indicates a turn in the trail (in some cases, the top marker is positioned in the direction of the turn).

If the instructions tell you to follow the markers during a certain portion of a walking tour, don't change trails unless directed to do so by the markers. If you're not sure you're on the right trail, retrace your steps until you pick up a marker, then turn around and resume your walking tour, keeping an eye out for the next marker. Some areas have no markings, and you will need to pay close attention to the walk directions.

PRECAUTIONS

Although most of the itineraries require no special athletic abilities, all travelers should dress appropriately and wear shoes or sneakers designed for walking. Always carry the clothing you'll need for a worst-case change in the weather. Don't be caught without lightweight rain gear, a wool or fleece layer of clothing, a small first-aid kit, and water. A daypack generally can handle whatever clothing and accessories two people might need, plus drinks and a picnic; these small packs, when empty, fit easily into your suitcase. Please remember to carry out whatever you bring in.

You will want to bring insect repellent, at least in spring and summer, and take precautions against deer ticks. Wear light-colored clothing, pull your socks over your pants legs, and be sure to shower thoroughly after your walk.

▼

The usual forest and countryside obstacles—such as muddy and rocky trails, fallen trees, and poorly cut footpaths—pose the greatest risks. Since you can accomplish the longest of these itineraries in just over a half day, there's no need to race through your walking tour. Take the time to enjoy the beauty, and watch your step. Be sure to pay attention to any warnings or advisories in the Walk Directions.

Poisonous snakes are rare in southern New England, and they are not found in the northern portions of the region. You will have no problem if you take the same precautions you would in just about any forest: Watch where you sit down or place your feet and hands, especially on sunny outcroppings in cool weather. If you encounter any animals, watch them from a safe distance and do not interfere with their activities.

Finally, the deer hunting season varies but generally lasts for several weeks in late autumn. There is usually no hunting on Sundays. In each chapter, you'll find the number of a local tourist office or park ranger who can provide specific dates for hunting in the area you're visiting. You should wear bright-colored clothing if you're walking through a forest during hunting season.

WEATHER

The weather in New England is far from predictable. "If you don't like the weather, wait ten minutes" has been a common observation about the region. Mark Twain, who lived in New England for half his life, reported that "in the spring I have counted 136 different kinds of weather inside of 24 hours." Travelers in New England should be prepared for anything, including rainy, cool, and windy weather at any time of the year, or snow and freezing temperatures in fall, winter, and spring. In southern New England (Connecticut, Rhode Island, and Massachusetts), summer temperatures often exceed 90 degrees, though evenings are generally cooler. In the northern portions of Vermont, New Hampshire, and Maine, summer evenings can occasionally be downright cold. Generally, the latter part of summer and autumn are the region's best seasons for walking. Autumn, of course, offers one of the world's great foliage spectacles. The foliage color peaks from mid- to late September in the north to mid-October in the south. In spring and early summer, temperatures are comfortable, but you may have to contend with mud and insects. Snow may also pose an obstacle in the higher elevations until well into May.

The itineraries in this book were selected because they offer other options besides walking. Travelers will find these in the Other Places Nearby section of each chapter and by contacting the local tourist office. If you encounter poor weather on one of your journeys, you can find a lot of other interesting things to do.

GETTING THERE

Although those who travel by car have the greatest and most flexible access to the area's hidden treasures, train travelers can enjoy some of these short escapes. Although none of the walks have direct train access, hotel and bed-and-breakfast owners will often be able to make arrangements for their guests to be picked up and dropped off at stations or trail heads. You will need to call ahead to see if this is possible.

If you are driving to a short escape, use the directions in the Getting There section and the small regional map alongside the walking tour map. A more detailed, commercially available road map will also help.

Almost all itineraries have been selected in regions already popular with travelers. So if you plan on going to a popular tourist attraction as well, you won't have to travel far out of your way to enjoy one of these short escapes.

OTHER PLACES NEARBY

For those who prefer to tour by car, we've provided suggestions on how to visit the high points of the experiences and have pointed out other places of interest in the region that are often

▼

overlooked by tourists. This way, you can enjoy the highlights of our itineraries and uncover other special places without driving more than a short distance.

DINING & LODGING

For those who want to continue the mood created by the day's experience, we've selected a few restaurants, inns, and bed-and-breakfasts in the countryside near our itineraries.

To be included in *Short Escapes Near Boston,* a restaurant must be near the walk, have an excellent view, be rustic or historic, or serve good food that's popular with locals. Restaurants fall into four categories based on the average cost of dinner for one person (including appetizer, main course, and dessert, without drinks, taxes, and tip):

Very expensive	**More than $50**
Expensive	**$31-$50**
Moderate	**$16-$30**
Inexpensive	**$15 or less**

Keep in mind that you may be able to spend less, depending on your order. And be sure to make a reservation, especially on weekends and holidays.

All country inns, bed-and-breakfasts, and other lodging establishments were chosen because they either are rustic or historic, have character or an excellent view, are near the walk, or are a great value.

Most of the lodging choices listed have less than 20 rooms and are located in quiet areas or in the downtown areas of pretty New England villages. Almost all rooms have private bathrooms with shower and/or bath. Each one was checked for cleanliness and up-to-date maintenance. Most bed-and-breakfasts include at least a continental breakfast in the price, and many offer gourmet breakfasts. Be sure to inquire when you book.

In general, you should request a reservation well before you go, because many of these small inns and bread-and-breakfasts fill up

▼

fast on popular weekends in spring, summer, and fall. Lodging prices are double-occupancy for a single night and are designated as:

Very expensive......................**More than $180**
Expensive.................................**$111-$180**
Moderate.................................**$76-$110**
Inexpensive............................**$75 or less**

Prices are based on weekends and peak periods; you can often save money by staying during the week or off-season, or by getting a smaller or otherwise less desirable room. Many of the places listed have two-day minimum-stay requirements on weekends during peak periods.

TOURIST OFFICES

Most of the areas featured in this book have tourist booths or chamber of commerce offices that can provide you with the latest information on restaurants, hotels, and other attractions. Contact these offices before your visit.

FOR SERIOUS WALKERS

New England offers some of the finest walking and hiking in the United States. The Appalachian Trail passes through all of New England except Rhode Island. The Long Trail of Vermont spans the entire state, and the hut system of the White Mountains is a magnet for foreign tourists. Information about walking and hiking opportunities may be found in the many hiking guides and maps for sale in outdoors stores.

For information on hiking in Maine, New Hampshire, Massachusetts, and Rhode Island, contact the Appalachian Mountain Club, 5 Joy St., Boston, MA 02108; tel. 617-523-0636. For information on hiking in Vermont, contact the Green Mountain Club, 4711 Waterbury-Stowe Rd., Waterbury Center, VT 05677; tel. 802-244-7037.

Up on Connecticut's Roof

EXPERIENCE 1:
BEAR MOUNTAIN

On the borders of Connecticut, Massachusetts, and New York stands a cluster of high mountains called the Southern Taconics. They rise well above the plains surrounding them and, from certain perspectives, appear taller than much higher ranges in Vermont and New Hampshire. Two north-south ridges, with a high valley between them, establish the structure of this plateaulike mountainous mass. The western ridge is traversed by the South Taconic Trail, the eastern by the Maine-to-Georgia Appalachian Trail, upon which you will walk.

The Highlights: A walk through varied forests to a high summit offering superb vistas, an optional descent into a rugged ravine.

Other Places Nearby: Charming New England villages filled with art galleries and antique shops, car races and boat rentals, great walking on the Appalachian and other trails.

Taconic is an Algonkian word meaning "vast wilderness." Today, these Taconic highlands remain mostly wild, penetrated by only a few tiny roads. However, the towns in the nearby lowlands rank among the most desired destinations for tourists seeking the history and charms of old New England.

▼

n the 1920s, efforts began to create a tri-state park with the goal of acquiring some 60,000 acres between New York, Massachusetts, and Connecticut. New York created Taconic State Park and Massachusetts the Mount Everett Reservation, Bash Bish Falls, and Mount Washington State Forest. Connecticut got a few landlocked parcels from a lumber company and created the completely undeveloped Mount Riga State Park. In addition, the National Trails Act of 1979 led to the federal government's acquisition of even more land to protect the Appalachian Trail. Today, protection of this tri-state semi-wilderness seems pretty much assured.

The Connecticut towns of Lakeville and Salisbury lie at the southern foot of this southern Taconic plateau (locally referred to as simply Mount Riga), each offering a wide array of accommodations, restaurants, and other attractions. Quaint New England villages today, they were mining boom towns long ago, with scenes not unlike that of the California Gold Rush in 1849. It wasn't gold that was discovered, though, but high-quality iron, valuable enough to attract the interest of many well-known colonial capitalists.

Prospectors found the mother lode of hematite (iron ore) in a hill near Lakeville that came to be known as Ore Hill. Once the workers had mined the iron ore, they had to transport it to a huge blast furnace that required much timber turned to charcoal (*see* Experience 16, Little Rock Pond) to fuel the fires. The vast forests of the nearby Taconic highlands, a portion of which is traversed in the walk, supplied the wood. One blast furnace was located near Riga Lake, which straddles the two parallel ranges of the Southern Taconics. Another, called the Salisbury Furnace, Connecticut's first, was located in today's Lakeville. Ethan Allen, the Vermont patriot, owned and managed this furnace, which no longer stands.

Although most people associate Allen with Vermont and the Green Mountain boys, he was born in nearby Litchfield, Connecticut. In 1762, at the age of 24, he became involved with the iron-making business in Salisbury and was part of the team that constructed the Salisbury furnace.

▼

The huge blast furnace made cannons. The iron ore was dumped into the top of the furnace, which was fired by charcoal made from the trees on the mountain, fanned by a water-powered bellows, and poured into molds set vertically into the ground. When the iron cooled and the molds broke open, the solid metal cannons were placed onto a water-powered drill that bored a straight shaft into the metal. You can find artifacts and information about cannon-making at the Salisbury Cannon Museum and the Holley-Williams House in Lakeville. The mine in Ore Hill has since flooded and now lies under a lake.

I n this former iron-making region, Under Mountain Road runs along the eastern edge of the Southern Taconic plateau. It was once a Native American path and now offers a beautiful drive past farms to the east and high mountains to the west. A series of peaks top the eastern ridge of these highlands. Starting in Connecticut, the first major peak is Lion's Head. To the north lies Bear Mountain. It is the highest summit in Connecticut that lies wholly within the state and is the first mountain on the Appalachian Trail north of Virginia with an elevation over 2,000 feet. It stands 2,316 feet above sea level and an impressive 1,500 feet directly above the Twin Lakes below, a site you will appreciate from Under Mountain Road. Atop Bear Mountain, a large stone monument reads "This monument marks the highest elevation in Connecticut, 2354 feet above the sea. Built in 1885. Owen Travis, mason." Later surveys revealed that a shoulder of Mount Frissell, which straddles the Connecticut-Massachusetts border, actually is higher.

The climb up Bear Mountain is a delight, especially in June when the mountain laurel is in bloom or during October at the height of fall foliage. The mountain abounds with chipmunks, birds, and other more discreet animals. On the summit, there are open ledges lined with scrub oak and pitch pines that struggle to maintain a foothold on the windswept crest.

▼

The many summit vistas, which together offer a 360-degree view, look out at other majestic mountains. Below to the east sit the Twin Lakes, Washinee and Washining, meaning "smiling" and "laughing water."

North of Bear Mountain you can see the crest of Mount Race and between the two, in a deep gap, Sages Ravine. In the dark ravine, Sages Brook cascades down the mountain, creating many waterfalls. Beyond Mount Race lies the top of the Southern Taconics, Mount Everett, also known as The Dome. The tower on its summit makes it unmistakable.

GETTING THERE

By car:

Drive to Salisbury, located on Rte. 44 in the northwestern corner of Connecticut, just south of the Massachusetts border. From Salisbury, proceed 3.3 mi. north on Rte. 41 (Under Mountain Rd.) to the Under Mountain Trail parking area on your left. If you reach Beaver Dam Rd., you've gone too far.

Walk Directions

TIME: Up to 4 hours
LEVEL: Moderate to difficult
DISTANCE: Up to 5.4 miles
ACCESS: By car

The trails to the summit of Bear Mtn. are well-used footpaths. Much of the first half of this walk is steadily uphill but not steep. If you take your time to enjoy the scenery, it should not present a problem. You'll follow the Under Mountain Trail to the Appalachian Trail, which leads to the summit. You come back the same way. If you wish to go further, you'll encounter a steep descent on the north side of Bear Mtn. The summit of Bear Mtn. offers many vistas away from the trail. Even on a busy summer or fall weekend, you can find great places for solitude and good places to picnic.

▼

TO BEGIN

From the parking area, find the trail head that begins near the northwest corner of the lot. Follow the trail a short way toward an information directory.

1. At the directory, follow the well-worn path of the Under Mountain Trail, marked with light blue blazes, west into the forest. The trail will soon

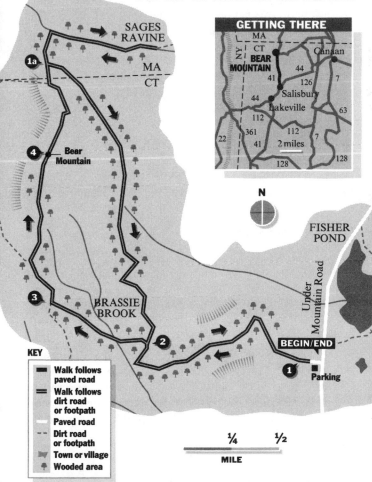

GETTING THERE

N

▼

begin a steady climb and then swing to the left onto government land acquired for protection of the Appalachian Trail. From here the trail is less steep, and it leads you past boulders, through thick stands of mountain laurel (watch for blooms in late June) and under tall hemlocks.

2. After walking 30 to 40 minutes, you reach a junction with the Paradise Lane Trail. (This may be your return route if you take the extended hike.) Keep left, staying with the Under Mountain Trail, now less steep, through a magnificent forest of hemlock, laurel, and dogwood. Pass by a few streams (some may be dry).

3. Arrive at Riga Junction to meet the Appalachian Trail. (The Under Mountain Trail ends here.) Turn right onto the Appalachian Trail, following white blazes. In a few minutes, you arrive at a junction. Ignore the path that heads straight (and to the left) and instead turn right, following only white blazes. Walk about 30 minutes over numerous boulders and rock faces to the summit of Bear Mtn. The route is not too steep and offers many fine vistas from rocky ledges. *As you rise in elevation, the vegetation thins out until only short scrub oak, pitch pine, and plenty of blueberry bushes (ripe in July and August) line the path.*

4. Arrive at the summit of Bear Mtn. and its tall rock monument. *Mt. Everett's tower and nearby Mt. Race are to the north, the twin lakes to the east. Sages Ravine sits in the cleft between Bear Mtn. and Mt. Race.* From this summit area, follow unmarked paths due west to find other ledges that offer vistas to the west. *Mt. Frissell, the shoulder of which is actually the highest point in Connecticut, is the large summit to the west.*

Return to your car the way you came. Follow the Appalachian Trail (white blazes) south to Riga Junction, then left onto the Under Mountain Trail (blue blazes) to the parking area.

▼

Walk 2 Directions

TIME: An extra 1 1/2 hours
LEVEL: Difficult
DISTANCE: An extra 1.5 miles

This extra walk is recommended for those who wish to explore Sages Ravine and feel comfortable negotiating a steep descent. The extension adds at least an additional 1.5 mi. to Walk 1, depending on how far you wish to go into the ravine, but you won't have to return by way of the summit of Bear Mtn.

TO BEGIN

Follow Walk 1 to Point 4. Follow the white markers of the Appalachian Trail north and descend from the summit of Bear Mtn. **Caution! The descent is very steep in places and will require the use of your hands.** The trail will turn left along the mountainside, then turn right, passing a trail that comes in from the left.

1A. Arrive at a trail junction (just beyond the state line between Connecticut and Massachusetts) marked by a sign. On the right is the trail head for the Paradise Lane Trail. Ahead, through a deep hemlock forest, is Sages Ravine, an environmentally sensitive area that is closely monitored by the Appalachian Trail Club, which owns the land.

Continue to descend into Sages Ravine on the Appalachian Trail and explore the many falls and cascades. The Appalachian Trail follows Sages Ravine Brook downstream. Proceed as far as you want, then return to Point 1A, the junction with the Paradise Lane Trail, and turn left onto this trail, following the blue blazes.

Follow the Paradise Lane Trail for about 45 minutes through picturesque forest. The trail is mostly level and offers some views of Bear Mtn. along the way.

▼

Arrive at Point 2, which is the junction with the Under Mountain Trail. Turn left and follow the blue blazes for about 30 minutes to the start of the walk and the parking area.

OTHER PLACES NEARBY

The area south of Salisbury and Lakeville contains many scenic stretches of road. For a beautiful drive from Salisbury, take Rte. 44 to Lakeville, Rte. 41 to Sharon, Rte. 4 to Cornwall Bridge, Rte. 7 to Canaan, and back on Rte. 44 to Salisbury. South of Cornwall Bridge on Rte. 7 are the picturesque towns of Kent Falls, and further on, Kent, an art center.

■ **Holley-Williams House & Salisbury Cannon Museum.** The Salisbury region's iron-making history is told through displays and the restored Holley family residence, a 19th-century house brought to life by period-dressed guides. The Salisbury Cannon Museum also is here. Both museums are designed for families and feature many children's activities. *15 Millerton Rd., Lakeville, CT 06039; tel. 860-435-2878. Open weekends 1-5 mid-Jun.-mid-Sep. and by appointment. Admission. On Rte. 44 near the center of Lakeville.*

■ **Lime Rock Park.** A major East Coast racing center that features sports car races on a track that winds through the hills. *Rtes. 7 and 112, Lime Rock, CT 06039; tel. 800-722-3577. Open summer weekends through Sep. Admission.*

■ **Collin's Diner** (inexpensive). Concrete tables and benches frame the entrance to this authentic 1941 railroad car diner on the National Registry of Historic Places. An old clock stands over the entrance. Breakfast is served all day. *Canaan, CT 06018; tel. 860-824-7040. At the historic Canaan Depot, at the junction of Rtes. 7 and 44.*

DINING

Besides the restaurants below, many more can be found about 15 miles north in Egremont and Great Barrington, Massachusetts (*see* Experience 8, Bartholomew's Cobble).

▼

■ **Charlotte** (expensive). Making its debut in 1999, this newcomer in a lovely 1775 clapboard house has garnered quick praise from locals. The menu, which has featured such dishes as Thai-marinated grilled shrimp and scallops with Chinese black rice, steamed red cabbage, and a lemon grass beurre blanc, has reinvigorated the local restaurant scene. Other entrées have included cassoulet, thyme-roasted halibut, and seared mushroom ravioli. A downstairs wine bar offers a dozen wines by the glass. *223 Main St., Lakeville, CT 06039; tel. 860-435-3551. Open daily for lunch and dinner May-Christmas; open Tue.-Sat. for lunch and dinner the rest of the year.*

■ **The Cannery Cafe** (moderate). Everything coming out of the kitchen is meticulously prepared at what many considered the area's finest restaurant. A sophisticated storefront eatery, the Cannery offers new American cooking with French influences. Look for such dishes as pistachio-crusted salmon, roasted free-range duck breast, and eggplant, caramelized onion, and walnut ravioli. Don't miss the garlic soup. *85 Main St., Canaan, CT 06018; tel. 860-824-7333. Open daily for dinner. Near the junction of Rtes. 44 and 7.*

■ **The Boathouse** (moderate). This new, attractive American Bistro with a boat house mural on an interior wall has an eclectic menu, including raw clams, fried calamari, shrimp po'boy sandwiches, and sushi. The restaurant says it doesn't specialize in seafood, however, and offers such entrées as roast free-range chicken and local quail. There's an extensive wine list. *349 Main St., Lakeville, CT 06039; tel. 860-435-2111. Open daily for lunch and dinner, and Sun. breakfast buffet.*

■ **The Woodland** (moderate). This compact, modern eatery serves good food in big portions. A tasty sandwich is the portabello mushroom with goat cheese and sun-dried tomatoes. There are also burgers, beef stew, and a shrimp quesadilla. For dinner, expect such fare as blackened tuna, lobster ravioli, and filet mignon. *192 Sharon Rd., Rte. 41, Lakeville, CT; tel. 860-435-0578. Open Tue.-Sat. for lunch and daily except*

▼

Mon. for dinner. On the east side of Rte. 41, south of Lakeville.

■ **Keilty's Depot** (moderate). At the nation's oldest continuously active railroad station, this family restaurant/pub offers a variety of sandwiches for lunch and an assortment of dinner entrées. Try the roast leg of lamb sandwich or choose between such main courses as lobster ravioli, crab cakes, shepherd's pie, and T-bone steak. *Canaan Union Station, Canaan, CT; tel. 860-824-4848. At the junction of Rtes. 7 and 44.*

■ **The Ragamont Inn** (moderate). You'll recognize this establishment (which also rents rooms) by its white pillars and terrace dining on Salisbury's Main Street. There are also two attractive indoor areas. The chef prepares continental and Swiss specialties, and fresh berry pies. No credit cards. *8 Main St., Salisbury, CT 06068; tel. 860-435-2372. Open for dinner Wed.-Sun., lunch Sat.-Sun. Closed Nov.-Apr. In the center of Salisbury.*

■ **Chaiwalla** (inexpensive). This unique restaurant offers a a wide selection of teas, sandwiches, and light meals. The kitchen is separated from the main room by only a counter, which allows for conversation between the friendly owner and the patrons. *1 Main St., Rte. 44, Salisbury, CT; tel. 860-435-9758. Open Wed.-Sun. Near the junction of Rtes. 41 and 44.*

LODGING

■ **Manor House** (very expensive). A romantic hideaway, this English Tudor mansion built in 1898 features stained-glass windows and has 10 guest rooms, each with a private bath. The decor is relaxed and understated. About half the rooms are large, including the master bedroom, which has a fireplace and a private balcony. Two rooms have Jacuzzis. *69 Maple Ave., Norfolk, CT 06058; tel. 860-542-5690. Off Rte. 44, about 15 mi. east of Salisbury.*

■ **The White Hart** (expensive). Much of the downtown action revolves around this 19th-century country inn at a major intersection in Salisbury. The 26 elegant guest rooms have all the amenities (including private bath, AC, and cable TV). There's a great little pub and a garden room for breakfast or light lunch. The

▼

American Grill restaurant offers such dishes as nut-crusted rack of lamb and filet mignon. Salisbury's shops are a short walk away. *P.O. Box 545, The Village Green, Salisbury, CT; tel. 860-435-0030, 800-832-0041. At the junction of Rtes. 41 and 44.*

■ **Under Mountain Inn** (expensive). The rural setting of this 18th-century farmhouse is charming, classic New England. The house has seven guest rooms and is loaded with antiques and artwork. There's also a restaurant, open to the public on weekends, offering English-style dining, including game. No credit cards. *482 Under Mountain Rd., Rte. 41, Salisbury, CT 06068; tel. 860-435-0242. 4 mi. north of Salisbury on Rte. 41.*

■ **The Earl Grey B&B** (expensive). On a hill looking down at Sailisbury and out to the Litchfield Hills, this 1850s Italianate house offers two guest rooms, each with a private bath. The largest room, located on the first floor, contains a four-poster queen-size bed, a wood-burning fireplace, and French doors that lead to a private garden terrace. The other room has an 1840s sleigh bed and a 19th-century quilt on a wall. *P.O. Box 177, The Lockup, Salisbury, CT 06068; tel. 860-435-1007.*

FOR MORE INFORMATION

Tourist Office:

■ **Salisbury Chamber of Commerce.** *P.O. Box 704, Salisbury, CT 06068; tel. 860-435-0740. Open Mon.-Fri. 8-5.*

For Serious Walkers:

The Southern Taconics abound with hiking trails, including the 15.5-mile South Taconic Trail and a 16.5-mile section of the Appalachian Trail. The latter actually passes through Salisbury.

■ **New York-New Jersey Trail Conference.** This hiking group publishes what is probably the area's best map. Ask for map 14, South Taconic Trails. More information can be found in their book, the *New York Walk Book. 232 Madison Ave., New York, NY 10016; tel. 212-685-9699. Open Mon.-Fri. 11-5:30.*

A Gift to a Town

EXPERIENCE 2: WHITE MEMORIAL FOUNDATION

Litchfield is fortunate to have such a large percentage of its acreage preserved as a wildlife refuge and conservation center. This great asset had little to do with government but, instead, resulted from the generosity of private citizens.

The Highlights: A preserve with wide lanes, peaceful forests, a pond, and a lake.

Other Places Nearby: Great dining and lodging in a quintessential New England town, a recreated Native American village.

Early in this century, Litchfield resident Alain C. White and his sister May W. White became convinced of the need to preserve the natural beauty of Bantam Lake in Litchfield, the largest natural lake in Connecticut. They saw it as being vulnerable to disorderly development. The Whites had family money that originally came from the fur industry—beaver for hats and coats. Later, the family money was generated from New York City real estate investments. Beginning in 1908, the Whites began to acquire large tracts of land. In 1913, they created a foundation, the endowment for which is still linked to the family investments in New York City.

The original White estate in 1863 was not particularly large, perhaps only 20 acres. The surviving buildings include

▼

the museum next to the parking area (which was the main house), the carriage house, and the barn. The dedication of the Whites to conservation and preservation was such that today the foundation owns more than 4,000 acres of forest, ponds, and fields. It is a wonderful place for walkers because it includes a wide variety of environments and settings, and a sizable portion of the walkways (there are 35 miles of trails) are old lanes, not narrow footpaths. Passing through the property is one of Connecticut's long-distance blue-blazed trails, the Mattatuck, a portion of which is used in the walk. Today, the White Memorial Foundation, open to the public, carries on the work of meeting its three basic goals: recreation, education, and conservation.

The walk described below explores only a small percentage of the White Foundation's land. One of the features of the walk is an observation platform on the shore of Bantam Lake at the site of an old ice-harvesting operation. Ice cutting was a business on the north bay of Bantam Lake for years during the last century and as late as 1929. Two companies operated there: Berkshire Ice and Southern New England Ice.

Walkers will see the remnants of some ingenious methods of taking blocks of ice out of the lake and moving them to an ice house. Just beyond the observation platform are the remains of a concrete sluiceway channel for sliding blocks to the ice house, which was located just off the Lake Trail. Later, a conveyor system was built of wood and concrete that transported blocks of ice to the ice house. The observation platform was built with the remains of this system.

The origin of the name "Bantam" is not clear. Although Windsor, Hartford, and Wethersfield were founded in 1635, the area that is now Litchfield remained a wilderness until the early 18th century. In 1715, the land was purchased from the Native Americans for 15 pounds, the Native Americans retaining a

▼

small reservation near Mount Tom for hunting. The area was first called Bantam, a name retained by the large lake reached in the walk. Some say the name is a corruption of "Peantam," a Native American name.

Others have suggested that it comes from a slang word used during colonial times to describe wild places inhabited by barbarians. Whatever the case, Bantam was the first name of the township within which Litchfield was located. Today, Bantam is a small village west of Litchfield, a name taken from an English town and located on the top of a broad hill.

Litchfield had some good fortune during the Revolutionary War. It prospered on the inland route that linked Boston with New Jersey and Philadelphia—where much of the action was taking place. For four years, Litchfield was a major depot for military provisions, and several buildings were erected for that purpose. A local jail housed war prisoners.

Ethan Allen was among the many famous and successful individuals who came from Litchfield. Besides Allen's near-legendary exploits in the American Revolution as leader of the Green Mountain Boys, and his involvement as an entrepreneur in the iron industry, he was also something of a radical thinker and writer. He published a 200-page work entitled "The Oracles of Reason," which attacked the doctrines of Christianity. This radical theological writing (imagine the courage this must have taken in Puritanical New England) was attacked vehemently by preachers and poets. Allen's response to this roar of disapproval was, "I defy the whole artillery of hell fire."

Doctrinal conflicts raged in Litchfield from time to time. Two preachers who were on opposite sides of the debate over predestination versus free will (one of them Lyman Beecher, Harriet Beecher Stowe's father) agreed to exchange pulpits. On the day of the exchange they passed each other, one saying to

▼

the other, "Is it not marvelous that our exchange has been ordained since the beginning of time?" The other immediately replied, "Then I won't do it."

Another conflict flamed between those who wanted heat in the church and those who didn't. When a wood stove was set up in the church, the leader of the pro-heat group warmed his hands over the stove. During the sermon, those opposed broke into a sweat, took off coats, and some even fainted from the "heat." After the sermon, the leader placed his bare hands on the stove to show the congregation that it was never lit.

The first law school in the country opened in Litchfield in 1784. Tapping Reeve was the founder and principal for the first 40 years. The school lasted until 1833, producing a vice president, 5 cabinet members, 17 senators, and 53 congressmen.

Another famous Litchfielder was Harriet Beecher Stowe, best known for her book *Uncle Tom's Cabin,* a major best-seller in America and abroad.

GETTING THERE:
By car:

From the center of Litchfield, located southwest of Torrington in northwestern Connecticut, drive 2.2 mi. west on Rte. 202. The entrance to the White Memorial Foundation is found on the left. Drive another 1/2 mi. on the entrance road to the parking area.

Walk Directions

TIME: 2 1/2 hours
LEVEL: Easy
DISTANCE: 3.5 miles
ACCESS: By car

The more than 35 mi. of trail and woods roads in the White Memorial Foundation can be confusing at first. There are so many trails that junctions seem to occur nearly every 1/10 mi. You should pay close attention to the text so you don't miss important trail junctions.

▼

TO BEGIN

From the parking area, follow a wide path past the museum's front door. Continue on the path past a field that's on your right and proceed into the woods.

1. At a junction, where stone gate pillars face you, turn left onto a lane marked with blue blazes. *If, instead, you walk straight ahead at Point 1, you will come to Catlin Woods, an area of old-growth forest.* You are now on the Mattatuck Trail. This lane crosses a wetland (ignore a nature trail to your left) and then swings around alongside the Bantam River under evergreens.

2. Cross paved Bissell Rd. and continue ahead, following the blue markers on a lane under hemlocks. After a minute or two, you arrive at a double blue blaze, where you make a sharp left turn (almost a U-turn). *If you reach a junction with a red trail, you've gone too far.* Continue through the woods, following blue blazes. Ignore a trail on your right. Walk for two minutes and stop at a clearing, with marshland (Duck Pond) to your right.

3. Turn sharply to your right (actually a U-turn) at the edge of the marshland and step onto a boardwalk, leaving the blue trail. Continue on to the first junction and turn left. Cross a footbridge. *The Pine Island area was long ago a potato farm, and Duck Pond was once a wood duck nursery. Alain White raised wood ducks during the 1930s, when the wood duck population was low.*

At the next junction, turn left, leaving the Pine Island Trail. *Signs of beaver activity are found in the vicinity.* At the following junction, turn right, rejoining the blue Mattatuck Trail. A short walk will bring you to paved Bissell Rd. again.

4. At Bissell Rd., turn right, **keeping on this busy road's**

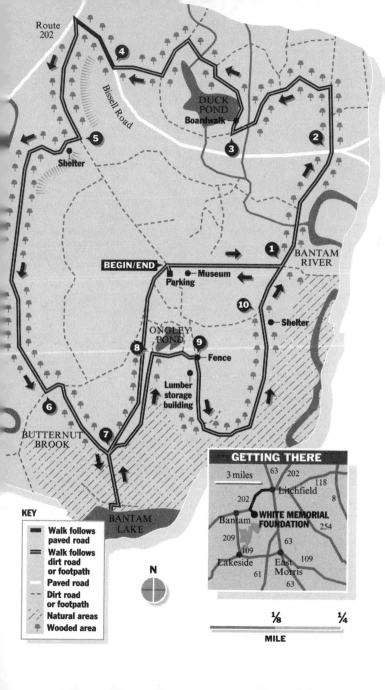

Route 202

4

Bissell Road

DUCK POND
Boardwalk

3

2

5

Shelter

1

BANTAM RIVER

BEGIN/END

Museum

Parking

10

Shelter

ONGLEY POND

8

9

Fence

Lumber storage building

6

BUTTERNUT BROOK

7

BANTAM LAKE

KEY

▬▬▬	Walk follows paved road
═══	Walk follows dirt road or footpath
▬▬▬	Paved road
- - -	Dirt road or footpath
⁄⁄⁄	Natural areas
🌲	Wooded area

N

GETTING THERE

3 miles

63   202

Litchfield   118

202   8

Bantam   WHITE MEMORIAL FOUNDATION   254

209

109

Lakeside   63

East Morris   109

61   63

⅛   ¼

MILE

▼

shoulder. Just before Rte. 202, cross the road, pass a rock wall, and turn left onto the White Memorial Foundation entrance road. Walk past a house that's on your left and a "Welcome" sign that's on your right. Proceed up a slight uphill grade.

5. Turn right onto a gated lane designated as Pine Grove I. This is the green-blazed Windmill Hill Trail. At a junction just before a shelter with picnic tables, turn right as the lane descends and swings to the left. For the next 10 to 15 minutes, follow this mostly level green-blazed lane through hardwoods. Some sections may be wet. *The land to your left rises up to Windmill Hill, where a windmill once pumped water for all the buildings of the White estate.*

6. Arrive at a junction. Turn left, walk about 20 yards, and make a right into the woods. Follow green markers.

7. At a junction for the yellow-blazed Lake Trail, turn right and walk toward Bantam Lake. At the next junction, follow the path to the right. Within seconds, turn left at a stone marker and step onto a boardwalk to a wooden observation platform. *The concrete pillars were formerly part of an ice-harvesting operation. More remains of this business are found farther along the trail.*
To continue the walk, retrace your steps to Point 7. Here you have two options. *At this point, if you wish to cut short the walk and return to your car, walk straight ahead on a lane, following yellow markers.* To continue the walk, turn right following green markers onto a footpath that parallels the lane. Cross a footbridge.

8. At a junction just before another footbridge, bear right and cross the footbridge, following orange markers into a hemlock forest. On your left is Ongley Pond. Follow orange markers and proceed on the path between the trees. Turn left up a small bank and walk straight, leaving the orange markers. Pass a lumber storage building and a fence on your right. Ignore a dirt road to your left.

▼

9. Turn right in front of small trees and follow the lane past two buildings and around the perimeter of a field. Then turn right into the woods onto a lane blocked by two huge tree trunks. Follow the lane as it bends around and heads north. Pass through a pine forest and pass a shelter to the right.

10. Turn right onto a gravel road and walk a short distance to a junction (Point 1). Turn left and walk by the museum to your car.

OTHER PLACES NEARBY

■ **Tapping Reeve House and Law School.** America's first law school had many notable graduates, including Aaron Burr and John C. Calhoun. *Rte. 63 South, Litchfield, CT 06759; tel. 860-567-4501. Open Tue.-Sat. 11-5, Sun. 1-5 mid-Apr.-mid-Nov. Admission.*

■ **The Institute for American Indian Studies.** This is a good place to learn about New England's original inhabitants. An indoor museum includes excellent displays and a gift shop. Outside is a recreated Algonkian village consisting of wigwams and a longhouse. *38 Curtis Rd., Washington, CT 06793; tel. 860-868-0518. Open Mon.-Sat. 10-5, Sun. 12-5. Closed Mon.-Tue. Jan.-Mar. Admission. Take Rte. 47 south through Washington, then turn right on Rte. 199.*

■ **White Flower Farm.** This nursery is well-known as a mail-order company specializing in perennials and bulbs. The 25 acres of grounds are open to the public and include many display gardens and a retail store. *Rte. 63, Litchfield, CT 06759; tel. 860-567-8789. Open daily 9-6 Apr.-Oct; 10-5 Nov.-Mar. 3 mi. south of Litchfield.*

DINING

■ **The Birches Inn** (expensive). The finest restaurant in the area, this renovated inn has a beautiful setting next to Lake Waramaug. You can look at the water through picture windows

▼

or get a view from the porch. The menu has included such top dishes as grilled marinated leg of lamb with parmesan polenta and grilled Atlantic salmon with a casserole of barley and winter squash, grilled asparagus, and crawfish reduction. Recommended appetizers are grilled head-on shrimp with a sweet chili and peanut crust, and roasted red beet tartar. *233 West Shore Rd., New Preston, CT 06777; tel. 860-868-1735. Open Thu.-Mon. for dinner. Closed Jan.-mid-Mar.*

■ **The Boulders** (expensive). The country dining room looks out impressively over Lake Waramaug, as do the outside dining terraces. Try appetizers like smoked pheasant quesadilla and black truffle risotto. For an entrée, choose such fare as sesame-crusted sushi-grade tuna with mango-ginger sauce or venison loin with spicy sweet potatoes. *East Shore Rd. (Rte. 45), New Preston, CT 06777; tel. 860-868-0541. Open daily except Tue. for dinner Jun.-Oct. (opens at noon Sun. in Oct.); Thu.-Sun. for dinner Jan.-Apr.; Wed.-Sun. for dinner May, Nov.-Dec.*

■ **The Mayflower Inn** (expensive). The setting is a country inn on a large estate where elegant dining rooms and porches overlook a Shakespeare garden. The salmon, smoked in-house, is a great appetizer. For an entrée, you might find grilled veal chop with potato parsnip gratin and red wine shallot sauce, or, for dessert, some Mayflower tapioca with fresh raspberries. All is served by a most courteous staff. *118 Woodbury Rd. (Rte. 47), Washington, CT 06793; tel. 860-868-9466. Open daily for lunch and dinner. South of the Washington Green.*

■ **West Street Grill** (expensive). Owner James O'Shea loves his job. He travels to expand his knowledge of the culinary arts and returns to Litchfield with novel ideas that keep his restaurant where he likes it to be—out in front. For a dinner appetizer, try the grilled Parmesan aioli bread or the Thai shrimp with noodle salad. Scrumptious grilled entrées may include Atlantic salmon, marinated leg of lamb, or curried chicken breast. The lunch menu can feature such unique items as tempura soft-shell crab on foccacia roll and pan-seared Cajun

▼

catfish filet. *43 West St., Litchfield, CT 06759; tel. 860-567-3885. Open daily for lunch and dinner.*

■ **The County Seat** (inexpensive). Relax on sofas and padded chairs and catch up on the news. Enjoy the light-fare menu at a table or maybe sip gourmet coffee or tea at the counter. Soups, salads, and creative pastas and sandwiches are served all day, and there's a full ice cream parlor for dessert. On the way out, pick up a gift basket and some gourmet foods. *3 West St., P.O. Box 7, Litchfield, CT 06759; tel. 860-567-8069. Open daily for breakfast, lunch, and dinner. On the town common.*

LODGING

■ **The Birches Inn** (very expensive). This Adirondack-style inn in a lovely Lake Waramaug setting abounds with country elegance. There are five guest rooms in the inn and three in a separate lake house. Try to book the inn rooms, particularly Rooms 6 and 7, which have big picture windows. A full breakfast, as well as wine and cheese in the evening, is served to all guests. The restaurant is a food-lover's delight. *233 West Shore Rd., New Preston, CT 06777; tel. 860-868-1735.*

■ **The Boulders** (very expensive). The inn, with its fine restaurant, is located at the foot of Pinnacle Mountain and faces Lake Waramaug. The 17 rooms are either in the main inn, a carriage house, or in small, very private guest houses on the mountain's slopes. The country guest rooms have fireplaces, AC, full baths, and views of lake and forest. *East Shore Rd. (Rte. 45), P.O. Box 2575, New Preston, CT 06777-0575; tel. 860-868-0541. North of New Preston, across from Lake Waramaug.*

■ **The Mayflower Inn** (very expensive). Originally a private school, the Mayflower became an inn in 1920. Everything about this English-style country inn is first class. The 25 rooms in three buildings have fireplaces, marble bathrooms, brass fixtures, and mahogany wainscoting. The inn sits far off the road on 28 acres and has a fitness center. *118 Woodbury Rd., Rte. 47, Washington, CT 06793; tel. 860-868-9466. South of the Washington Green.*

▼

■ **Toll Gate Hill** (expensive). In 1745, this inn began as the Captain William Bull Tavern, a stop on the road between Albany and Hartford. Today, the restored tavern is a restaurant and inn, with two new buildings also providing guest rooms. There are a total of 20 antique-style rooms, including five suites, and all offer a hotel's amenities—private bath, TV, AC, and phone. Some have fireplaces. Fine dining is offered in the tavern building. *Rte. 202 and Toll Gate Rd., Litchfield, CT 06759; tel. 860-567-4545.*

■ **Abel Darling B&B** (moderate). You can stay in town in a historical 1782 house named for its original owner. Two spacious guest rooms—each with a private bath—face south and are bright, cheerful, and decorated to match exposed beams and wide floorboards. A continental breakfast is served each morning. *102 West St., Litchfield, CT 06759; tel. 860-567-0384. Near the village green.*

■ **The Hopkins Inn** (inexpensive). The inn, an 1847 boarding house that faces Lake Waramaug, draws many senior citizens and is a good bargain. Seven of 11 modest guest rooms have private baths, and several have water views. The Hopkins Inn offers a restaurant specializing in Austrian and Swiss cuisine. There's a private beach for guests on the lake, and right next door is the Hopkins winery. *22 Hopkins Rd., New Preston, CT 06777; tel. 860-868-7295 From Rte. 202, go 2 mi. north on Rte. 45 (which is also East Shore Rd.), then left on North Shore Rd.*

FOR MORE INFORMATION
Tourist Office:
■ **Litchfield Hills Visitors Bureau.** *P.O. Box 968, Litchfield, CT 06759; tel. 860-567-4506. Open Mon.-Fri. 10-6.*

For Serious Walkers:
Walkers will no doubt wish to tour the town of Litchfield and its historic houses. The tourist office has walking maps. More strenuous hiking may be found at the "five ponds" sec-

▼

tion of the White Memorial Foundation (trail heads located on Route 63 south of Litchfield near the junction with Route 61) and at Steep Rock Reservation in Washington Depot. Write the Steep Rock Association, Washington Depot, CT 06759.

See Experience 1, Bear Mountain, for extensive hiking opportunities.

■ **Connecticut Forest & Park Association.** This private association maintains and documents 700 miles of trails—a number of which are in Litchfield County. You can order the association's book, *The Connecticut Walk Book*, for $21 including postage. *16 Meriden Rd., Rockfall, CT 06481; tel. 860-346-2372.*

An American Hero

EXPERIENCE 3:
MASHAMOQUET BROOK

This walk takes you through the area called the "quiet corner" of northeastern Connecticut. Quiet in the sense of no big cities, no malls, no unsightly rows of condominiums monopolizing fields that should have been left for farming. And quiet in the sense of respect

The Highlights: Forested lanes where a war hero walked, a wolf's den, a scenic, peaceful trail, a jumble of rocky outcrops.

Other Places Nearby: Old Sturbridge Village, a great restaurant, a gristmill, and a blacksmith museum.

for the past. But this was not always such a peaceful locale. Long ago, the towns of Pomfret and Brooklyn were home to rebellious patriots and their excellent leader, Israel Putnam.

Putnam's legend began shortly after he moved to this corner of Connecticut from Massachusetts. It was 1735 when his farm was established, and only one wolf remained in the area. This clever she-wolf denned in a remote and rocky valley, living off the rich farms of Pomfret and beyond. For several years, she'd ravaged farms and homes, covering an immense territory that was said to have extended all the way to the Connecticut River. Although her cubs were shot, she always

24

▼

survived her encounters with humans. One night the she-wolf killed 70 of Israel Putnam's sheep and goats. A man of action, he joined with five other neighbors to hunt her down in the winter of 1742.

By tracking the wolf's prints in a light snow, the men discovered her lair, a 40-foot-long narrow tunnel through the side of a hill, and trapped her there. Hounds were sent in, but they came out wounded and terrified. Night was near, and many feared that, under the cover of darkness, the wolf would make an escape. When fires failed to dislodge her, Israel Putnam quickly volunteered his services, establishing a legendary reputation for bravery.

He tied a rope around his body, grabbed a torch, and crawled into the small opening of the den. At the end of the tunnel, he saw the glaring eyes of the wolf and signalled his colleagues to pull him out of the den by the rope. Now with his gun and a torch, he re-entered the cave and shot the wolf at close range as she prepared to attack. Putnam, again dragged out by the rope, appeared with the dead wolf.

All of this action occurred in what is now Wolf Den State Park, originally acquired by the Daughters of the American Revolution in 1899, and the contiguous Mashamoquet Brook State Park through which much of this walk passes. You'll walk by the wolf den, now a famous site and frequently visited by locals, and also through the jumble of rocks and forest that kept the den hidden.

But the wolf incident is nothing compared to this hero's other exploits. Putnam is surely one of the most colorful characters in Colonial history, if not in all American history, so it's not hard to understand why our forefathers named a town after him.

In 1755, Putnam was called up to fight with the Connecticut army in the French and Indian War. When the main army disbanded in the fall, he stayed as a guerilla fighter—one of Roger's Rangers. Once, with his boat's course

▼

blocked by huge waterfalls, and surrounded by a large force of Indian enemies, Putnam steered the craft through a quarter mile of dangerous rapids. The feat was so incredible that the Native Americans, thinking him a god, let him go.

Putnam was not as fortunate a few years later when the Indians took him prisoner. They tortured him and tied him to a tree to be burned alive, but at the very last minute, he was "rescued" by the French and became their prisoner of war. After a prisoner exchange, he was back in action, saving Fort Edward from burning.

When the war shifted to the Caribbean and Putnam was taking part in the capture of Havana, his ship was wrecked by a hurricane. His company survived the storm but was decimated by sickness. Still, Putnam plugged on, and in 1774, he sailed through the Gulf of Mexico and up the Mississippi exploring what was then the West. Then he retired to his farm—for a very short time.

Putnam was already an active member of the Sons of Liberty when hostilities between the British and Massachusetts came to a head. On April 20, 1775, Putnam was working his farm when he heard the news of Paul Revere's ride. He dropped everything and set off to gather the local militia, who made him their leader. Then, without changing his clothes, he rode the 100 miles to Boston in under 18 hours.

At the Battle of Bunker Hill, he was a commanding general, but Putnam's zeal was not well-received by the undisciplined Massachusetts regiment and its touchy military leaders. He was labeled a hot head, but no one could question his courage. Before the battle, he and his Connecticut men attacked a British ship that was grounded at low tide by wading out to it under gunfire. They eventually captured the boat, took its guns, and burned it. The 57-year-old Putnam, affectionately called "Old Put," reported that he "wished there were more of this sort of work to do everyday."

Putnam helped plan the battle of Bunker Hill, incessantly digging fortifications with his men. It was Putnam who gave the

▼

famous command ordering his men to withhold their fire until they could see the whites of the enemy's eyes. During the battle, he stationed himself on the top of Bunker Hill, exposed to cannon and gunfire. He alternately rushed to the front on his horse to urge the men on and to the rear to order deserting militia back to their places. If Old Put could have been fully in charge, he would have probably stormed Boston as well, which was held by the British.

Putnam's friend, George Washington, put him in command at the Battle of Long Island, where he was forced to retreat—albeit successfully. Washington later ordered Putnam to the Hudson Highlands to select a strategic site for fortifications, now known as West Point. He was next placed in command of a portion of the Continental Army stationed in Connecticut. Once, in a surprise encounter with the British, Putnam escaped by riding his horse down a rocky ravine. The British wouldn't follow him and wondered how he managed the descent.

A stroke in 1779 paralyzed his right side and ended his extraordinary military career at the age of 61. He returned to his farm between Pomfret and Brooklyn, where he lived until 1790.

Be sure to visit the imposing equestrian statue beneath which he is buried, located on Route 169 in Brooklyn. You can also pay your respects to "Old Put," a real American hero, at Putnam Memorial State Park in the town of Redding in western Connecticut, where he was in command of the right wing of the Continental Army during the brutal winter of 1778-79.

GETTING THERE

By car:

From exit 93 on I-395 in northeastern Connecticut, drive 6 mi. west on Rte. 101 to Rte. 169. Continue ahead on Rte. 101 and turn left onto Wolf Den Dr., just before the junction with Rte. 44. (Alternately, at the junction of Rtes. 44 and 101, you will find Wolf Den Dr. almost immediately as you turn onto

▼

Rte. 101.) Drive 7/10 mi. down Wolf Den Dr. and turn left into the park entrance and campground. There is parking to the right just beyond the park office or in the campground's overflow lot across from the office.

Walk Directions

TIME: 2 1/2 to 3 hours
LEVEL: Moderate
DISTANCE: 4 1/2 miles
ACCESS: By car

The walk is a loop that follows blue markers. The first half is relatively easy, on footpaths and old woods roads. The second half has many ups and downs and is rocky in places. The best picnic spots can be found at Point 6.

TO BEGIN

From the parking area, walk back toward Wolf Den Dr.

1. Cross Wolf Den Dr., following the blue markers to a footpath leading into a woods where rock walls seem to close in on you. Cross a wooden bridge spanning a brook and continue through the woods for about 15 minutes.

2. Turn right at a junction with a red trail. Follow this lane (marked with both blue and red markers) to another junction where the red trail turns off to the left. Ignore the red trail and continue on to the right.

3. Just past a point where the red trail turns off, you arrive at a junction marked with a post. Turn left, following blue markers. *If you wish to explore Masamoquet Brook or the Old Red Mill, turn right. After exploring, return to this point.*

During the next mile, you cross a brook, then keep left at a trail marker. Continue to a junction and turn left. Follow the

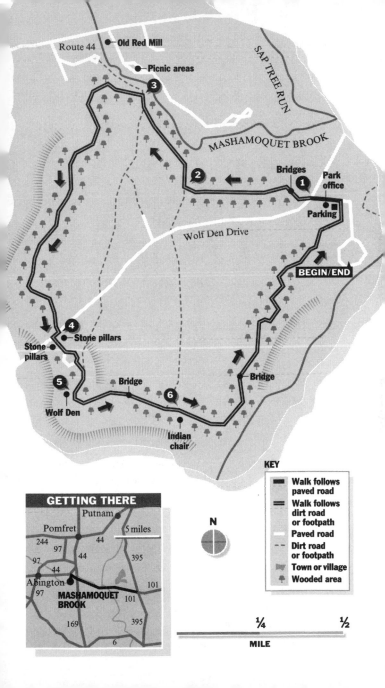

Route 44 •**Old Red Mill**

Picnic areas

SAP TREE RUN

3

MASHAMOQUET BROOK

2 **Bridges** **1** **Park office**

Parking

Wolf Den Drive

BEGIN/END

4 **Stone pillars**

Stone pillars

5 **Bridge** **6** **Bridge**

Wolf Den

Indian chair

KEY

	Walk follows paved road
	Walk follows dirt road or footpath
	Paved road
	Dirt road or footpath
	Town or village
	Wooded area

GETTING THERE

Putnam

Pomfret

5 miles

244 97 44 395

97 44

97 44

Abington

97 **MASHAMOQUET BROOK** 101 101

169 395

6

N

¼ ½

MILE

▼

blue trail as it gradually climbs a hill, reaches a field's edge, and traverses high ground covered with mountain laurel.

4. When you reach a gravel road, turn right and then left, entering the Wolf Den area marked by two stone pillars. At the parking circle, keep left and follow the drive almost halfway around the loop. Near a marker for the Wolf's Den, turn left onto a footpath that leads downhill over rocks. Red markers will rejoin the blue that you are following. Continue down to the right, following the Wolf Den marker.

5. About halfway down the slope, on your right, you arrive at the Wolf Den. *A plaque placed here tells the near-mythical story of Putman's encounter with the wolf.*

Follow the blue markers down a steep hill to the bottom of the valley. Cross the brook on a long bridge, and climb up slabs of rock to a junction. The red trail turns to the left here, but continue ahead, following blue markers.

6. Just past the junction, you arrive at a ledge that's to the right a few yards off the trail. *This rock formation, known as "Indian Chair," is a good place to rest or picnic.*

To continue, follow the blue markers downhill, across a boulder field, which can be wet. You cross a bridge and climb back up to higher ground. *The next mile of trail is very rugged and scenic, passing through a pine forest with wild rock outcrops. Notice why it was so hard for settlers to find the wolf den.*

Follow the trail to the left over a rock outcrop. Continue on as the trail turns right between two outcrops. Go through an opening in a rock wall and head back to the parking area.

OTHER PLACES NEARBY

■ **Brayton Grist Mill and Marcy Blacksmith Museum.** A well-preserved small mill at the entrance to Mashamoquet State Park, it operated from 1890 to 1928, grinding corn and grain.

▼

Upstairs is a blacksmith museum. *Rte. 44, Mashamoquet Brook State Park, Pomfret, CT 06259. Open Sat.-Sun. 2-5 May-Sep.*

■ **Old Sturbridge Village.** Old Sturbridge Village is an 1830s New England village frozen in time. Every detail is perfectly recreated in a large living museum with town center, shops, sawmill, working farm, homes, and much more, populated by a cast of hundreds who dress in period clothing and do what they would have been doing 165 years ago. Special events (Spring Militia Day) and celebrations (Fourth of July) are held from time to time. *1 Old Sturbridge Village Rd., Sturbridge, MA 01566; tel. 508-347-3362. Open daily 9-5 end of Mar.-Oct.; Tue.-Sun. (Sat.-Sun. only Jan.-mid-Feb.) 10-4 Nov.-end of Mar. Admission. Take Mass. Tpke. exit 9 or I-84 exit 2 to Rte. 20.*

■ **Statue of General Israel Putnam.** This powerful equestrian statue, created in 1887 and erected by the state of Connecticut, towers 20 feet over the grave of Israel Putnam. The law offices behind the statue are those of a descendant. The Brooklyn Historical Society has its museum here also. *Brooklyn, CT. On Rte. 169, just south of Rte. 6 junction.*

DINING

■ **The Golden Lamb Buttery** (very expensive). Considered one of Connecticut's better restaurants, the 110-year-old barn holds not only tables, but also totem poles and a 1953 XK-120 Jaguar. The fixed-price ($60) dinner consists of appetizers, herb soups, a choice of entrées that normally includes duck, lamb, and salmon, vegetables, and desserts. Also provided: a predinner hay ride with a drink, wine at dinner, and live entertainment by folk singer Susan Lamb. Lunch is much simpler. No credit cards but checks are accepted. *Bush Hill Rd., Brooklyn, CT; tel. 860-774-4423. Open Tue.-Sat. for lunch, Fri.-Sat. for dinner mid-Apr.-Jan. 1. Off Wolf Den Rd., 2.8 mi. south of Rte. 101, or 2 mi. north of Rte. 6.*

■ **The Inn at Woodstock Hill** (expensive). The dining room overlooks rolling countryside. You'll find an

▼

American/continental menu that's strong on seafood, including the popular appetizer Cajun-style soft shell crab. Entrées include mushroom strudel, sautéed striped bass, and rack of lamb Dijon. Reservations are necessary. *94 Plaine Hill Rd., South Woodstock, CT 06267; tel. 860-928-0528. Open daily for lunch and dinner (closed Mon. lunch). Just off Rte. 169, north of South Woodstock.*

■ **The Harvest** (expensive) Request the alcove table in the main dining room of this recently renovated mid-1700s farmhouse, which also offers moderately priced lunches. The eclectic dinner menu may feature such specials as Asian broiled sesame tuna, Danish lamb chops, and southwestern grilled calamari. Don't miss the top-notch wine, beer, scotch, and vodka lists. *37 Putnam Rd., Pomfret, CT 06258; tel. 860-928-0008. Open Tue.-Fri. for lunch, Tue.-Sun. for dinner (closes 7 p.m. on Sun.), and Sun. brunch. On Rte. 44 at the Lemuel Grosvenor House.*

■ **The Vine Bistro** (moderate). This small, off-the-street restaurant serves contemporary American cuisine—a mix of Italian, French, and southwestern styles. A popular appetizer is portobello mushrooms sautéed with spinach and tomatoes and roasted red peppers. About eight regular dinner entrées are supplemented by six daily specials. Rack of lamb is prepared differently each night. Desserts, including some that are imported from Italy, are a specialty. *85 Main St., Putnam, CT 06260; tel. 860-928-1660. Open Tue.-Sun. for lunch and dinner.*

The Vanilla Bean Cafe (inexpensive). This cafe has a casual, artistic atmosphere. On a recent visit, fiddlers were jamming outside as a chef prepared lunch on a barbecue grill. One room inside has plush chairs and a sofa. The menu focuses on sandwiches, soups, and baked goods—many vegetarian. You'll also find gourmet ice cream. The chili was voted best in Northeast Connecticut. On weekends, there's live jazz and folk music. *Corner of Rtes. 169, 44, and 97, Pomfret, CT 06258; tel. 860-928-1562. Open daily for breakfast, lunch, and dinner.*

▼

LODGING

■ **The Inn at Woodstock Hill** (expensive). Set on high ground overlooking farms and hills, this handsome 22-room country inn has large common areas, a restaurant, and a wide range of guest accommodations, some at moderate prices. Rooms have private baths, TV, and AC, and some have four-poster beds and fireplaces. A continental breakfast is served indoors or in the courtyard. *94 Plaine Hill Rd., P.O. Box 98, South Woodstock, CT 06267-0098; tel. 860-928-0528. Just off Rte. 169, north of South Woodstock.*

■ **Friendship Valley** (moderate). Abolitionist William Lloyd Garrison and Friendship Valley resident Helen Benson were married in the living room by Samuel May, a local pastor who was author Louisa May Alcott's uncle. Today, this 18th-century Georgian country house on 12 wooded acres offers four guest rooms, each with a private bath. Ask for the elegant Tyler Room or splurge for the cathedral-ceilinged Prince Suite, which includes a queen-size bed, a whirlpool, and a private entrance. A full breakfast, as well as afternoon tea or evening dessert, is served. *P.O. Box 845, Brooklyn, CT 06234; tel. 860-779-9696. On Rte. 169, just north of the intersection of Rtes. 6 and 169.*

■ **Wintergreen** (moderate). This B&B is an 1888 Victorian set on six parklike acres well off the main road. The large 18-room house has two spacious guest rooms with private baths and two with a shared bath. Guests have the run of the parlor and sitting room, the country kitchen, and a cozy porch that overlooks the lawn, distant woods, and farmlands. A full breakfast is served. *354 Pomfret St., Rte. 169, Pomfret, CT 06259; tel. 860-928-5741. On Rtes. 169 and 44.*

■ **Cobbscroft** (moderate). Three rooms with private baths and one suite with a fireplace are available to guests of this 18th-century farmhouse. In the barn, you'll find an art studio and a gift shop. The grounds may sometimes need a manicure, but the interior of the house is nice. A full breakfast, which can feature apple crisp, quiche, or blueberry cobbler, is served. *349*

▼

Pomfret St., Rte. 169, Pomfret, CT 06258; tel. 860-928-5560. 1 mi. south of the junction of Rtes. 169 and 44.

■ **Karinn B&B** (moderate). This large 20-room house was once a girl's school and later the Old Pomfret Inn. Today, it's a six-unit B&B, all with private baths. Two rooms have fireplaces and can be combined into suites. Large common areas include a TV room, a bar, and a huge, relaxing porch with garden views. There's an impressive breakfast menu. Well-mannered pets are welcome. Call before you arrive because, at press time, the house was for sale. *330 Pomfret St., Rte. 169, Pomfret Center, CT 06259; tel. 860-928-5492. 1 mi. south of the junction of Rtes. 44 and 169.*

■ **Tannerbrook** (inexpensive). This colonial saltbox built around 1750 features two large guest rooms with private baths and fireplaces. One room has a four-poster bed, the other antique twin beds. In back, 10 acres of private land include a fishing lake with a trail around it. A full breakfast is served. *Rte. 169, Brooklyn, CT; tel. 860-774-4822. On Rte. 169, north of Brooklyn.*

FOR MORE INFORMATION
Tourist Office:
■ **Connecticut's Quiet Corner.** *P.O. Box 598, Putnam, CT 06260; tel. 860-928-1228. Open Mon.-Fri. 9-5.*

For Serious Walkers:
Walking in Northeast Connecticut is a tradition, especially on Columbus Day weekend, which is known as the "walking weekend." At that time, the trees are at full foliage, and more than 50 walks are led by experienced leaders. There are many interesting trails, including the Natchaug in nearby James Goodwin State Forest and the Nipmuck further west.

Last of the Coastline

EXPERIENCE 4:
BLUFF POINT

I t's a pity that only at Bluff Point can the public experience what the Connecticut coastline was once like. This peninsula, ending abruptly where rocks meet the sea, is

The Highlights: Sand and rock beaches, woods teeming with deer, the remains of a former governor's home.

Other Places Nearby: Mystic Seaport, a world-class aquarium, Foxwoods Casino.

covered with vines and a forest of hardwoods, including sassafras, that is home to many deer. To the west is the Poquonock River estuary where you may see herons, swans, and other waterbirds. On the bluff are views over Long Island Sound toward Fishers Island, which is part of New York State, and to the east, Watch Hill in Rhode Island. Mumford Cove sits on the east side of the peninsula where, close up, you may see huge jellyfish and other ocean creatures. On the other side of the bay are rows of houses—now the dominant feature of the Connecticut coast.

The area around Bluff Point was home to one of the most formidable Native American tribes in New England, the Pequots. In the Algonquin language their name means "destroyer." They were particularly powerful in the area near the Thames River

▼

and, most likely, occupied or at least hunted and fished on Bluff Point. In this area, relations between English settlers and Native Americans became so tense that they ignited their first major war in New England, generally known as the Pequot War.

I n 1633, a small group of traders on their way upriver to the Dutch trading station at Hartford were murdered by Native Americans subject to the Pequot chief Sassacus. The chief promised to deliver the murderers to the English in Boston, but he failed to do so. Three years later, the Block Island tribe killed explorer and pioneer John Oldham, an incident that added pressure to an unresolved (at least as far as the English were concerned) situation. The Governor of Massachusetts then sent out a force, commanded by John Endicott, that attacked first Block Island and then Pequot territory, killing Native Americans and burning their homes. These actions upped the ante. During the winter of 1636-37, the Pequots attacked the Connecticut settlements, killing settlers and keeping the rest in a state of constant alarm. By May 1637, a force of 20 men from Boston and Hartford led by John Underhill and 90 from Connecticut led by John Mason, along with 70 Mohegans and more than 200 Narragansetts (all enemies of the Pequots), assembled and marched on the Pequot stronghold near present-day Mystic.

The English and their Native American allies launched a surprise attack on the Pequot walled village, burning the lodges and killing those trying to escape. Only 5 of the 700 Pequots in the village survived this brutal attack, while only 2 of the English were killed. The remaining Pequots in Connecticut were driven out; their leader was killed by the Mohawks, who sent his scalp to Boston as a peace offering. The site of this attack is northeast of Mystic, at the John Mason monument.

After the Pequot Wars, the remaining Native Americans in the Groton/Bluff Point area were removed to Noank, and the English took over their former lands. John Winthrop, son of the

▼

Massachusetts governor, took the piece that included Bluff Point. This 1648 land grant stayed within the Winthrop family until 1818. Winthrop served as governor of Connecticut from 1657 to 1676, and his son Fitz-John did the same from 1698 to 1707. Although both men owned the Bluff Point site, neither ever lived there but leased the land to others.

In 1690, the first house was built there by Anthony Ashley; apparently, it was not built well—it fell down in 1725. In the late 1600s, another house was built under the direction of Fitz-John: This was a 16-room house with many outbuildings for livestock. The remains of these buildings, along with many stone walls, are passed along the walk. There is a cistern and a tunnel that ran from the house to a barn.

The Winthrop title to the land was sold in 1818 and again in 1856. The land continued to be leased to a series of farmers. During the 1930s, about 200 cabins were built around the tip of the bluff, and a casino was erected near the sand beach. The 1938 hurricane flattened these fragile structures. The Winthrop house survived the storm, but it burned in 1962, about the time the land was (fortunately) being acquired by the state of Connecticut to be preserved as a state park.

Today things are better for everyone. Bluff Point is open to the walking and bike-riding public, who visit the preserve in large numbers. From their near-annihilation, the Pequots made a slow and difficult recovery. Through lawsuits and legislation in the 1970s, they reclaimed much of their original lands and now own over 5,000 acres, including the successful Foxwoods Resort Casino (*see* Other Places Nearby).

The director Steven Spielberg filmed a portion of his 1997 movie, *Amistad,* in the area around Bluff Point.

GETTING THERE

By car:

From exit 88 on I-95 in southeastern Connecticut, take Rte. 117 south for 1 mi. to a junction with Rte. 1. Turn right

▼

and drive 3/10 mi. and turn left at the first light onto Depot Rd. Follow Depot Rd. for another 3/10 mi. and then bear right under a railroad bridge. Continue following the unpaved road to a large parking area.

Walk Directions

TIME: 2 hours
LEVEL: Easy
DISTANCE: 4 miles
ACCESS: By car

The many trails in this park are not marked. However, the loop described below utilizes the main pathway, a woods road that can handle a vehicle if necessary. Ignore the many side paths that intersect it along the way. Be aware that this park, being as beautiful as it is and close to major population centers, can become quite crowded with walkers, mountain bikers, and equestrians during summer and weekends. It is recommended that you take this walk during the weekdays, off-season, or early in the morning.

You should also **be aware that deer ticks, which are carried by the many deer that inhabit the park, may be found here, and some may carry Lyme disease.** The disease derives its name from the nearby town of Old Lyme, where the disease is thought to have originated. You are far more likely to pick up ticks if you leave the trail and bushwhack through the wooded thickets. Since the trail is quite wide, the chances of picking up a tick are very low if you stay on it. Still, you may wish to take the standard precautions: Wear lightcolored pants tucked into your socks, spray your shoes and pants with tick repellent, and check yourself carefully for ticks after the walk. Deer ticks are very small, the size of a speck or a pin head. The larger ticks that you are more likely to see—wood ticks, not deer ticks—are the size of match heads.

▼

TO BEGIN

From the parking area, walk toward the entrance gate, where you find the main trail, a dirt lane wide enough to accommodate a single vehicle. There is a box with maps.

1. From the entrance gate, follow the lane southward, with the waters of the Poquonock River on your right and the woods on your left. You pass the dirt lane that will be your return route. On the way, you pass footpaths and woods roads coming in on your left; ignore them, and keep to the main lane. Just after a point where the path rises, you find primitive rest rooms on your left. Follow the path to a clearing, where a casino once stood. A sandy beach is on the right.

2. About one hour after you began the walk, you reach a spit of land on your right that extends about a mile west into Long Island Sound. *You may wish to explore this long, narrow beach which culminates at Bushy Point. If you do explore the full length of the spit, you will add an additional 2 mi. to the walk, including retracing your steps to Point 2. In any case, you'll probably want to walk down to the water and enjoy the view.* When finished exploring, return to the main path, turn right, and follow the path gently uphill. In only a minute or so, you approach Bluff Point.

3. From Bluff Point, follow one of the paths that parallel the edge of the bluff, or descend to the rocky shoreline and explore the shoreline up close, working your way east.

If you choose to follow the edge of the bluff, you may either follow the main dirt lane or take one of the side paths that parallel the main lane.

If you follow the shoreline, you will come to a very large boulder. From here, walk about 100 yards, then leave the shoreline and follow one of several paths that will bring you back toward the main dirt lane.

Parking
BEGIN/END

Gate

①

POQUONOCK RIVER

⑤ Winthrop
site

②

③

Bluff
Point

④

LONG ISLAND SOUND

¼   ½
MILE

GETTING THERE

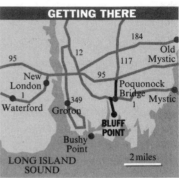

95   12   184
                                  Old
                         117   Mystic
New   95
London   Poquonock
1   Bridge
Waterford 349   1   Mystic
        Groton

        BLUFF
        POINT

Bushy
Point

LONG ISLAND
SOUND   2 miles

KEY

▬	Walk follows paved road
═	Walk follows dirt road or footpath
▭	Paved road
- - -	Dirt road or footpath
🌲	Town or village
🌲	Wooded area

N

▼

4. Rejoin the main dirt lane, which will swing around Mumford Point, and then head north into the interior of the peninsula. After another 20 to 30 minutes of walking through woods, you begin to see stone walls.

5. When you reach a junction with a road coming in from the left, you are near the site of the former Winthrop complex. Follow the road as it swings to the right and then to the left (do not go straight here), passing the foundations of the old house that's off to the right. *You may explore them if you wish*. Continue along the main pathway past stone walls and under hickory trees. Arrive at Point 1 after another half hour of walking.

OTHER PLACES NEARBY

■ **Foxwoods Resort Casino.** The Mashantucket Pequots have made one of the most spectacular comebacks in the history of New England. Surviving a massacre and government efforts to strip them of their territory and identity, they made it into the 20th century, were awarded damages, and have reclaimed their land. In addition to their casino, which is one of the largest anywhere, the resort includes hotels, a spa, and various entertainment facilities. *P.O. Box 3777, Mashantucket, CT 06339; tel. 860-312-3000. Open daily 24 hours. About 10 mi. north of Mystic.*

■ **Mashantucket Pequot Museum.** With the profits from their casino, the Pequots have constructed an elaborate museum with dramatic displays depicting their history and culture. *110 Pequot Trail, Mashantucket, CT 06339; tel. 860-396-6800. Open daily 10-6, except Tue. About 10 mi. north of Mystic. About 10 mi. north of Mystic.*

■ **Mystic Marinelife Aquarium.** More than 2,500 creatures are housed in this world-class aquarium. Don't miss the daily dolphin and whale shows in the theater, or the seals, penguins, sharks, and local sea creatures, all in wonderfully designed enclosures. The museum shop alone is worth a visit.

55 Coogan Blvd., Mystic, CT 06355-1997; tel. 860-572-5955. Open daily 9-6 Jul.-Labor Day, 9-5 the rest of the year. Admission. Exit 90 on I-95.

■ **Mystic Seaport.** This multifaceted living museum, known for its tall ships, also offers boat rides, demonstrations by working craftspeople, and even an entire 19th-century village. The whaling ship *Charles W. Morgan* is the centerpiece. Plenty to do and learn about here—there's even a children's museum. Several shops in the complex are open without admission. *75 Greenmanville Ave., Mystic, CT 06355; tel. 860-572-5315. Open daily 9-5 in summer, 9-4 in fall and spring, 10-4 in winter. Admission. From exit 90 on I-95, take Rte. 27 1 mi. south.*

DINING

■ **Flood Tide Restaurant** (very expensive). The Flood Tide, at the Inn at Mystic, is one of the most elegant restaurants in town. On the menu you'll find items like whole roast pheasant, broiled scallops with fresh basil crust, and roast duckling with glaze *du chef.* Desserts like bananas Foster (bananas and walnuts on vanilla ice cream covered with banana liqueur and flamed tableside) shouldn't be missed. The dining room overlooks the bay. *Rtes. 1 and 27, P.O. Box 216, Mystic, CT 06355; tel. 860-536-8140. Open Mon.-Sat. for breakfast, lunch and dinner. At the junction of Rtes. 1 and 27.*

■ **Restaurant Bravo Bravo** (expensive). In addition to the spare and roomy main dining room, this restaurant includes an outdoor cafe where lunch is served in summer. The dinner menu is contemporary Italian with such interesting choices as fusilli with vodka sauce and shrimp seasoned with sundried tomatoes and basil. Many Italian wines, at reasonable prices, are stocked. *20 E. Main St., Mystic, CT 06355; tel. 860-536-3228. Indoor dining room open Tue.-Sun. for dinner year-round, and for lunch Oct.-Apr. Outdoor cafe open daily for lunch and dinner May-Sep.*

▼

■ **Abbott's Lobster in the Rough** (moderate). You stand in line and place your order, then wait until your number is called at the counter. There's a simple indoor dining area as well as plenty of picnic tables overlooking the boat zoo in Mystic harbor. Bring your own beer or wine. A great place to go for fresh lobster on a nice summer day. *117 Pearl St., Noank, CT; tel. 860-572-9128. Open daily for lunch and dinner May-Columbus Day.*

■ **Seahorse Tavern** (moderate). This local eating spot, a bar and family restaurant, offers inexpensive to moderate meals mostly centered around seafood: broiled flounder, fish-and-chips, linguini with mussels, grilled chicken, and the like. *65 Marsh Rd., Noank, CT 06340; tel. 860-536-1670. Open daily for lunch and dinner. Off Groton Long Point Rd.*

■ **The Fisherman** (moderate). The dining rooms in the restaurant face an inlet, allowing for some very pleasant boat-watching. The menu, while strong on seafood, also includes pork chops, steaks, and pasta. The lunch menu features a variety of sandwiches at reasonable prices. A bar with its own dining area offers a different, tavern-like atmosphere. *937 Groton Long Point Rd., Noank, CT 06340; tel. 860-536-1717. Open daily for lunch and dinner. Near junction of Rte. 215 and Groton Long Point Rd.*

■ **Trader Jack's** (moderate). According to the blurb on the back of the menu, Trader Jack survived a shipwreck, learned the culinary secrets of the world, and opened one of the first restaurants in Mystic. The menu today is pretty standard—seafood, pasta, veal, poultry, and steaks—nothing particularly exotic. *14 Holmes St., Mystic, CT 06355; tel. 860-572-8550. Open daily for dinner. In downtown Mystic, near the drawbridge.*

LODGING

■ **Applewood Farms Inn** (expensive). Four generations of the Gallup family worked this farm. The main house, built in 1826, offers six guest rooms, including four with fireplaces.

▼

With three common rooms, gardens, and 33 surrounding acres, there's plenty of room. Full breakfast is served. Polite pets are allowed. *528 Colonel Ledyard Hwy., Ledyard, CT 06339; tel. 860-536-2022. I-95 to Exit 89, north on Cow Hill Rd., left on Rte. 184, and right onto Colonel Ledyard Hwy. for 2.7 mi.*

■ **Red Brook Inn** (expensive). Two restored 18th-century buildings, one (a former tavern) set back from the road, make up this Colonial-style inn. The decor is historically correct; guest rooms have period furnishings (canopy beds, stenciled floors), and seven have fireplaces. Some rooms contain whirlpools. The common rooms are roomy and house collections of glass and pewter. *P.O. Box 237, Old Mystic, CT 06372; tel. 860-572-0349. Exit 89 on I-95, north on Allyn St., right on Gold Star Hwy. to first left.*

■ **The Palmer Inn** (expensive). It's a mansion, hidden behind a wall of hedges, with tall columns that greet you at the front door. You enter into a spacious living room, almost museumlike with its collections of hats, stuffed toys, and other period antiques. The six upstairs guest rooms have private baths, and some have balconies. Continental breakfast is served. The inn is located in the small town of Noank, which offers excellent walking past seafront and historical homes. *25 Church St., Groton, CT 06340; tel. 860-572-9000. Call for specific directions.*

■ **Charley's Harbour Inne and Cottage** (moderate). Here's a simple, unpretentious place that may appeal to those interested in getting a feel for the local scene. Charley, by all accounts a colorful local character, has converted a house and garage near a water treatment plant to a B&BYOB (bring your own breakfast). There are four rooms, plus a cottage with private baths. The place is immaculate, there's a kitchen to use, it's on the water and within walking distance of downtown Mystic. Amenities include piano, fireplace, gazebo, Jacuzzi, and cable TV. Pets are welcome. *Edgemont St., Mystic, CT 06355; tel. 860-572-9253. One block from the train station.*

▼

■ **The Whaler's Inn** (moderate). This large recently reno-vated inn has rooms in a main building and three others, including the 1865 house, which has the feel of a B&B. All 41 rooms have private baths (some with only bathtubs) and TV. The location is right in town by the drawbridge, good for exploring and shopping, but not especially quiet. *28 Cottrell St.,P.O. Box 143, Mystic, CT 06355; tel. 860-536-1506, 800-243-2588; fax 860-572-1250.*

FOR MORE INFORMATION

Tourist Office:

■ **Mystic Chamber of Commerce.** *16 Cottrell St., P.O. Box 143, Mystic, CT 06355; tel. 860-572-9578. Open Mon.-Fri. 9-5. Office located near the drawbridge in the center of Mystic.*

For Serious Walkers:

Trail walking opportunities in the area are few, but good beach walking is possible at Napatree Point in Watch Hill, Rhode Island. In summer, get an early start because parking is limited.

The Power of Water

EXPERIENCE 5: ASHTON

Most of the walks in this guide focus on places of great natural beauty, or places that have been sculpted by great landscape artists. Here, along the Blackstone River, is an historic walk in Ashton, an

> **The Highlights:** A walk on the tow path of an 18th-century canal, views of falls over a dam on the Blackstone River, 19th-century factory towns.
>
> **Other Places Nearby:** An old mill that's now a museum, a state park with a large lake.

area shaped by the Industrial Revolution. Don't expect to find a well-manicured trail system or great B&Bs nearby—at least for now. What you should anticipate is a pleasant walk on a path between river and canal in a state park in the making. Ten years from now, you may find part of a statewide bikepath, trails along the river bank, and more historic buildings open to the public. For now, be content with a lesson in river power, a glimpse of a blue heron cruising just above the canal, and a look at life in a mill town long after its heyday.

The Blackstone River Valley is named for William Blackstone, not only the first settler in the area, but also the first English settler in both Boston (1623) and Rhode Island (1634). He arrived in New England just three years after the Pilgrims

▼

landed at Plymouth, and settled on land that is now part of Boston. His neighbors, the Puritans, were so fanatical that he moved 35 miles south just to get away from them, to a place near today's Woonsocket, Rhode Island. The river he lived near—one that would eventually take his name—was called the Patucket by the Indians.

Blackstone, a preacher who pioneered the Anglican-Episcopalian religion in America, was known as "the Sage of the Wilderness." Apparently a very serious man, he was well-educated, and always reading and studying. His home was called Study Hill, and he lived there for 40 years, raising cattle and planting. He was the first person to cultivate apples in America.

Roger Williams, a champion of religious tolerance and a friend to the Native Americans, arrived in Rhode Island two years after he did, and invited Blackstone to preach in Providence on a regular basis. When Blackstone was 64, he married 34-year-old Sarah Stevenson with whom he had one child. He died in 1675, after his Study Hill farm was destroyed during the King Philip Indian war. A large granite monument marks the approximate site of his grave in Cumberland.

The Blackstone River begins in Worcester, Massachusetts, and runs 46 miles to Pawtucket (a "w" was added to the name by the settlers) and Providence, Rhode Island, where it becomes the Seekonk River and empties into Narragansett Bay. The river drops steeply in places, a factor that was noticed by manufacturing pioneers. In 1790, the Brown and Almy Mill in Pawtucket became the first textile mill in America (Slater Mill Historic Site), and soon after, more mills were established upstream. Water power turned the mills, and textiles of wool and cotton were manufactured. A new way of life for many in New England, and for many immigrants, had begun.

In the Ashton area, the focus of the walk, the first textile mill was built between 1810 and 1815. The mill's name was the

▼

Smithfield Woolen and Cotton Manufactury, and the small settlement that grew up around the mill was called Old Ashton. Wilbur Kelly, a sea captain who foresaw the demise of shipping and the rise of manufacturing, bought the mill in 1825. Kelly eventually let his son Christopher run the Old Ashton mill, and moved on to run the Lonsdale Company mills three miles south. A small Greek Revival house was built for his use that is now being renovated and will become an interpretive center. It's located near the start of the walk. Only four other houses from the Old Ashton era survive on Lower River Road. The mill itself was demolished in 1930 in order to make way for the Route 116 bridge (the George Washington Highway Bridge).

One of the challenges that early manufacturing presented was transporting mass quantities of goods. Mills were built along rivers that had falls, and were therefore unnavigable. Railroads were not yet in existence, and simple carts and wagons were too small to handle this dramatic increase in production. Canals, which were dug parallel to and fed by rivers, were the best solution. The Blackstone Canal was one of the last canals built in New England. It was 45 miles long with 49 locks (large holding tanks that could fill to raise boats moving upstream, or drain, for downstream travel). Along the towpath, teams of horses were used to pull boats up or down the canal.

The Blackstone Canal was not a great success. Although the canal served to link the smaller mill towns with the big cities of Worcester and Providence, the manufacturers who used it were in a catch-22 situation, since it siphoned off the water they needed to drive their mills. There were also problems due to ice, lack of water during drought, and too much water during wet periods. When the railroad came to the Blackstone River Valley in 1847, it quickly killed the canal.

During the 1860s, another mill town sprung up on the other side of the river. Called Ashton, it was basically an expansion project of the mills of the Lonsdale Company three miles downstream. This town is typical of the mid-19th-century mill village,

▼

with its big brick factory buildings and rows of identical brick houses built for the workers, all down by the river. On higher ground is the upper village, mostly built of wood, where the supervisors lived. And, of course there is the waterfall—the source of the power for every mill town—that turned the machinery that spun the cloth.

Ashton, like other mill towns up and down the Blackstone River, supplied jobs for workers and kept the Industrial Revolution going. But, by the early part of this century, the mills were no longer profitable, and the rivers had become polluted. Mill owners found cheaper labor and lower capital costs down south. Textile production in Ashton ceased in 1935, and the Blackstone Valley, which had become so dependent on one industry, entered a time of economic hardship.

In 1986, Congress passed legislation that created the Blackstone River National Heritage Corridor. The National Park Service is now establishing a unique kind of park, one that links various surviving pieces of the previous century's industrial history. Administered by state and local agencies as well as the Park Service, the "corridor" consists of 21 towns in Massachusetts and Rhode Island grouped together with the common theme of historic preservation and recreational attractions. Plans call for walking trails, a long bikeway, restored historic sites, and other attractions. Some of these are already in place.

Our walk is in the newly created Blackstone River Park, which includes a three-mile section of the Blackstone Canal (the best preserved section in Rhode Island) and its towpath.

GETTING THERE

By car:

From Providence, RI, go north on Rte. 146. Exit onto Rte. 116 north (Ashton/Albion exit). Drive 7/10 mi. to the junction with Rte. 126, where you will turn right (south), and then immediately bear left onto River Rd. Drive 1.7 mi. and turn left

▼

onto Simon Sayles/Cullen Hill Rd. After another 1/2 mi., turn left at a junction onto Lower River Rd. There is a sign for Blackstone River State Park 7/10 mi. ahead, where the road crosses over the canal and ends under the highway bridge. The parking area is located between the canal and the river, under the Rte. 116 bridge.

Walk Directions

TIME: 2 hours
LEVEL: Easy
DISTANCE: 3 1/2 miles
ACCESS: By car

The walk explores the river, the canal, and the towpath through this historic industrial area. You may encounter some people fishing, canoeing, mountain biking, or even dirt biking. The area is not patrolled by rangers.

TO BEGIN

Leave the parking area and begin walking north along the land between the canal and the river. The canal should be to your left.

1. Pass a wooden pedestrian bridge that spans the canal.

2. After another minute or two of walking, you arrive at the point where the river feeds the canal. *Here you can examine the stone handiwork of the canal builders who were mostly Irish immigrants.* Turn around and return to Point 1. Cross over the bridge and turn right, following the lane uphill.

3. When you reach the crest of the river bank just past a junction, keep right. *There are rock outcrops offering a fine view over the river, the dam, and the canal.* Retrace your steps to Point 1, and then your starting point at the parking area, and continue walking south on the towpath.

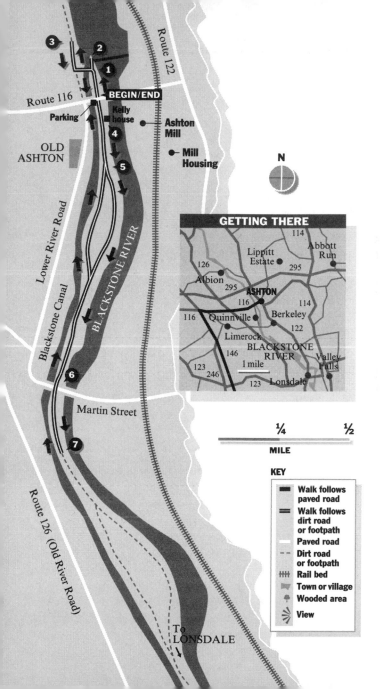

Route 122

Route 116

BEGIN/END

Parking

Kelly house

OLD ASHTON

Ashton Mill

Mill Housing

N

Lower River Road

BLACKSTONE RIVER

Blackstone Canal

GETTING THERE

114

Lippitt Estate

Abbott Run

126

Albion

295

ASHTON

116

114

Quinnville

Berkeley

122

Limerock

146

BLACKSTONE RIVER

Valley Falls

123

246

1 mile

123

Lonsdale

Martin Street

Route 126 (Old River Road)

To LONSDALE

¼   ½

MILE

KEY

	Walk follows paved road
	Walk follows dirt road or footpath
	Paved road
	Dirt road or footpath
	Rail bed
	Town or village
	Wooded area
	View

▼

4. Pass the Wilbur Kelly house. *The buildings of the Ashton Mill are visible on the far side of the river.*

5. Turn left at the fork, leaving the towpath. Follow a lane that swings out onto former farm fields and then bears right, paralleling the towpath. After another five minutes, the path turns to the right, and you enter a wooded area, and then swing around toward the towpath bank. Follow the lane as it climbs the bank. Turn left to join the towpath and continue walking south on it. *In this section, the canal flows through a rock cut. The river is immediately to your left, much lower than the canal. Sassafras lines the towpath in this section.*

6. After about 1/2 hour of walking, cross Martin St. and continue walking south on the towpath.

7. In another 20 minutes or so, you come to a rounded concrete spillway that allows the canal to overflow and drain into the river. This makes a convenient turnaround point for the walk. *Some walkers may wish to continue for another 1.5 mi. to the end of the towpath in Lonsdale.* To return, retrace your steps along the towpath all the way back to the parking area.

OTHER PLACES NEARBY

■ **Slater Mill Historic Site.** This was the first factory to produce cotton yarn with water power, the birthplace of the Industrial Revolution in America. Built in 1793 by Samuel Slater and two Providence merchants, the mill now operates as a museum, illustrating the use of water power and the production of textiles. *Roosevelt Ave., P.O. Box 696, Pawtucket, RI 02860; tel. 401-725-8638. Open daily 10-5 Jun.-Nov.; Sat.-Sun. afternoons Dec.-May. Call for tour times. Admission. From I-95 heading south, take exit 27 and follow signs. From I-95 heading north, take exit 28, go left off ramp, cross Main St. Bridge, and follow signs.*

▼

■ **Blackstone River and Canal Heritage State Park.** A 3.75-mile towpath trail follows a section of the Blackstone River Canal and passes locks, dams, and other remnants of 19th-century industry. *287 Oak St., Uxbridge, MA 01569; tel. 508-278-6486. From the Massachusetts Tpke., take exit 11 and then Rte. 122 south to North Uxbridge. Turn left onto E. Hartford Ave. and follow signs.*

DINING

The restaurants in these parts offer a family—rather than a fine—dining experience. What you can expect is standard fare and good value.

■ **Cantina Di Marco** (moderate). This restaurant, with Formica tables, booths, and a bar, offers many seafood, Italian, and meat entrées, some at bargain prices. Their clam chowder (Manhattan or New England), a local favorite, is featured on Wednesday and Friday only. *405 Mendon Rd., Rte. 122, Cumberland, RI 02864; tel. 401-722-4170. Open daily for lunch and dinner. South of Ashton.*

■ **Crickets** (moderate). Crickets is a family restaurant (booths and tables) serving Italian-American cuisine. Sautéed fish, chicken, and meat, and pastas are their specialty. There's dancing to a live band in the lounge Wednesday through Saturday nights. *280 George Washington Hwy. (Rte. 116), Smithfield, RI 02917; tel. 401-232-0300. Open daily for lunch and dinner and for brunch on Sun. Near the Susse Chalet hotel.*

■ **Davenport's Restaurant** (inexpensive). This family restaurant has booths, a bar, and serves a wide variety of foods—sandwiches, steaks, and seafood. Pizza is their specialty and you'll find a number of other Italian entrées on the menu. *1070 Mendon Rd. (Rte. 122), Cumberland, RI 02864; tel. 401-334-1017. Open daily for lunch and dinner. South of Rte. 116, just past the Ashton section of Cumberland.*

▼

LODGING

You won't find elegant B&Bs in this part of Rhode Island, but you still will enjoy your stay. The people are friendly and down to earth, and costs are low.

■ **Susse Chalet Inn** (inexpensive). This is the only hotel in the area. You'll find the usual chain hotel-decor and amenities (swimming pool, free in-room movies, etc.) and also a complimentary continental breakfast in the coffee shop. *355 George Washington Hwy. (Rte. 116), Smithfield, RI 02917; tel. 401-232-2400. Exit 8 on I-295.*

FOR MORE INFORMATION

Tourist Office:

■ **Blackstone Valley Tourism Council.** *171 Main St., Pawtucket, RI, 02860 (mailing address: P.O. Box 7663, Cumberland, RI 02864); tel. 401-724-2200, fax 401-724-1342. Open Mon.-Fri. 8:30-5. Visitors center open daily. There's a 24-hour information line.*

For Serious Walkers:

Nearby Lincoln Woods State Park, very popular with walkers, joggers, and equestrians, has ten miles of wide bridle paths and a large lake. It's open year-round and easily accessible from both Route 146 and Route 123. Diamond Hill Park on Route 114 in Cumberland has quartz ledges that offer vistas over the Blackstone Valley. The Monastery, with an entrance on Route 114 near Ashton, is the site of a former Cistercian monastery that burned in the 1950s. The grounds are still nicely maintained.

Much Ado About Architecture

EXPERIENCE 6: NEWPORT

When you visit the town of Newport, you are simply bombarded with fascinating history. Some experiences—such as a walk down Thames Street at the height of tourist season, or a glance at the array of TV screens at the visitors information center—can be almost

The Highlights: A busy seaport, historic buildings, fantastic mansions, the church where the Kennedys married, a mysterious tower, the Tennis Hall of Fame.

Other Places Nearby: An oceanfront cliff walk, mansions, a bird sanctuary, great shops, restaurants, and B&Bs.

overwhelming. There's the attractive harbor and all the yachts, the mansions on Bellevue Avenue, the rocky coast along which snakes the Cliff Walk, and the hundreds of historic homes. In summer, Newport is too tourist-jammed to qualify as an "escape," but in spring and fall the place is simply a walker's delight. Nearly everything is within a few miles and, unlike many other urban areas with historic features, it's safe.

How did Newport, a town on an island with a small but excellent harbor, come to be what it is today? In 1639, it was founded by a group of dissenters. The Puritans in Boston were making life difficult for the future founders so they set off for a

▼

better neighborhood. Roger Williams in Providence pointed them toward Aquidneck Island where they set up an agricultural community with strong religious (Anabaptist) and collectivist overtones. About 20 years later, many Quakers came to the island, which had now been renamed Rhode Island. The peaceful Quaker influence was quite strong and helped keep the colony from involvement in the Indian conflicts of the time. Later in the century and well into the next, a sizable Jewish community, largely from Spain and Portugal, was established in Newport, which had become a haven of religious tolerance. On the walk you'll pass the Touro Synagogue, built in 1763—the oldest synagogue in the United States.

By the 1670s, Newport had become a major commercial power. Exports of lumber, livestock, butter, and cheese were shipped to the British Caribbean islands in exchange for sugar, molasses, cotton, candles, rum, and other items. In 1681, Newport was bigger than Providence, and by 1730, it was one of the largest Colonial towns, with 400 houses. By then, Newport merchants had established a profitable shipping pattern: Rum from Newport was shipped to West Africa, slaves from West Africa were brought to the West Indies, and sugar cane and molasses (used to make rum) from the West Indies were shipped to Newport. Newport's commercial success had much to do with the slave trade, but there were other enterprises, including whaling, that were also carried on during its economic prime. On the brink of the American Revolution, Newport was second only to Boston as a seaport and was far more prosperous than New York. The biggest towns in Colonial America at that time were Boston, Newport, New York, Philadelphia, and Charleston.

The attempts by Great Britain to regulate trade were resisted in Newport, and when the War for Independence broke out, the British responded by blockading the harbor, effectively shutting down commerce. Without supplies, the town was in trou-

▼

ble. The wharfs were burned for firewood during the following cold winter. Newport's commercial seaport economy never fully recovered from the blockade. After the war, commerce shifted to the mills on the Blackstone River, and Newport slumbered.

But then, during the late 19th century, wealthy New Yorkers discovered Newport and built extravagant mansions (which they called "cottages"), for which the town is probably now most famous. Far from being cottages, these mansions are huge. Most are along Bellevue Avenue, a nice street to walk on with its brick sidewalks and decorative utility poles. One such mansion, The Elms, is passed on the walk; its grounds are particularly beautiful. The largest and perhaps the most famous "cottage" is The Breakers. This architectural extravaganza was modeled after a northern Italian palace and was built for Cornelius Vanderbilt in 1895. The ceiling of its Great Hall towers 45 feet above the floor. The Breakers overlooks the ocean just above the popular Cliff Walk, a paved 3.5-mile walking path along the rocky shoreline.

Visitors to Newport will be practically bombarded with information on these mansions, a number of which are open to the public. But for the moment we will look carefully at another kind of architecture in this historically rich town.

Possibly the most controversial architectural structure in America is located in the center of Newport. It could very well be the oldest as well. In Touro Park stands a 24-foot-high cylindrical stone tower, originally covered with plaster, set on eight columns joined by arches. Its origins are unknown and have been heavily debated for years. One side of the debate says that it is a windmill built by an early governor. The other side says it was built around the 12th century by Vikings.

The earliest-known Newport reference to the structure is Governor Benedict Arnold's will which states that he must be buried between his house and his "stone built wind-mill." Notice that he didn't say he built it himself. This was in 1677. It is generally assumed that Arnold (a relative of the traitor) built the mill

▼

after a storm in 1675 destroyed Newport's only windmill. As for the strange design, some say he patterned it after a mill in Chesterton, England, which it resembles. Many old paintings prove the structure was indeed used as a mill during the 18th century.

On the other hand, a 1630 document preserved in England suggests that the tower was already there at that time, several years before Newport was settled. The document describes the various commodities of the land (in the Rhode Island vicinity) that would benefit the King. It suggests a "round stone tower" as the prospective location for a possible small colony that might be sent to trade with the Native Americans Also, 100 years earlier, Italian explorer Verrazano reported a "Norman Villa" on the east side of Narragansett Bay near its mouth—right where Newport is.

There are a number of strange features in the tower that hint it was either an astronomical observatory, a lighthouse, or a church built by Vikings—or all of the above. It is precisely aligned to north and south and has windows aligned to significant astronomical events. There's a fireplace built into what would be a second-story wall that lies directly across from a window opening to the port. Theoretically, the light of the fireplace would be visible from the bay. There are niches in the second-story walls that suggest an altar.

The structure is very similar to a type of round church built in Norway and Denmark during the Middle Ages. This church design, which is usually surrounded by an ambulatory (missing in Newport's), was inspired by the Church of the Holy Sepulcher in Jerusalem. A runic inscription was found on a rock near the top of the Newport Tower. The inscription has been interpreted as a date, somewhere in the 11th or 12th century. Add to this the fact that the Vikings are known to have been in this part of the world, which they called Vinland, around this time.

The debate about the tower has raged for more than 150

▼

years, with each theory having devoted, well-educated support-ers. During the 1840s, several writers argued the two sides pub-licly, both distorting the truth, which lowered and cheapened the level of the debate. Since that time, the topic is generally avoided by those in academia who value their reputations. Today, tourists are told to decide for themselves.

A few other possible explanations have been put forward. One says that the tower was built by Sinclair of Scotland, who in 1399 sailed west to start a colony, presumably in Vinland. Another is that it was built in the 16th century by Portuguese who visited the coast. A recent dating of the mortar between the rocks yielded a date between 1500 and 1630. Whatever the answer, there's no doubt the Newport Tower is an anomaly. As you walk past it, think of it as the earliest of the many architec-tural relics and wonders found throughout this historic town.

GETTING THERE:

By car:

Newport, located in southeastern Rhode Island, is reached from the west via Rte. 138, which begins at Rte. 1. Two bridges are crossed to reach the island (the Newport Bridge has a $2 toll). From the northeast, take I-195 to Rte. 24, then Rte. 114 to Newport. Public parking is available at the Newport visitors center or at numerous small lots nearby. Full-day parking at the visitors center may be more costly than at other lots.

Walk Directions

TIME: 2 hours
LEVEL: Easy
DISTANCE: 4 miles
ACCESS: By car

The walk described below is an urban walk, entirely on sidewalks along streets. It covers much of what Newport is known for, and also passes many of the restau-rants listed in the Dining section. Although it can be walked easily

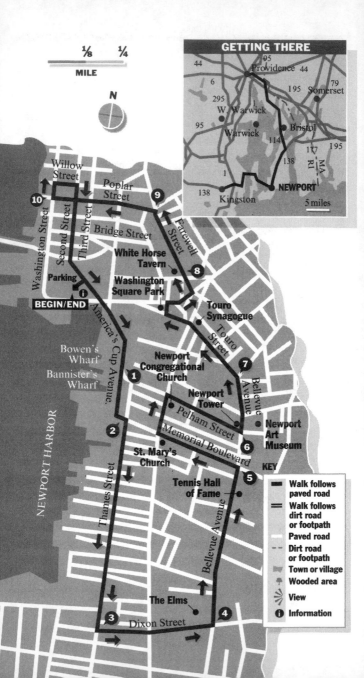

GETTING THERE

95 Providence
44   44
6
I 95   Somerset
295   79
I
W. Warwick
95
Warwick   Bristol
114
138
1   117   I 95
138   MA
RI
1
138   NEWPORT
Kingston
5 miles

⅛   ¼
MILE

N

Willow Street

Poplar Street   ⑨

Second Street
Third Street
Bridge Street

Washington Street

White Horse Tavern

Washington Square Park   ⑧

Farewell Street

Parking

ℹ

BEGIN/END

America's Cup Avenue

Touro Synagogue

Touro Street

Bowen's Wharf

Bannister's Wharf

①

Newport Congregational Church

⑦

Bellevue Avenue

Newport Tower

②

Pelham Street

⑥   Newport Art Museum

Memorial Boulevard

NEWPORT HARBOR

Thames Street

St. Mary's Church

KEY

Tennis Hall of Fame   ⑤

Bellevue Avenue

The Elms

③   Dixon Street   ④

	Walk follows paved road
	Walk follows dirt road or footpath
	Paved road
	Dirt road or footpath
	Town or village
	Wooded area
	View
ℹ	Information

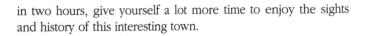

in two hours, give yourself a lot more time to enjoy the sights and history of this interesting town.

TO BEGIN

From the Newport Gateway Transportation and Visitor's Center, walk to America's Cup Ave. and turn right, passing the Marriott Hotel. To your right is the harbor area. Follow the sidewalk as it swings to the left and resumes its course.

1. Arrive at the wharf area. First is Bowen's Wharf, then Bannister's Wharf. *You may wish to explore this area. Several of the restaurants listed in Dining are located here.*

2. Where America's Cup Ave. joins Thames St., at the Newport Bay Club and Hotel, turn right. Proceed down Thames St. *On this street are many boutiques and specialty shops; to the right are lanes that extend to the waterfront.*

3. After about 25 minutes of walking, turn left onto Dixon St., passing some residences. Continue on Dixon across Spring St., now walking alongside the high stone walls of mansions.

4. Turn left onto Bellevue Ave. *On your left is one of the great mansions of Newport, The Elms, built in 1899. This mansion is an example of 18th-century French architecture—modeled after the Chateau d'Asnieres near Paris. Inside, it is museumlike, with some period furniture on loan from art museums. Its grounds, considered perhaps the finest of all the Newport mansions, include fountains, a sunken garden, and many interesting trees and shrubs. To your right is Salvia Regina University. Ahead, on the right, is the Tennis Hall of Fame, where tennis games are held daily.* Continue on Bellevue toward the first traffic light.

5. Turn left onto Memorial Blvd. Walk down to St. Mary's Church *(where John and Jacqueline Kennedy were married in*

▼

1953). Begun in 1848, this is the oldest Catholic church in Rhode Island. Turn right onto Spring St., passing numerous antique shops. At the Newport Congregational Church, turn right onto Pelham St. *Ahead, on the left is Touro Park where the controversial Newport Tower (or Old Mill) is located.*

6. Turn left onto Bellevue Ave. in front of the Newport Art Museum, which exhibits historic and contemporary art of the region. Pass the Redwood Library, *the nation's oldest functioning library. Designed by architect Peter Harrison (who also designed the Touro Synagogue), it's modeled after a Roman temple, but it's made of wood coated with sand paint. Inside is a collection of rare books and early American paintings, including some by Gilbert Stuart and Rembrandt Peale.* Continue on past the Viking Hotel.

7. Bear left onto Touro St. Pass the Newport Historical Society building and then the 1763 Touro Synagogue, *the oldest Jewish house of worship in America. This Georgian-style structure seems plain but well-proportioned on the outside. In contrast, the interior is ornate; 12 columns support a gallery that separates men from women in accorance with Orthodox tradition.* When you arrive at a complex intersection, continue straight ahead on the continuation of Touro St. (marked with two "do not enter" signs). Then turn right into Washington Square Park, *the center of activity in Colonial times. Here there is a statue of Oliver Hazzard Perry the naval hero of the 1813 Battle of Lake Erie.* Cross the park in front of the courthouse, turn right, and make a left onto Farewell St.

8. Pass the White Horse Tavern. *Built some time before 1673, this is claimed to be the oldest continuously operated tavern in the country. State legislators used to meet here in the days when Newport was Rhode Island's capital.* Continuing on Farewell St., you enter the old Colonial district of Newport.

▼

9. Make a left onto Poplar St., near a grocery store. Cross America's Cup Blvd. and continue straight ahead, now passing through an unusually dense concentration of historic homes. *Most of these small houses date to the 17th century, making this an unusual residential neighborhood. Few New England towns can boast as many Colonial homes as there are in just one block of this section of Newport. Many of these houses have intricate private (secret) gardens in their small backyards or adjacent lots.*

10. At Washington St. (where Poplar St. ends), turn right. Pass the Congregational Church and turn right on Willow St. Make the next right onto Second St. and continue straight ahead to the visitors center. *Another option: From Second St., turn left onto Bridge St. Pass the Rhumb Line Restaurant and Tavern, then turn right onto Third St. and walk back to the visitors center.*

PLACES ALONG THE WALK

The number of historic or interesting places passed on this walk is astounding. Besides those listed below, consider visiting the Newport Art Museum, which has a collection of New England paintings, old and new; the Redwood Library, which also houses historic paintings; and Trinity Church, built in 1724 and a block off the walk's route (corner of Spring and Church streets). The architecture alone is worthy of a careful look.

■ **The Elms.** One of seven mansions open to the public through the Preservation Society of Newport County (*see* Other Places Nearby), The Elms was built in 1901 by Edward J. Berwind, who made his fortune in Pennsylvania coal. Don't miss the surrounding grounds. *Bellevue Ave., Newport, RI 02840; tel. 401-847-1000 (Preservation Society). Open daily May-Oct., weekends only in the off-season. Admission.*

■ **The International Tennis Hall of Fame.** Besides a tennis museum, there's the stunning architecture of the

▼

Newport Casino, where the U.S. Open was first held in 1881. Amateur and professional matches are held here during summer, and educational programs (including lessons) are ongoing. *194 Bellevue Ave., Newport, RI; tel. 401-849-3990. Open daily 9:30-5. Admission.*

■ **Touro Synagogue.** The nation's oldest Jewish house of worship, dedicated in 1763, is plain on the outside but has a beautiful interior. *85 Touro St., Newport, RI 02840; tel. 401-847-4794. Open Sun.-Fri. 10-4 in summer, Sun. 1-2:30 in the off-season.*

OTHER PLACES NEARBY

■ **Other mansions.** The Preservation Society of Newport County operates six turn-of-the-century mansions (including The Elms and The Breakers), one colonial mansion built in 1748, and a topiary garden. Call the society for tour information and admission tickets (you can save money with combination packages for multiple sites). *424 Bellevue Ave., Newport, RI 02840; tel. 401-847-1000. Society open Mon.-Fri. 9-5. Mansions' schedules vary.*

■ **Norman Bird Sanctuary.** About 450 acres contain habitat for many kinds of birds and mammals. Rocky ridges in woodlands—including rugged Hanging Rock—create an interesting landscape. There are seven miles of trails, ocean views, ponds, marsh, and a science center. *583 Third Beach Rd., Middletown, RI 02842; tel. 401-846-2577. Open daily in summer 9-5, Wed. evenings until dusk. Other seasons open Tue.-Sun. 9-5.*

DINING

■ **Le Bistro Newport** (expensive). This restaurant offers casual dining in bright second-floor rooms overlooking the wharf. The dinner menu includes seafood and country classics but also some unusual items like grilled south Texas antelope steak with dried cherry *poivreade*, and medallions of wild boar with apples and calvados. In autumn, look for the

▼

wild-game menu. *Bowen's Wharf, Second Fl., Newport, RI 02840; tel. 401-849-7778, 401-849-7750. Open daily for lunch and dinner.*

■ **The Black Pearl** (expensive). Located on the wharf, the tavern portion of this restaurant offers a wide selection of meals ranging from sandwiches to serious entrees. Grilled fish and meats are featured. More formal dining is offered in the Commodore's Room, where you will find choice items like soft-shell crabs and roast duckling. *Bannister's Wharf, Newport, RI 02840; tel. 401-846-5264. Open daily for lunch and dinner. Closed Jan. 15-Feb. 15.*

■ **The White Horse Tavern** (expensive). You walk into this restaurant and enter another time: The building dates to 1673 and has operated as a tavern for most of its long life. Fine   dining is offered in the dining room and drinks in an old bar room. Selections on the dinner menu include appetizers like saute of wild mushrooms, and entrées like baked Atlantic salmon coated in red onions and fried capers, and individual beef Wellington with pâté de fois gras, wrapped in puff pastry and served with *Perigourdine* sauce. Reservations and jacket are required. *Marlborough and Farewell St., Newport, RI 02840; tel. 401-849-3600. Open daily for dinner; Thu.-Sat. for lunch, and Sun. for brunch. A block from Washington Square Park.*

■ **Asterix & Obelix** (moderate). In a converted garage, with outdoor sidewalk tables in summer, this new restaurant serves a unique mix of Mediterranean and Asian cuisine. Popular lunch items are the grilled swordfish club sandwich with sun-dried tomato, and Maryland crab cakes with *rémoulade* sauce. For a dinner appetizer, try firecracker   spring rolls with peanut dipping sauce. Dinner entrées include tandoori chicken, sautéed swordfish, and a Lebanese-style rack of lamb. *599 Thames St., Newport, RI 02840; tel. 401-841-8833. Open daily for dinner. On Lower Thames St. near Wellington Ave.*

▼

■ **Franklin Spa** (inexpensive). Here's a very casual and inexpensive place for breakfast/lunch that is popular with the locals. This classic luncheonette serves a wide variety of omelets and sandwiches (including a fresh turkey sandwich). *229 Spring St., Newport, RI 02840; tel. 401-847-3540. Open daily for breakfast and lunch. On the corner of Franklin St.*

LODGING

Newport has many fine B&Bs, and they are in demand. Prices are high, and weekends typically require minimum stays of two or three days. Other options include hotels in town or chain hotels closer to the main highways.

■ **Elm Tree Cottage** (very expensive). If your fantasy is to stay in a Newport mansion, this B&B is a good choice. The rooms in this 1882 "summer house" vary in decor from opulent to restrained elegance. All six rooms have queen- or king-size beds, private baths, and AC; five have fireplaces. A gourmet breakfast is served at private tables in a large, sunny dining room. The common rooms are huge and offer views over the bay; the parlor has a grand piano (and a guitar). The property is near the Cliff Walk. *336 Gibbs Ave., Newport, RI 02840; tel. 401-849-1610, 800-882-3356; fax 401-849-2084. Closed Jan.-mid Feb. Off Memorial Blvd.*

■ **Sanford-Covell Villa Marina** (expensive). An early Victorian house, located on the shoreline with excellent water views, this B&B is also something of a museum. Inside are antiques (including a dollhouse), ancient clocks, a grand staircase, ceiling paintings, and floors and walls made of various hardwoods. Of the ten rooms, six have private baths, some have fireplaces, and some have water views. Room rates vary considerably—from very expensive to moderate. Breakfast is "full" continental. *72 Washington St., Newport, RI 02840; tel. 401-847-0206. On the harbor north of the visitors center.*

▼

■ **The Francis Malbone House** (very expensive). Built in 1760 and located on the main town road along the harbor, the Francis Malbone House offers exquisite Colonial-style guest rooms. All rooms have private baths and antique furnishings; some have working fireplaces. There's a lot of room in the parlors and in the dining room. A new building matches the style of the old. *392 Thames St., Newport, RI 02840; tel. 401-846-0392, 800-846-0392; fax 401-848-5956.*

■ **The Victorian Ladies** (expensive). Located between the start of the Cliff Walk and downtown, this 11-room Victorian B&B offers large rooms with private baths, comfortable common rooms, an outdoor patio, and friendly hosts. The decor is balanced—it's Victorian without the "flounce." Lodging includes a full breakfast. Rates are considerably lower off-season. *63 Memorial Blvd., Newport, RI 02840; tel. 401-849-9960. Closed Jan.-mid-Feb.*

■ **The Pilgrim House** (moderate). This 11-room, three-story inn is located right in town, close to everything. Rooms have AC and are decorated in Victorian style; 9 have private baths. Although the atmosphere is more like that of an inn, guests can meet in a living room with a fireplace, the upstairs dining room, and a rooftop deck with views of the harbor. A continental breakfast is served. *123 Spring St., Newport, RI 02840; tel. 401-846-0040, 800-525-8373.*

FOR MORE INFORMATION

Tourist Office:

■ **Newport County Convention & Visitors Bureau.** This large and unique visitors center has everything you could want: a film about Newport, tons of flyers, maps, menus, books, gifts, etc. *23 America's Cup Ave., Newport, RI 02840. tel. 800-976-5122. Open daily 9-7 May-Sep., 9-5 Oct.-Apr.*

▼

For Serious Walkers:

The famed Cliff Walk is a magnet for many tourists. It's a 3.5-mile paved path along the rocky edge of the sea, in back of the mansions. Parking is at Easton Beach on Memorial Boulevard, for a fee, or free on town streets. The start is behind the Cliff Walk Manor hotel (117 Memorial Boulevard), though you can access it from Narragansett Avenue. A good 7-mile loop is the Cliff Walk and then back on Bellevue Avenue.

A Remnant of the Ice Age

EXPERIENCE 7: BLOCK ISLAND

Block Island sits between Long Island Sound and the Atlantic Ocean, a location that catches the full force of the ocean's waves as they push into the Sound. Like Nantucket and

---

The Highlights: A charming harbor, beautiful beaches, a lighthouse, dramatic cliffs, old stone walls, and Victorian architecture.

Other Places Nearby: Great nature trails, picturesque inns.

Martha's Vineyard, Block Island is a product of the Ice Age—a pile of sand and stones dumped into the sea by the glacial ice sheet when it melted away.

Three main features distinguish this island: low hills, ponds, and a lack of trees. From the hills, one can see the sea in every direction. In between are as many as 365 freshwater ponds. Before the arrival of Europeans, the island was covered with trees. They were long ago cut down. Today, a few planted trees, and houses and rock walls built from granite boulders loosely mixed in the sandy loam, stand in relief before wide open vistas.

Native Americans inhabited Block Island long before the Europeans. They called it Manisses, the "little island of the god Manitou," a name retained by one of the hotels on the island

▼

today. In 1524, the explorer Verrazano passed by, noting that it was tree-covered, hilly, and occupied. He likened it to the island of Rhodes, a comparison that led to the naming of the state it now belongs to. Almost another century went by before the Dutch fur trader, Adriaen Block, landed there and named it "Adriaen's Eylant." Over the years, it became known by his last name.

Early contacts between the native inhabitants of Block Island and the settlers did not go well there. Captain John Oldham from Boston landed there in 1636 and was killed. The Massachusetts Bay Colony responded by sending in soldiers to punish the Native Americans. Colonel John Endicott, the commanding officer, and his troops spent a few days burning villages, destroying gardens, and stealing baskets; they also killed 14 braves. These actions pushed relations to the breaking point (see Experience 4, Bluff Point). Within a year, control of the island fell to the Bay Colony at Boston.

Title to the island changed hands several times until a small group of settlers bought the island for 400 pounds in 1661 and moved in with families, tools, and livestock. In 1672, they incorporated their settlement as New Shoreham. They shared the island with about a thousand Native Americans, who had their own problems with tribes on the mainland and felt caught between a rock and a hard place. The settlers and the Native Americans established a delicate peace. During the King Philip War, a potential conflict was defused without injury and the island did not see the warfare that occurred on the mainland.

Being well out to sea, Block Island was vulnerable to pirates who would periodically land and plunder. Legend has it that Captain Kidd himself hid treasure here. The islanders were even harassed by the French fleet. Finally, in 1740 and after much prodding, the state issued Block Island a 20-soldier garrison and a six-gun battery for defense.

During the War for Independence, which Block Island supported at the beginning, the General Assembly of Rhode Island decreed that all people should leave the island with their

▼

possessions. Most of the settlers refused to leave, and they continued to live their intensely self-sufficient lifestyle. For this they suffered. The British harassed them, and the mainland refused to trade with them but still taxed them. During the War of 1812, the islanders took a different tack: They declared neutrality. They were free from tax and war duty and made a little profit by selling produce to the British.

Over the years, Block Islanders have lived a rugged, independent life with the sea a constant danger and challenge. To navigate a sailing ship through the strong ocean currents that surge into Long Island Sound requires expert skills and knowledge, and Block Island was well-known for its ship pilots. The youngest master mariner in the Merchant Marine, Rob Lewis, age 25, was from Block Island. Pilot Hill, a high point near Old Harbor and on the walk, is so-named because it is a vista from which ships at sea could be seen. A number of sea pilots are memorialized on an historical marker there.

One important fact about Block Island, one that inhibited rapid full-scale settlement, was that it had no real harbor. During most of its history, boats were tied onto poles set into the Atlantic and had to be removed when storms hit. Not until 1870 was a breakwater built at Old Harbor, and a few years later New Harbor was constructed out of the Great Salt Pond. At the same time, New Shoreham changed its name to Block Island, and the tourist wave began to "The Bermuda of the North." Steamers from New York and major New England cities arrived on regular schedules. The grand hotel era was on.

The rise of automobile travel, World War I, and the Depression killed the resort business, and soon the island lapsed back into its traditional self-sufficiency. During World War II, the island was a watchpost for enemy ships and submarines. Five concrete lookouts were built on the island that could relay any sightings to the mainland, where

▼

16-inch guns stood ready with a shelling range of 25 miles. On the last day of the war, a German U-boat was sunk right off Block Island. The wreck of this submarine is now a favorite diving area.

After World War II, the tourists came back. In 1960, a proposal to allow gambling on the island troubled the residents so much they threatened to secede. The measure was defeated. In 1971, residents enacted a moratorium on subdivisions. Today, 25 percent of Block Island is preserved in its natural state or protected from development. Three main groups work together toward this end: the private Block Island Conservancy, the public Block Island Land Trust, and the national Nature Conservancy. The result is beautiful scenery and outstanding walking opportunities.

GETTING THERE
By ferry:
The walk described below assumes that you've taken a ferry from the Rhode Island mainland to Block Island's Old Harbor. The most frequent ferry service, from Point Judith, arrives there, as does the service from Newport and Providence., as well as from New London, CT. For ferry information, *see* For More Information.

Walk Directions

TIME: 2 1/2 hours
LEVEL: Easy
DISTANCE: 3 1/2 miles
ACCESS: By ferry

This walk begins and ends at the ferry landing in Old Harbor. The first segment of the walk is quite popular with tourists, primarily because a car is not needed and few travelers bring their car to the island. The walk first follows a paved road that may be more congested with walkers (for the 1.5-mile walk to Southeast Lighthouse) than with cars. Direct contact with the sea is possible in two places: near the beginning of the walk at Pebbly Beach (just past the Spring House Hotel), and at Mohegan Bluffs. The walk back is partly on a gravel road and is much quieter. Throughout its length, the walk gives exposure to some of the scenic delights of Block Island. There is much more to see for the traveler who stays for a few days. Other points of interest on the island require, in most cases, a taxi, a moped, or a bicycle. The walk route also is suitable for bicycles.

TO BEGIN

Depart the ferry at the docks and walk straight ahead to Water St., the main street on which you'll find most stores and hotels. Turn left here and walk to the three-way junction where, in the center of the intersection, you'll see the statue of Rebecca. *Her troughs formerly served water to animals but today are planted with flowers.*

1. At this junction, proceed ahead onto Spring St., keeping the Harbor Church on your left. Ahead, on your right will be the Hotel Manisses. As you crest the hill, the Spring House Hotel will be on your right. Continue following the road that gains in elevation and becomes South East Light Rd. As you walk along a stretch of stone walls and rose bushes, you see the lighthouse straight ahead.

2. Arrive at a path to Southeast Lighthouse. *Alongside the road, near the path to the lighthouse, is a historical society marker commemorating the many ships that have gone down in this area of navigational danger. The lighthouse was recently moved to prevent its falling off the continuously eroding cliffs (see Places Along the Walk).* After examining the lighthouse, go back to the road, turn left, and walk for only a minute or two down the road.

KEY

Walk follows paved road

Walk follows dirt road or footpath

Paved road

Dirt road or footpath

Town or village

Wooded area

Old Harbor

Water Street

BEGIN/END

Harbor Church

Ballard's Beach

1

6

7

Spring Street

Pebbly Beach

High Street

Pilot Hill Road

Pilot Hill

Historical Marker

5

BILL PAYNE'S SWAMP

JOHN E. TUG HOLE

Historical Marker

2

The Whale Swamp

3

4

Southeast Lighthouse

Mohegan Bluffs

ATLANTIC OCEAN

¼   ½

MILE

N

GETTING THERE

RI
CT

95

112

1

2 West Kingston

108

Jamestown

1

Newport

108

Point Judith

Ferry

5 miles

BLOCK ISLAND

▼

3. Make a left onto the dirt path to Mohegan Bluffs. *Here, 163 feet above the ocean, at the Edward S. Payne Overlook, are your best views of the eroding cliffs.* A wooden set of stairs brings you down to the pebbly shoreline. *This natural area is owned and maintained by the Nature Conservancy. The erosive action of the sea is steadily chipping away at the bluffs, where one can see the various types of soil and loose rock that make up the island. A historical monument commemorates a battle in 1590 when a war party of Mohegans were driven off these cliffs by the Manissean Block Island Indians.*

After visiting the bluffs, walk back out to the paved road and turn left.

4. After five or ten minutes of walking, you come to a place where the road makes a sharp turn to the left. A small pond is on your left. Turn right onto a sand and gravel road, Pilot Hill Rd. Pass John E. Tug Hole, a pond on your left, as you walk along the quiet lane lined with stone walls and surrounded by pasture and an occasional house.

5. When you reach a high point, where you find the Pilot Hill historical marker, bear right onto pavement. Ahead is a vista of Old Harbor and the northeastern shore of the island. The Block Island School will appear on your left as you walk toward town.

6. After you pass a pond on your left, go right onto a lane marked by a sign for the Atlantic Inn and the Rose Farm Inn.

7. Arrive in front of the Atlantic Inn. Turn left and head down over a lawn toward a large animal pen, the farm zoo maintained by the Hotel Manisses and the 1661 Inn. Continue along the lane, now with the farm zoo's fence to your left, and arrive at the Hotel Manisses and Spring St. Turn left (Point 1) and walk back to Old Harbor.

PLACES ALONG THE WALK

■ **Southeast Lighthouse.** Built in 1875, this large brick lighthouse attached to a house was moved in one piece in 1993 about 250 feet from the steadily eroding cliffs that threatened to destroy it. The Coast Guard, the Army Corps of Engineers, the National Trust for Historic Preservation, the state of Rhode Island, the town of New Shoreham, and the Southeast Light Foundation contributed to the rescue effort. The light has a fresnel lens, originally imported from France for $10,000, and is visible for 45 miles at sea. At 204 feet above the sea, the Southeast light is the highest and strongest one on the Atlantic coast. *Tours are available several times daily, Jul. 4-Labor Day.*

DINING

■ **Hotel Manisses** (expensive). Considered by many to be Block Island's finest restaurant, the hotel serves dinner in two dining rooms and on the deck. A nearby garden supplies vegetables and herbs. The creative menu features smoked fish and meats for appetizers, as well as seafood, beef, pork, and veal entrées. *Spring St., Block Island; tel. 401-466-2836. Open daily for dinner. Closed Nov.-May 14. A short walk from Old Harbor.*

■ **Ballard's Inn** (moderate). Ballard's is an inn, a beach, a party place, and a restaurant. The dining room is monstrous, with flags hanging overhead, and there's a stage and a huge bar. Stop in for casual seafood dining (try lobster) and entertainment at night. *Block Island, RI 02807; tel. 401-466-2231, 401-334-1997. Open daily for lunch and dinner mid-May-mid-Oct. Turn left after you arrive on the ferry.*

■ **Mohegan Cafe** (moderate). Located on Water Street and facing the harbor, this restaurant is popular and usually quite busy. The menu features seafood, pasta, and steaks, with some very creative adaptations. The seafood chowder won the 1994 Block

▼

Island chowderfest cookoff. The dining area, while a little crowded, is casual and friendly. *Water St., Block Island, RI; tel. 401-466-5911. Open daily for lunch and dinner. Located in Old Harbor.*

LODGING

■ **The 1661 Inn and Hotel Manisses** (very expensive). The 1661 Inn (named for the year Block Island was discovered), the Hotel Manisses (after the Native American name for the island), and two cottages are owned by the same family. The 1661 Inn is a restored guest house, the Manisses a restored Victorian hotel. Everything is first class: precise restoration, fine dining, ocean views, an animal farm and garden, along with an excellent location. *1 Spring St., Block Island, RI 02807; tel. 401-466-2421, 800-626-4773, fax 401-466-2858. Just south of Old Harbor.*

■ **Eastgate House** (very expensive). One of the most luxurious, beautifully situated B&Bs anywhere in New England, with high prices to match. It offers two huge rooms, elegant decor, and great views. *433 Spring St., Block Island, RI 02807, tel. 401-466-2164. Open year-round. Located on the walk route.*

■ **The Sea Breeze Inn** (expensive). Once a boarding house, this collection of small wood houses offers 10 rooms, five with private baths. A suite offers particularly good views, and patrons in the know request Room 10. *Spring St., Box 141, Block Island, RI 02807; tel. 401-466-2275. Located along the walk.*

■ **Helterline's B&B** (expensive). The quiet setting adjacent to a great area for walking, along with the ability to rent two very comfortable rooms together with a private entrance, make this a great choice for families. *Corn Neck Rd., Box 576, Block Island, RI 02807; tel. 401-466-2156. North of Old Harbor.*

■ **The Rose Farm Inn** (expensive). Two buildings—an 1897 farmhouse with eight rooms, and a new building, the Captain Rose House, with nine rooms—make up this inn. All rooms have private or semi-private baths, and some have whirlpools. The rooms in the Captain Rose House have private entrances. A light breakfast buffet is served. *P.O. Box E, Block Island, RI 02807; tel. 401-466-2034, fax 401-466-2053. Open May-Oct. Along the walk, off of High St.*

FOR MORE INFORMATION

Tourist Offices:

■ **Block Island Chamber of Commerce.** This office provides tourist information, including ferry schedules, and operates a booth facing the ferry dock. *Drawer D, Block Island, RI 02807; tel. 401-466-2982, 800-383-2474. Open daily year-round , except Sun. Booth open daily May-Sep. for ferry arrivals.*

■ **Interstate Navigation Co.** This company operates all the ferries to Block Island, from Point Judith (year-round), Providence/Newport (late June to early September), and New London, CT (early June to early September). You must call to make a reservation for a car on the ferry. *P.O. Box 482, New London, CT, 06320; tel. 401-783-4613.*

For Serious Walkers:

Block Island is a walker's paradise, with miles of gravel lanes and footpaths, outstanding vistas, and few cars. The island is so small that it can be explored entirely by foot. Especially recommended walking areas are the Clay Head nature trails in the northern part of the island, and the Black Rock Road area in the southwest.

The Colonel and the Cobble

EXPERIENCE 8: BARTHOLOMEW'S COBBLE

Most people traveling through the Berkshire Hills are looking to shop or enjoy the scenic villages, farms, and mountains. Many visitors never notice the Housatonic, the Berkshires' major river, which you'll walk alongside during this walking tour. The Housatonic flows

The Highlights: Luxuriant meadows and forest next to a river where Native Americans lived, pastoral vistas over valley and farmland.

Other Places Nearby: Stockbridge and other unique southern Berkshires towns, an antiques center, excellent B&Bs, fine dining, the Norman Rockwell museum, a botanical garden.

through Pittsfield and then turns south through Stockbridge and the southern Berkshires' largest town, Great Barrington, on its way to Connecticut. Native Americans lived along this river at what is now Great Barrington in a village called Mahaiwe—a name that today graces a movie theater downtown.

South of Great Barrington, the river comes to Sheffield, a very small village that's primarily a strip of colonial houses along Route 7. Sheffield has more antique shops than any other town in the region, as well as fine bed-and-breakfasts. It makes a wonderful base camp for explorations of the area.

▼

Below Sheffield, at the Connecticut border, the Housatonic passes the very small village of Ashley Falls, named for the most distinguished citizen of the region in colonial times, Colonel John Ashley. A Yale graduate, businessman, lawyer, and patriot, Ashley moved to the area when it was wilderness, after the Massachusetts court granted settlement petitions in 1722. The Native Americans were "compensated" for their land with 460 British pounds, 3 barrels of cider, and 30 quarts of rum. Ashley built his house in 1735 and became famous for his community involvement in Sheffield, his service in the French and Indian Wars, and his entrepreneurial activities.

Ashley is also remembered for an early "declaration of independence." Being pioneers, the residents of today's lower Berkshire County had little or no tolerance of British interference in their business. In 1773, Ashley chaired an 11-member committee that met in the study of his house and produced a list of statements that has come to be known as the Sheffield Declaration. This text, which preceded Jefferson's Declaration of Independence, became known throughout the colonies. In 1774, Ashley chaired a convention of 60 delegates in the region who met and wrote a "league and covenant" to boycott British goods and all merchants who didn't go along with the Sheffield Declaration.

Another story concerning Ashley involves an experience with one of his slaves. The slave, Mum Bet, took a blow on her arm from a shovel while defending her sister from Ashley's raging wife. The slave left the household and refused to return. Colonel Ashley took her to court but dropped his case after finding that the Massachusetts Bill of Rights—which stated "all men are born free and equal"—had been adopted. This was the first test of the law, and Mum Bet was the first Massachusetts slave legally set free.

Ashley's house still stands in excellent condition and is located within a half mile of Bartholomew's Cobble, the site of this walking tour. You can visit the house and its interesting

▼

rooms and period furnishings on a side trip from the walking route outlined below, or by car after the walk.

The Cobble was originally part of Ashley's property. In the late 19th century, the land was owned by George Bartholomew, whose name has been retained at the site. In 1946, the Trustees of Reservations, a group dedicated to preserving natural and historic areas of the state, acquired the property. It was designated a National Natural Landmark by the National Park Service in 1971.

The Cobble (an old English name for a rock outcropping) is basically a limestone rise overlooking the Housatonic River. From the Cobble and from other parts of the property are wonderful views of the river valley. Farming is an ongoing activity, and walkers should not be surprised to encounter cows or farmers haying in the pastures that alternate with woodlands.

Like many river valleys, Bartholomew's Cobble harbors many life forms. There are more than 800 species of plants and more forest types than anywhere else in Berkshire County. In early spring, you'll find exotic wildflowers such as the trillium and Dutchman's breeches, but many find the variety of ferns that grow in the shaded rocky clefts the most interesting. More than 240 species of birds have been sighted, lured by the Cobble's substantial amount of grassland.

From the high spot on Hurlburt's Hill that you'll ascend on this walking tour, it's clear why this area was chosen for settlement many years ago. It's a beautiful place with farmlands and a meandering river next to high mountains.

GETTING THERE
By car:

Drive to Great Barrington, which is located on Rte. 7 in the southwestern corner of Massachusetts. From downtown Great Barrington, drive south on Rte. 7 for 7.9 mi. and turn right onto Rte. 7A (Ashley Falls/Bartholomew's Cobble). Drive 1/2 mi.

▼

and turn right onto Rannapo Road (cross over railroad tracks). Go 1.4 mi. to a junction at Cooper Hill Rd. Turn left, proceed 100 yards, and then turn right onto Weatogue Rd. Parking for the Cobble is located 0.1 mi. ahead on the left.

Walk Directions

TIME: 2 1/2 hours
LEVEL: Easy
DISTANCE: 3 miles
ACCESS: By car

You'll walk on a level footpath up to Point 4 and then proceed up a hill. If you want to shorten the walk, continue straight ahead (instead of turning left) at Point 4, and you'll be back to your car in a few minutes. At Point 7, you can picnic in a clearing on the Massachusetts-Connecticut border while savoring the mountain and valley views. Buy picnic provisions in Sheffield or Great Barrington shops. **Throughout the walk, stay on the footpath because poison ivy abounds in the fields nearby.**

TO BEGIN

From the parking area, go to the visitors center, pay a fee, pick up a map, and proceed to the left of the visitors center to the beginning of a wide trail.

1. At a junction, take the Ledges Trail straight, which leads into the Cobble. Continue ahead through the woods, ignoring a trail on your left. *The air temperature will suddenly drop as you enter this unique hemlock forest dominated by limestone outcrops alive with ferns. The visual effect of the combination of evergreen trees, gray rock, and light green ferns is that of a tall rock garden.* Follow the steps with a handrail that lead you down and closer to the Housatonic River.

2. Arrive at the junction with the Cedar Hill Trail.

▼

Continue on the Ledges Trail which again follows close to the river. *The trail is lined with jewelweed, a natural remedy for **poison ivy that also grows in the vicinity**. A "cow-proof" opening alongside the path allows for exploration of the river's edge.* Proceed up steps. Ignore a trail on the left and follow a trail to the right of a bench.

3. At a clearing, arrive at a sign for the Bailey Trail (that goes off to the left). **Stay on the trail because poison ivy abounds in the field.** You will return to this junction later, but now continue straight ahead along the Ledges Trail. *The big mountain to your left in the distance (with a tower on the summit) is Mt. Everett, or "The Dome."*

4. At a trail junction adjacent to a road, leave the Ledges Trail and turn left (crossing the road) onto the trail for Hurlburt's Hill. Ignore the Boulder Trail to your left. Follow the lane along the edge of a field and re-enter the woods, following a sign pointing to Borland Trail.

5. Arrive at a junction with the Borland Trail. *This trail leads to the right and downhill, arriving in about a half mile at the Colonel Ashley House. Some walkers may wish to take this side trip, but the house is more easily reached by a road walk or by car after this walk.*

If you decide not to head directly to the house, ignore the Borland Trail and continue straight ahead on the lane that climbs Hurlburt's Hill. You cross an edge of a field.

6. At a clearing, notice the junction with the Tulip Tree Trail. This will be your return trail. Ignore it and continue up the hill. Proceed across a field of tall grass.

7. Arrive at benches on Hurlburt's Hill. *The vista from this point, located just several yards from the Connecticut border,*

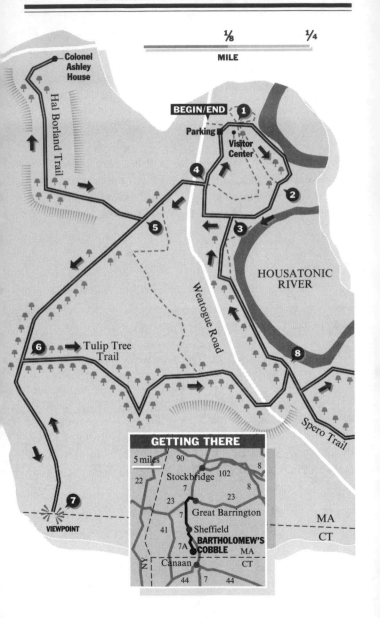

⅛   ¼
MILE

Colonel Ashley House

Hal Borland Trail

BEGIN/END ①

Parking

Visitor Center

④

②

③

⑤

HOUSATONIC RIVER

⑥ → Tulip Tree Trail

Weatogue Road

⑧

Spero Trail

⑦

VIEWPOINT

GETTING THERE

5 miles   90

22   Stockbridge   102   8

7   8

23   23

7   Great Barrington

41   Sheffield

7A   **BARTHOLOMEW'S COBBLE**   MA

MA

CT

NY   Canaan   CT

44   7   44

▼

includes Mt. Race and Mt. Everett to the west and the Housatonic Valley to the north. In late June, you'll often see haying activities. After taking in the views, return to Point 6, the junction with the Tulip Tree Trail.

N

KEY

- **Walk follows paved road**
- **Walk follows dirt road or footpath**
- **Paved road**
- **Dirt road or footpath**
- **Town or village**
- **Wooded area**

Turn right onto the Tulip Tree Trail. This trail has some square white markers and leads you into deeper woods. When the trail turns sharply to the left, *notice a monster tulip tree, said to be 120 feet tall.*

Continue downhill past the junction with the Boulder Trail, cross the road, and continue downhill to a trail junction.

8. When you reach a junction with the Bailey Trail, turn right onto the Spero Trail, a loop trail that explores an open area along the river and a wooded area above it. At a Spero Loop sign, turn left and follow another white-blazed trail. When you emerge out of the woods at a clearing, turn right and take the Sterling and Louise Spero Trail, following white markers. Pass the Spiro Loop sign.

Return to the junction at Point 8 and go straight on the Bailey Trail along the river to the Ledges Trail at Point 3, encountered earlier in the walk. Turn left at this junction and walk parallel to the road, passing Point 4 back to the parking area.

PLACES ALONG THE WALK
■ **Colonel John Ashley House.** Look for the walls with carved paneling in the upstairs study, where the Sheffield

Declaration was written. *Cooper Hill Rd., Ashley Falls, MA 01222; tel. 413-229-8600. Open weekends and Mon. holidays Memorial Day-Columbus Day. Guided tours 1-5. Admission.*

OTHER PLACES NEARBY

■ **Stockbridge.** A focal point for many tourists, the Stockbridge area has several "cottages" (former summer homes of the wealthy) and other historic homes that are open to the public for a fee. Among them are Chesterwood, the summer estate of sculptor Daniel Chester French, and Naumkeag (with its extensive gardens), which was built for Joseph Choate, a lawyer and an ambassador to England. *On Rte. 7, 18 mi. north of Ashley Falls.*

■ **The Berkshire Botanical Garden.** There are herb and perennial gardens, a daffodil meadow, and a woodland trail. Picnickers are welcome. *Rtes. 102 and 183, Stockbridge, MA 01262; tel. 413-298-3926. Open daily 10-5 May-Oct. Admission. West of Stockbridge near the Norman Rockwell Museum; 20 mi. from Ashley Falls.*

■ **The Norman Rockwell Museum at Stockbridge.** Norman Rockwell lived much of his life in Stockbridge, and this museum, which includes his studio, contains the world's largest collection of his paintings and illustrations. *Rte. 183, Stockbridge, MA 01262; tel. 413-298-4100. Museum open daily 10-5 May-Oct.; weekdays 10-4 and weekends 10-5 Nov.-Apr. Rockwell's studio open May-Oct. Admission. Near the junction of Rts. 183 and 102, 20 mi. from Ashley Falls.*

DINING

There are many fine places to dine in the southern Berkshires, particularly along Route 7 and Route 23. Listed below are only a sampling.

■ **Castle Street Cafe** (expensive). The emphasis in this casual streetside restaurant is clearly on the food. Chef-owner Michael Ballon uses only fresh ingredients from local producers. Entrées include game hen, trout, and scallops. There are

▼

several vegetarian meals on the menu, homemade desserts, and a fine bar featuring a good wine selection. *10 Castle St., Great Barrington, MA 01230; tel. 413-528-5244. Open daily except Tue. for dinner. Off Main St., next to the movie theater.*

■ **The Old Mill** (expensive). The main dining room of this restored 1797 gristmill is a former blacksmith shop. With exposed beams and high-backed wooden chairs, the restaurant is Spartan, yet appealing. Expect entrées such as grilled salmon over penne, pan-roasted cod, filet mignon, and grilled mixed vegetables with polenta cakes. *Rte. 23, South Egremont, MA 01258; tel. 413-528-1421. Open daily for dinner. West of Rte. 7.*

■ **The Painted Lady** (expensive). There's high-quality northern Italian and continental cuisine in this small but comfortable Victorian-style restaurant that's considered the area's best by many locals. There's an eight-item menu, including grilled filet mignon with herb sauce, that changes every few weeks. No credit cards. *785 South Main St., Great Barrington, MA 01230; tel. 413-528-1662. Open daily for dinner. On Rte. 7, between Sheffield and Great Barrington.*

■ **Barrington Brewery & Restaurant** (moderate). This pub brews quality beer in what appears to be sacred tanks, visible to bar patrons. The beer is the attraction (don't miss the bargain sampler), but hungry customers can choose from a menu that includes various sandwiches, burgers, and salads, and after 5 p.m., dinner entrées such as Porterhouse steak and tuna steak. Try the brewer's pocket—spinach, turkey, bacon, sprouts, blue cheese dressing and melted Swiss cheese on a pita. *Jenifer House Commons, Rte. 7, Great Barrington, MA; tel. 413-528-8282. Open daily for lunch and dinner. North of Great Barrington.*

■ **20 Railroad Street** (inexpensive). Open for two decades, this pub is popular with locals and tourists. On the menu are salads, sandwiches, and burgers. There's an old 28-foot mahogany bar that once graced the Commodore Hotel in New York City. *20 Railroad St., Great Barrington, MA; tel. 413-528-9345. Open daily for lunch and dinner.*

▼

LODGING

Sheffield, about four miles north of Bartholomew's Cobble, is home to many B&Bs, most catering to the antique-buying crowd. Guest houses accustomed to walkers and hikers are found along Under Mountain Road, which runs from Egremont to Salisbury. You can also choose one of the nearby lodging options in Experience 1, Bear Mountain.

■ **Ivanhoe Country House** (moderate). A fresh-mowed lawn, a pool, and Golden Retrievers greet you at this inn with its back to a mountain. All nine rooms have private baths, including three with a fireplace and two with a kitchenette. A continental breakfast is brought to the room. Guests can read or converse in the expansive Chestnut Room with its library table and fireplace. Dogs are welcome. *254 S. Under Mountain Rd., Rte. 41, Sheffield, MA 01257; tel. 413-229-2143. Just south of Berkshire School Rd.*

■ **Race Brook Lodge** (moderate). A large restored barn is the centerpiece of this rustic 21 guest-room (all with private bath) country retreat surrounded by a brook and a forest. Rooms are decorated with quilts and rugs, and some have lofts that are suitable for children. Cottages are available for larger groups. A hearty buffet breakfast is served, and light lunches or dinners can be arranged for groups. *864 Under Mountain Rd., Rte. 41, Sheffield, MA 01257; tel. 413-229-2916. Between the Connecticut border and Berkshire School Rd.*

■ **Stavleigh House** (moderate). Built in 1821, this house is kept in top condition. The ambience is delightfully old-fashioned, and the five guest rooms are decorated in traditional style. A full breakfast and afternoon tea are served. Enjoy the shade under the huge trees on the wide lawn. No credit cards. *South Main St., Rte. 7, Sheffield, MA 01257; tel. 413-229-2129. Next to the town green.*

■ **The Berkshire 1802 House** (moderate). The 1802 House is historic but casual, and the hosts are friendly. A full breakfast (with a few choices) is served in either the dining room or the screened-in porch. There are seven air-conditioned

▼

bedrooms, five with private bathrooms. *P.O. Box 395, 48 South Main St., Sheffield, MA 01257; tel. 413-229-2612.*

FOR MORE INFORMATION
Tourist Office:
■ **Southern Berkshire Chamber of Commerce.** *362 Main St., Great Barrington, MA 01230; tel. 413-528-1510, 413-528-4006 (lodging information). Open Tue.-Sat. 9-5.*

For Serious Walkers:
There are many places to explore, particularly in the Taconic plateau region (*see* Experience 1, Bear Mountain). Recommended are the hike to Alander Mountain (with its excellent views over the Hudson River valley and the not-so-distant Catskills) and Bash Bish Falls. Monument Mountain, another Trustees of Reservations property (on Route 7, about four miles north of Great Barrington), makes a great day hike.

A Mountain for Everyone

EXPERIENCE 9: MOUNT GREYLOCK

As you walk on lush Mount Greylock, notice that it has several summits, including one at just under 3,500 feet—the highest elevation in Massachusetts. Along its southern ridge, called Saddle Ball Mountain, stands a three-mile

> **The Highlights:** Magnificent vistas from the state's highest point, the mountain that inspired *Moby Dick,* a boreal forest.
>
> **Other Places Nearby:** Two art museums, a science center, an aquarium, top restaurants, an historic college.

stretch of boreal forest (a northern forest consisting mostly of spruce and fir), the only one in the state. Through this moist evergreen woods in Massachusetts' northwestern corner, the Appalachian Trail passes on its way north to Maine. The wild, remote forest suddenly terminates at a clearing atop Greylock's highest peak, which often teems with visitors who have arrived by car. It's a stark contrast, pointing out that both preservationists and developers—who have warred with each other for a century—have their places on this huge mountain.

Before Greylock, the mountain was called Grand Hoosac—the name of the Native Americans who were a sub-tribe of the Mahicans. Pittsfield settlers, however, called the mountain

▼

Saddleback because of its appearance. How Greylock came to be the accepted name is unclear. One tradition says that the name of an Indian chief, Gray-Lock, was bestowed on the mountain. Another states that mists around the summit, a common occurrence, gave rise to the name. Apparently, the gray clouds were likened to a lock of hair.

There are a number of interesting features on the Greylock massif that have interesting names. On the west side is an enormous gulf or valley called the Hopper, which is closed in on three sides by mountains. It was so named because its shape looks like a coal or grain hopper. Although it is a product of drainage, it was probably enlarged by glacial ice during the Ice Age. Today, most of the Hopper is a natural area that's open to hikers. Nearby Money Brook was named for a counterfeit gang that supposedly worked in the area. Bellows Pipe, the hollow between Greylock and Ragged Mountain, is a natural conduit for the winds, hence its name. Jones Nose, the starting point of your walk, was named for the man who cleared and farmed the land.

At an elevation of 2,500 feet, Jones Nose is quite high for a farm. But farming took place on Mount Greylock well into the 19th century, and much of the lower portions of the mountain were cleared. By the middle of that century, the demand for wood pulp and charcoal was running high, and many more trees were cut down. After the logging led to severe erosion, local business people formed the Greylock Park Association in 1885 and bought the summit area for recreational purposes. The group was not environmentally conscious but solely interested in saving the mountain to generate revenue from recreation.

As early as 1830, an observation tower stood on Mount Greylock's summit. It was built in one day by a hundred or more Williams College students who cut a trail up from the

▼

Hopper. (Williams College has long had a special relationship with the mountain; many geology professors have taken students there to study nature.) A second tower—three stories high—was built in 1841. By then, the summit was attracting many visitors, including Henry David Thoreau, who slept on the summit in 1844. Other New England writers and artists also noticed Greylock. Ralph Waldo Emerson called it "a serious mountain," and Nathaniel Hawthorne hiked through the Bellows Pipe. Herman Melville's home in Pittsfield looked out to Greylock, which looks like an enormous white whale in winter. Melville, the author of *Moby Dick*, dedicated one of his lesser-known novels to "Greylock's most excellent majesty."

In Williamstown—just a short distance from Greylock—the first organized hiking club in America was formed in 1863. Of the 12 founding members of the Alpine Club, nine were women, and one was a founding member of the Appalachian Trail Club 13 years later. The Alpine Club, which existed for three years, hiked and camped on Greylock, in Vermont, and in New Hampshire's White Mountains.

During the same era, a toll road from the north was built to Greylock's summit. By 1896, with the support of the Greylock Park Association, a road to the summit from the south was built, and a new metal tower, a house, outbuildings, and tennis courts were constructed on the summit. The park association wasn't able to generate enough money from visitors, however, and gave the mountaintop to the State of Massachusetts. The Mount Greylock Reservation became the first state-owned mountain park, although it was run by appointed commissioners from Berkshire County.

One of the commissioners was John Bascom, who put tremendous energy into the creation of a summit lodge for hikers. Unfortunately, he died before the lodge that is named for him was built during the 1930s by the Civilian Conservation Corps. Other commissioners improved the roads to the summit and built a new tower—a lighthouse dedicated to the fallen soldiers of World War I.

During the 1930s, the sport of Alpine skiing also began to take form in the United States—on the slopes of Greylock. Down the eastern slope, the Civilian Conservation Corps built a ski run named the Thunderbolt Trail that descended 2,175 feet in 1.6 miles. For 20 years, major ski races were held there.

In 1964, conservationists began a battle against businessmen seeking to develop the mountain. The commissioners of Greylock Reservation, who were supposed to protect the mountain, leased part of it to a group that intended to transform the mountain into a major resort with full-scale Alpine skiing. The world's largest aerial tramway was to take visitors to the summit. Lawsuits followed, and they dragged on for decades. Today, the controversy still hasn't been settled. Both developers and townspeople in nearby Adams and North Adams, hard hit by the decline of industry, look to the mountain as a source of revenue. But walkers, hikers, and conservationists want to leave the mountain alone. On your walk, you'll see the results of both perspectives.

GETTING THERE
By car:
Drive to Lanesboro, located north of Pittsfield in northwestern Massachusetts. To reach the Jones Nose parking area from Rte. 7 in Lanesboro—3 mi. north of the Pittsfield town line—pass signs for the Mt. Greylock Reservation and Bascom Lodge and turn right onto North Main St. Coming south from Williamstown, you make a left at this turnoff, located 12 mi. south of the junction of Rtes. 2 and 7. After you have turned onto North Main St. from either direction, make a right, following signs for Rockwell Rd. and Greylock Reservation. Then turn left onto Rockwell Rd. Follow the road past the visitors center, which offers various publications and maps, and proceed 3.8 mi. to the large parking area at Jones Nose on the right side of the road.

▼

The long spine of Mt. Greylock is also traversed by paved road: Notch Rd. from the north to the summit, and Rockwell Rd. from the south to the summit.

Walk Directions

TIME: 4 hours
LEVEL: Moderate to difficult
DISTANCE: 7.2 miles
ACCESS: By car

The beginning is rocky and steep, but you don't have to be an expert to complete this walk. The trail levels off, and the footing is sure. After you reach the mountaintop, you will retrace your steps back to the car. If you'd like to shorten the walk, proceed to Point 2 or Point 4 and then head back to your car. You can also cut the walk in half by leaving a car (or arranging pickup) at the summit. If you prefer walking downhill, reverse the directions below, starting atop Greylock at Point 7 and leaving a vehicle at the Jones Nose parking area. At the summit, visit the Bascom Lodge which is owned by the state but run by the Appalachian Mountain Club. You can buy maps and books or stop at a small kitchen that sells sandwiches. It's a good place for lunch in a rustic setting with a vast panorama out the window.

TO BEGIN

Find the trail head for the Jones Nose Trail on the north side of the parking area and walk through a cleverly constructed wooden gate that keeps vehicles off the path. A short walk uphill leads to an open field with spectacular views in every direction. *The ski area to the west is Brodie Mountain, which is famous for making lots of green snow on St. Patrick's Day. Facing you to the north is the abutment of Jones Nose. The eastern vista includes the Kitchen Brook ridge and drainage area.*

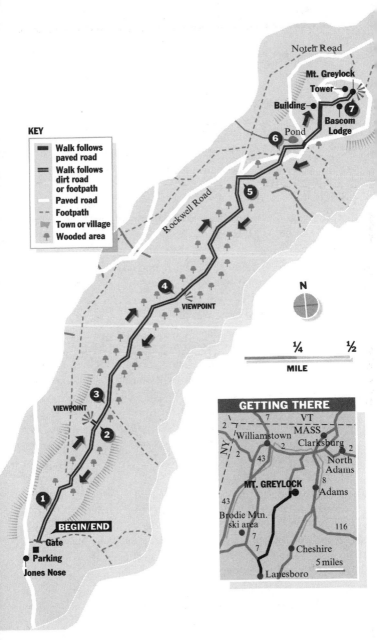

KEY

- Walk follows paved road
- Walk follows dirt road or footpath
- Paved road
- Footpath
- Town or village
- Wooded area

Notch Road

Mt. Greylock
Tower
Building
Bascom Lodge
Pond

7

6

5

Rockwell Road

4
VIEWPOINT

N

¼   ½
MILE

3
VIEWPOINT

2

1

BEGIN/END

Gate
Parking
Jones Nose

GETTING THERE

7   VT
2   MASS
Williamstown   Clarksburg
2   2
43
North Adams
8
MT. GREYLOCK   Adams
43
Brodie Mtn. ski area   116
7
7   Cheshire
5 miles
Lanesboro

▼

Follow the pathway north through the field.

1. When you reach the edge of the forest, follow the blue-marked Jones Nose Trail into the woods. Continue on the trail as it turns and ascends steeply. When the trail levels off somewhat, you reach a junction with the C.C.C. Dynamite Foot and Ski Trail. Continue on the Jones Nose Trail, following signs to Greylock's summit. Proceed on the trail as it climbs steeply into the boreal forest.

2. At the next level area, leave the trail and walk on a short footpath on the left that leads to an outstanding western vista of the Taconic Plateau, the Taconic Mountains, and, far in the distance, the Catskill Mountains. *This is one of the best viewpoints on Mt. Greylock, so be sure to absorb the beauty of the scenery.* Return to the trail and continue on as it climbs steeply to the top of the Saddle Ball Mountain ridge.

3. The Jones Nose Trail ends at a junction with the Appalachian Trail and Old Adams Rd., which is on the right. From this point, Greylock's summit is at least an hour away. Turn left and follow the white markers of the Appalachian Trail northward on the quiet, windy ridge top cloaked in boreal forest. *Clintonia, hobblebush, and milk-white quartz are a few of the features in this lush, green, and pleasant-smelling environment.*

4. Arrive at a small opening in the forest that offers a view of Greylock's summit. *If you wish to shorten the walk and return to the Jones Nose parking area, this is a good turnaround point.* Continue on the path northward, occasionally on boardwalks that span sphagnum moss bogs and small streams. Pass a newly cleared vista facing the summit.

5. At a paved road, turn right. Ignore a dirt road on the

▼

right and then make the next right turn onto a footpath, following the white markers. When you meet the paved road in another 10 minutes, cross it.

6. Pass the junction with the Hopper Trail on your left. Continue on and pass a pond that is the water supply for the buildings at the summit. When you reach a junction of roads, turn left. Follow signs directing you to Greylock's summit and back onto the Appalachian Trail, which proceeds directly to the summit. Continue uphill for about 10 minutes.

7. When you pass a utility building that's on your left, follow the Appalachian Trail straight ahead. Cross a paved road and walk by trees and bushes for 150 feet. You arrive at a summit clearing, facing a monument and Bascom Lodge.

To return to your car, retrace your steps. Follow the white markers of the Appalachian Trail for about an hour and then turn right onto the blue-blazed Jones Nose Trail. If you need to descend Greylock quicker, you can return to the road intersection in Point 6 and walk on Rockwell Rd. to your car. Though this route offers several outstanding views and takes about 75 minutes, it's not recommended. The road can be loaded with cars, particularly in the summer.

OTHER PLACES NEARBY

■ **Williamstown.** This scenic town is home to Williams College, one of the nation's top liberal arts colleges. Besides visiting the art museum, the shops, and the restaurants, enjoy the views of farmland, forest, and mountains. *Northwest of Mt. Greylock at the junction of Rtes. 2 and 7.*

■ **Sterling and Francine Clark Art Institute.** This art museum contains a very large collection of French Impressionist paintings, including more than 30 by Renoir. You'll also find the works of American artists such as Homer and Cassatt, and a major art library. *225 South St.,*

▼

Williamstown, MA 01267; tel. 413-458-9545. Open Tue.-Sun. (daily Jun.-Jul.) 10-5. 1/4 mi. south of the junction of Rtes. 2 and 7.

■ **The Berkshire Museum.** This very interesting art, natural science, and history museum houses an outstanding collection of paintings, including many of the Hudson River School. The large science section has exhibits ranging from local animals to dinosaur fossils. Downstairs is an aquarium with more than 100 living aquatic species. There's also an art gallery featuring children's works. *39 South St., Pittsfield, MA 01201; tel. 413-443-7171. Open Tue.-Sat. 10-5, Sun. 1-5 (open Mon. Jul.-Aug.) Admission. On Rte. 7 in the center of Pittsfield.*

DINING

■ **The Mill on the Floss** (expensive). Most seem to agree that this is the place to go for fine dining in this part of the Berkshires. The classic French restaurant, next to a motel that shares its entrance, is in an old house with exposed beams, a fireplace, bookshelves, and paintings. The atmosphere is both casual and tasteful. The open kitchen with dangling copper pots adds to the dining experience. *Rte. 7, New Ashford, MA 01237; tel. 413-458-9123. Open Tue.-Sun. for dinner. Just north of Brodie Mountain ski area.*

■ **Wild Amber Grill** (moderate). The decor is traditional yet modern at this creative contemporary American eatery. Expect such appetizers as tempura soft shell crab and main courses such as sesame-seared yellowtail tuna, filet mignon, and lasagna *de Roma.* The dessert menu tantalizes with crepes Gauguin—mango-orange mousse wrapped in a crepe with mango and caramel sauces. *101 North St., Williamstown, MA 01267; tel. 413-458-4000. Open Mon.-Sat. for lunch and daily for dinner. Sometimes closed Tue. in winter.*

■ **Main Street Cafe** (moderate). This new Northern Italian restaurant with a professional, friendly staff has quickly gained a regular following. The ambience, from the music to the light-

▼

ing, is first-rate. Choose from such appetizers as grilled sea scallops or eggplant grilled with Fontina cheese and wrapped around marinated chicken breast. Main courses include shrimp and asparagus, spicy chicken, and vegetable cannelloni. The beer and wine lists are top-notch. *16 Water St., Williamstown, MA 01267; tel. 413-458-3210. Open daily for dinner. Brick-oven pizza served until midnight on weekdays and until 1 a.m. on weekends.*

■ **Hobson's Choice** (moderate). This popular, casual restaurant in an old house offers beef, fish, and a variety of sandwiches, including chicken teriyaki, blackened pork chop, and vegetarian pocket, on the lunch menu. The dinner menu features chicken Santa Fe, New York strip sirloin teriyaki, and Cajun barbecued shrimp. *159 Water St., Williamstown, MA 01267; tel. 413-458-9101. Open Tue.-Sun. for lunch and daily for dinner.*

LODGING

■ **Field Farm Guest House** (moderate). Built in 1948, this former home of an art collector and its 294 acres were deeded to the Trustees of Reservations. Furnishings from the 1950s, unusual art objects, balconies, and a magnificent view of Mount Greylock are all part of the experience. Five large guest rooms, each with private bath, are classic 1950s bedrooms. A continental breakfast is served. *554 Sloan Rd., Williamstown, MA 01267; tel. 413-458-3135. From Rte. 43, just past the junction with Rte. 7, turn right onto Sloan Rd. and drive 1.1 mi.*

■ **River Bend Farm** (moderate). Staying at this B&B is like going back in time. The house, built in 1770 by one of the founders of Williamstown, has been meticulously restored and contains antiques and a copper sink. A large fireplace with a well-worn hearth is the focus of the parlor. There are four guest rooms that share two baths. *643 Simmonds Rd., Rte. 7, Williamstown, MA 01267; tel. 413-458-3121, 800-418-2057. Open May-Oct. North of Williamstown.*

▼

■ **Steep Acres Farm** (moderate). Sitting next to the Vermont border in a very private location, this house has expansive views of the Berkshires—visible from an enclosed front porch with wicker furniture and singing canaries. There are four guest rooms that share two baths (one room has a half bath). A full gourmet breakfast is served. Spend some time at the farm's pond and on nearby walking trails that penetrate the Green Mountains in Vermont and Pine Cobble in Massachusetts. *520 White Oaks Rd., Williamstown, MA 01267; tel. 413-458-3774. Open most of the year. Call for directions.*

■ **The Williamstown B&B** (moderate). This B&B, a short walk from town and two art museums, has three guest rooms with private baths and sturdy oak, maple, and mahogany furniture. The house is a 110-year-old Victorian with a large front porch. Inside decor is elegant, yet restrained, with many period antiques throughout the house. A full breakfast is served in the dining room. *30 Cold Spring Rd., Williamstown, MA 01267; tel. 413-458-9202. Just off the traffic circle at Rtes. 2 and 7.*

■ **Bascom Lodge** (inexpensive). In the 1930s, the Civilian Conservation Corps built this stone and wood lodge to accommodate hikers and nature lovers. Today, the Appalachian Mountain Club offers Spartan accommodations: four private rooms and four co-ed bunk rooms, all with shared baths. Blankets, towels, and sheets are provided. Breakfast and dinner must be requested in advance. The views are superb, and the setting is very peaceful early and late in the day (when day-trippers have gone home). *P.O. Box 1800, Lanesboro, MA 01237; tel. 413-443-0011, 413-743-1591. Open daily mid-May-mid-Oct. On the summit of Mt. Greylock.*

FOR MORE INFORMATION
Tourist Offices:

■ **Northern Berkshire Chamber of Commerce.** Besides the main information office located at the address below, you can visit an information booth at Route 2 on Union Street in

▼

North Adams. *57 Main St., North Adams, MA 01247; tel. 413-663-3735. Main office open Mon.-Fri. 9-5. Booth open daily 10-4 Jun.-Columbus Day.*

■ **Berkshire Hills Visitors Bureau.** *Berkshire Common (plaza level), Pittsfield, MA; tel. 413-443-9186, 800-237-5747. Open Mon.-Fri. 8:30-5.*

For Serious Walkers:

Greylock, which is laced with trails, would take days to fully explore. Maps are available at the visitors center on Rockwell Road and at the summit. Nearby are other interesting hikes and walks, including Berlin Mountain in the Taconic range; Pine Cobble, just north of Williamstown, and the Dome and Broad Brook, across the border in Vermont. A hiking guide to the Williamstown area, published by the Williams College Outing Club, is available at local bookstores.

America's First Mountain Hotel

EXPERIENCE 10: MOUNT HOLYOKE

I n the 19th century, the great mountains of New England were rediscovered. Colonial settlers had previously considered mountains as things that were either in the way or too wild to be good for anything use-

> **The Highlights:**
> Sweeping vistas of the Connecticut River Valley, a restored mountain hotel.
>
> **Other Places Nearby:**
> Exciting college towns, good shops, excellent restaurants and B&Bs.

ful. During the 19th century, however, this attitude began to change: Mountains were seen as a source of cool, fresh invigorating air and spectacular vistas. The first mountaintop hotel opened its doors in the 1820s—atop Mount Holyoke in western Massachusetts, the setting for this walking tour.

Prior to 1820, Mount Holyoke was a popular destination for picnickers. Although its elevation is a mere 935 feet, it towers over the Connecticut River, which runs at its foot. From its summit, the extensive view of farms, towns, and hills leaves many visitors breathless. The sight is "the richest prospect in New England, and not improbably in the United States," declared Timothy Dwight, who published an early travel guide in 1821. The view was good enough to attract the attention of

▼

Thomas Cole, the central figure of the Hudson River School of landscape painting. New York City's Metropolitan Museum of Art owns Cole's *View from Mount Holyoke,* painted in 1836. Interestingly, Cole's painting depicts an oxbow, or bend, in the Connecticut River that no longer exists. It was cut off by an ice jam in 1840, leaving an oxbow lake that is now a marina.

By 1821, and possibly a few years earlier, a structure was built on the summit of Mount Holyoke that came to be known as the Prospect House. It wasn't much of a hotel, measuring 12 by 22 feet, but it was enlarged in 1822. This was one year before New York's famous Catskill Mountain House opened.

In the middle of the century, the Prospect House was acquired by a serious hotel owner. Renovation work began at once, and by 1851, the hotel was an eight-room, two-story structure. Roads were built and improved, and by 1854, a unique addition arrived—a tramway. Exactly what type of tramway it was is hard to say, but it provided a solution to the problem of getting guests effortlessly up the very steep face of the mountain. Previously, guests had arrived on foot— after climbing ladders on rugged places along the trail. With the tramway, they had only to step onto a chair and be lifted up to the hotel. Here's how the system worked.

Hotel guests who arrived by boat took a covered tramway from the steamboat dock on the Connecticut River to a building halfway up the mountain (the Halfway House). Then they entered a second, and even more unique, covered cable tramway. It carried guests, three at a time, 400 feet up the face of the mountain right into the hotel. At first, it was real horse power that turned the belts, but later steam and then electric. The first section of the lift, from the river to the Halfway House, didn't last long and was replaced by a simpler system—horse and carriage. The second and far more vertical tramway was changed and modified several times but operated until 1948,

▼

when it collapsed under heavy snow. Its route, directly in back of the Halfway House, can still be seen today.

By 1890, the Propect House had become a Victorian resort. Porches and balconies, many of which still exist, were built, and rooms were added. Many famous guests stayed at the hotel, including Alexander Graham Bell. But, by the end of the century, business began to decline. In 1908, when the hotel was purchased by Joseph A. Skinner, a silk manufacturer from Holyoke, and other local businessmen, it was four stories high and had expanded to well over 50 guest rooms. The era of mountaintop hotels was waning fast, but it took the 1938 hurricane to finally shut down the Prospect House. Some 35 rooms and an entire wing were destroyed. Skinner deeded the remaining part of the hotel, and 375 acres around it, to the state in 1940.

Today, the hotel is called the Summit House, but it is no longer open to guests. It is, however, open to the public on weekends between Memorial Day and Columbus Day, and also for special events. The Friends of the Holyoke Range, a local group that helped restore the hotel in the 1980s, holds many annual events at the Summit House, including a series of summer evening concerts. The section of the summit east of the hotel is parklike, with picnic tables on ledges, each offering a fine view of the Pioneer Valley (Massachusetts' part of the Connecticut River valley).

Mount Holyoke was not the only mountaintop hotel in this section of the valley. Nearby Mount Tom, near Holyoke, had one, and so did South Sugarloaf in South Deerfield and Mount Toby in Sunderland. None remain, although an observation building stands at the former hotel site on South Sugarloaf.

Walkers may wish to know some interesting facts about the range of mountains of which Mount Holyoke is a part. The Holyoke range and the Mount Tom range to the southwest are actually tilted lava beds. During the separation of continents

▼

long ago, the earth cracked and molten rock oozed out, forming basalt, also known as traprock. The beds of basalt were then tilted and uplifted. Erosion wore down the weaker rocks, leaving the basalt beds standing as mountains. These traprock ranges are found in Connecticut and Massachusetts on a north-south line, basically along the path of the Connecticut River. Mount Holyoke is unique because it runs east to west. In fact, east-west mountain ranges are rare anywhere.

Along the sides of the Holyoke and Mount Tom ranges are exposures of shale that preserve dinosaur footprints. In the vicinity of Mount Holyoke, the first dinosaur footprint fossils in America were described by scientist Edward Hitchcock of Amherst College. Hitchcock thought the tracks were those of giant birds. For many years, scientists discounted that observation because they believed dinosaurs were reptiles—cold-blooded and slow. Now this view is changing: Many believe dinosaurs were the ancestors of birds. Hitchcock may have been right about dinosaurs long before anyone else.

GETTING THERE

From I-91, take exit 19 to Rte. 9 east, Hadley/Amherst. After crossing over the Connecticut River, turn right onto Rte. 47. Drive just over 3 mi. to a large parking area on your left. A gate at the trail head blocks off a lane leading into the forest.

Walk Directions

TIME: 2 hours
LEVEL: Moderate
DISTANCE: 3 miles
ACCESS: By car

Although the first section of the walk does not follow the original route that visitors used years ago, it does bring you, without any serious climbing, to the Halfway House. The original route is now called the Tramway Trail. It is marked, but it doesn't have a parking area on Rte.

▼

47. From the Halfway House, a foot trail—perhaps the oldest in the park—leads you uphill via a switchback to the Summit House. Just east of the Summit House is a picnic area, an excellent place for lunch, with many vistas. Picnic provisions can be purchased in numerous shops in Amherst, Northampton, and Hadley.

TO BEGIN

From the parking area, walk through the gate and follow the lane uphill. You will find blue markers indicating that you are on the Halfway House Trail. A ravine is off to your right.

1. At the first junction, bear right, following yellow and blue markers. At the next junction, bear right and follow blue markers. At a third junction, bear right again. For the next 5 minutes, the trail parallels Rte. 47 (which can be heard through the forest). Ignore a trail heading upward on your left and then ignore a trail leading to a gate on your right. Cross a brook and pass under hemlock tress. At the next junction, turn left and follow blue markers uphill, ignoring the Deer Trail that heads off to the right. Continue on the blue trail for about 10 minutes.

2. At a paved road, turn right. Walk downhill for a few hundred feet and pass the Halfway House. *Behind and above the house is the tramway route and above it the Summit House.*

3. Turn left onto the steps of the Halfway House Trail, again marked in blue, and begin walking uphill. After a good climb, the trail switches back to the left and continues the climb on a recently stabilized trail. At a junction near the top, turn right and proceed up wooden steps.

4. You immediately reach another junction where you turn left and follow the Metacomet-Monadnock Trail uphill over rocks. Continue past the parking lot and then to the Summit House. To return, retrace your steps.

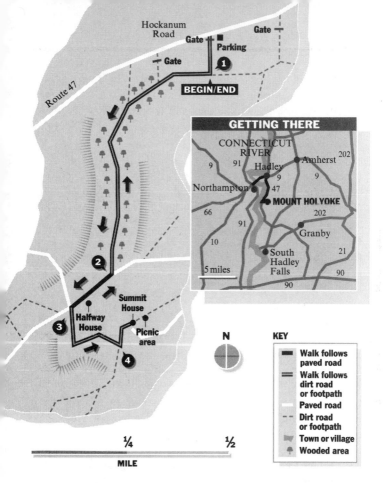

CONNECTICUT RIVER

Amherst 202

Hadley

9

Northampton

47

MOUNT HOLYOKE

202

Granby

South Hadley Falls

21

90

90

5 miles

N

KEY

Walk follows paved road

Walk follows dirt road or footpath

Paved road

Dirt road or footpath

Town or village

Wooded area

¼   ½

MILE

Hockanum Road

Gate

Gate

Gate

Parking

❶

BEGIN/END

Route 47

❷

❸

Halfway House

Summit House

Picnic area

❹

OTHER PLACES NEARBY

■ **Amherst, Northampton, and South Hadley.** Three neighboring towns house historic colleges—Amherst, Smith, and Mount Holyoke. The University of Massachusetts and Hampshire College also are in Amherst, which has top bookstores and fine restaurants. Most activity centers around Northampton, a great town for live music, dining, and shops.

■ **Deerfield.** One of the true pioneer settlements in western Massachusetts and the scene of two Indian massacres,

▼

Deerfield today is a museum village with 12 antique-filled houses. You can also visit the historic Deerfield Inn—still very much alive and open for guests and diners. *Historic Deerfield, Inc., P.O. Box 321, Deerfield, MA 01342; tel. 413-774-5581. Museum village open daily 9:30-4:30. Admission. Take I-91 to exit 24N or 25S and follow Rtes. 5 and 10. About 18 mi. north of Mt. Holyoke.*

■ **The Dickinson Homestead.** Emily Dickinson lived her life and wrote her poems in this historic house. Only guided tours are given; call for a reservation. *280 Main St., Amherst, MA 01002; tel. 413-542-8161. Open Wed.-Sun. 1-4 Jun.-Aug. (including Jul. 4); Wed.-Sat. 1-4 Sep.-Oct.; Wed., Sat. 1-4 Nov.- mid-Dec., Mar.; Wed.-Sat. 1-4 Apr.-May. Admission. About 5 mi. north of Mt. Holyoke.*

DINING

■ **Sienna** (expensive). Sensational, inventive dishes emerge from the kitchen of this small (46-seat) restaurant with classic French, southwestern U.S., and Thai influences. The chef whips up such appetizers as shrimp ravioli (rice pasta filled with shrimp, onion salad, Southwest curry sauce) and such entrées as tuna grilled with smoked jalapeno and lime juice marinade, served on white bean and sun-dried tomato salad with crispy taro root. Don't miss the beer list featuring world-class brews from a neighbor, the Berkshire Brewing Company. Reservations are required. *6-B Elm St., South Deerfield, MA 01373; tel. 413-665-0215. Open Wed.-Sun. for dinner. Take Rte. 116 to the center of South Deerfield.*

■ **La Cucina di Pinocchio** (expensive). Enjoy gourmet Tuscan meals and vintage Italian wines in one of several bright, ground-level dining rooms. Try the popular calamari *insalata* for an appetizer. Excellent entrées include penne *mare* and *monti* (shrimp, sun-dried tomato, portobello mushroom, olives, beans, and broccoli *di rapi* in a light tomato sauce), or *melan-zana al forno* (grilled eggplant layered with roasted peppers,

▼

spinach, and cheeses, in a light tomato-basil sauce). *30 Boltwood Walk, Amherst, MA 01002; tel. 413-256-4110. Open Mon.-Sat. for lunch and dinner, Sun. for dinner. Off Main St. in downtown Amherst, opposite town hall.*

■ **Eastside Grill** (moderate). This former Cajun restaurant still serves some dishes with a Louisiana accent but has turned more to "American fare with a twist." Favorites include pan-blackened scallops and beef tenderloin with gorgonzola and fried leeks. For dessert, look for the homemade chocolate mousse cheesecake or New Orleans bread pudding. *19 Strong Ave., Northampton, MA 01060; tel. 413-586-3347. Open daily for dinner. Off Main St.*

■ **Judie's** (moderate). Perched a few feet above the sidewalk in downtown Amherst, Judie's offers a variety of items, from munchies to entrées, from burgers to full meals—served all day. The key to many items on the menu is the popover: such as curry chicken sandwich in a popover, or popovers stuffed with shrimp or vegetables. For a snack, try potato skins supreme, or Judie's unique onion soup. The several dining rooms are intimate and decorated with art. *51 N. Pleasant St., Amherst, MA 01002; tel. 413-253-3491. Open daily for lunch and dinner.*

■ **Paul & Elizabeth's** (moderate). High ceilings, fans, and plants create the atmosphere in this gourmet natural-foods restaurant. Creative salads and homemade whole-wheat rolls begin a meal that might include a variety of vegetarian dishes or perhaps fresh fish, shrimp, or scallop tempura. People who are serious about what they eat will love this place. *150 Main St., Northampton, MA 01060; tel. 413-584-4832. Open daily for lunch and dinner. In Thorne's Market in downtown Northampton.*

■ **Sylvester's** (inexpensive) With breakfasts this good, it's easy to overlook the plain, modern decor of this small eatery in a bustling downtown area. Get a perfect start to the day with banana bread French toast, apple cinnamon pancakes or a Lox-Ness omelet—an omelet with herb cream cheese, onions, tomatoes, and smoked salmon. Sylvester's bakes its own bread and is a perfect pit stop for picking up sandwiches before a walk up Mount Holyoke. *111 Pleasant St., Northampton, MA 01060; tel. 413-586-5343. Open daily for breakfast and lunch.*

LODGING

In addition to the listings below, a number of bed-and-breakfasts with one or two guest rooms offer quality lodging in the Amherst area. Call the Amherst Area Chamber of Commerce (413-253-0700) for details.

■ **The Black Walnut Inn** (expensive). This recently renovated 1821 Federal-style brick house offers seven large and elegant rooms for guests. All rooms have a private bath, interesting period pieces, a queen-size bed, air conditioning, a TV, and a phone with a computer hookup. Ask for the sunny, quiet Poet's Room, which includes a sofa. If you want more space, request the Webster Room, a suite. Downstairs there's a parlor, a sunny side porch, and a dining room where a full breakfast (with hot apple pie) is served. *1184 North Pleasant St., Amherst, MA 01002; tel. 413-549-5649. In North Amherst at Rte. 63.*

■ **Allen House Inn** (moderate). An 1886 Queen Anne Victorian that has been meticulously restored, this B&B includes seven large guest rooms with private baths that feature period wall coverings. The house's exterior has been painted the way it was when it was new: in six colors! The inn—on a relatively busy street only a short walk away from the town's restaurants and shops—serves a full breakfast. Lower-priced rooms with shared baths are available in a separate building that's across from Emily Dickinson's house. *599 Main St., Amherst, MA 01002; tel. 413-253-5000.*

■ **The Lord Jeffery Inn** (moderate). This New England-style inn has 48 rooms with all the amenities of a major hotel. Rooms vary from economy class (inexpensive to moderate)

▼

to large suites (expensive). Breakfast does not automatically come with lodging, but it can be part of a package. The inn has a fine restaurant and also the Boltwood Tavern. Its location is very central, on the town common and near Amherst College. *30 Boltwood Ave., Amherst, MA 01002; tel. 800-742-0358, 413-253-2576.*

■ **Ingate Farms B&B** (inexpensive). Stay here and you'll experience a 250-year-old house that is part of a 400-acre equestrian center. There are four guest rooms, two with a private bath. The front porch overlooks a horse pasture, and there's an Olympic-size swimming pool on the premises. An expanded continental breakfast is served. *60 Lamson Ave., Belchertown, MA 01007; tel. 413-253-0440. South of Amherst off Bay Rd., 4 mi. east of Rte. 116.*

FOR MORE INFORMATION

Tourist Office:

■ **Amherst Area Chamber of Commerce.** Besides the main office, a tourist booth on the common (near the bus station) is open during the summer. *409 Main St., Amherst, MA 01002; tel. 413-253-0700. Office open Mon.-Fri. 8-5. Booth open Mon.-Fri. 10-4 in summer.*

For Serious Walkers:

The Amherst area offers outstanding hiking opportunities. The 120-mile Metacomet-Monadnock Trail runs along Mount Tom and the Holyoke Range, which are both laced with other hiking trails. In Amherst, you'll find the 33-mile Robert Frost Trail and many conservation areas with trails. The paved Norwottuck Rail Trail connects Amherst with Northampton and is well-used by walkers and bicyclists. Guidebooks and maps are sold at Hastings in downtown Amherst.

Before and After the Flood

EXPERIENCE 11:
QUABBIN RESERVOIR

n the center of Massachusetts lies a huge, irregular body of water surrounded by a wilderness that is more reminiscent of Maine. It's a new wilderness—one that made its appearance only about 50 years ago. As you walk on these lands in the Swift River Valley today, you

The Highlights: A vast island-filled reservoir and wilderness; beaver, moose, and other wildlife.

Other Places Nearby: Harvard University's forest, a bald eagle overlook, a lookout tower.

would never imagine that they once were occupied by four towns and several villages.

The region's centerpiece is now Quabbin Reservoir, created by the damming of three large streams that joined in the vicinity of the former towns of Greenwich and Enfield. Before Colonial times, these streams—the west, middle, and east branches of the Swift River—supported a small population of Native Americans from the Nipmuc tribe. Their name for the area was Quabbin (sometimes spelled Qaben), meaning "well-watered place." The first European settlements in the valley began around 1735, and the population grew steadily well into the 19th century. Farming was the primary way of life, but the presence of the streams gave rise to some

▼

water-powered manufacturing. For the most part, the towns of Dana, Greenwich, Prescott, and Enfield, and the smaller villages associated with them, developed at the same pace as other settlements in central and western Massachusetts. They were small towns populated by independent people.

A critical event occurred, however, in the middle of the 19th century. The age of railroads had arrived, but no tracks were laid to the Swift River valley, effectively isolating it from the mainstream of the Industrial Revolution. The valley's population declined as people moved to industrial centers to find work. Even agriculture was affected, because crops grown hundreds of miles away sold for less than the those that were produced by local farmers. By the early 20th century, the region had become quite backward. Roads had not been paved, and electricity was unavailable in some areas. These conditions only further discouraged commercial activity. On the positive side, outsiders discovered the area as a quaint and beautiful place for summer cottages. But it was too late.

More trouble came from Boston, a thirsty city that had been drawing its water from the Charles River. After the river became polluted, Boston obtained water for its growing population from neighboring towns. By 1895, the demand for water was such that the Metropolitan Water District Commission was created to find regional solutions. It decided to channel impounded water in aqueducts from pure sources west of Boston. The commission first targeted Wachusett Reservoir, but it wasn't enough to quench Boston's thirst. The next project was much bigger and more ambitious: the capture of the watershed of the Swift Rivers by flooding their valleys.

After years of hearings and investigations—during which people living in the valley began to move out—the decision to create the Quabbin Reservoir came in 1927. Work quickly began, and the towns were shut down. The town of Prescott ceased to exist officially on April 28, 1938. Bridges were dynamited, trees cut, and

▼

houses bulldozed. The devastation, as shown in photographs on display at the Quabbin Visitor Center, was massive. By 1939, the evacuation and dismantling of 200 years of Swift River valley life had been completed, and the streams began to back up behind the two enormous dams. By 1946, the reservoir was filled.

The creation of the Quabbin was one of the major engineering feats of the time. Two dams, each roughly a half mile in length, block two gaps in the hills. Since the valley floor was not bedrock but loose glacial deposits, the foundation of the dams extends more than 100 feet below ground level. The reservoir behind these two dams stretches for nearly 18 miles to the north. The Quabbin shoreline totals 118 miles (not including the islands), and the water surface area is 38.6 square miles, or about 25,000 acres. Sixty islands, formerly valley hills, are off limits (as is the Prescott Peninsula, home of bald eagles) to visitors.

During the last 50 years or so, the 61,000 acres of Boston-owned forest surrounding the Quabbin have reverted to wilderness. Wildlife is now abundant—so abundant that in recent years a controversial deer hunt has been held annually to stabilize the deer population. Moose live at the Quabbin, beaver and porcupine are very common, and there have been occasional sightings of cougar.

On your walking tour, you will enter the Quabbin lands after passing through the Federated Woman's Clubs State Forest. This forest was once a source for wood used in making matches by the Diamond Match Company, which sold the land to the state in the 1930s—about the same time the Federated Woman's Clubs made a donation of land. The tract was named for their contribution. Today the state forest is almost entirely undeveloped except for a primitive camping area, through which the walk passes.

Cellar holes, foundations, and old road markers are what walkers will find along the route. Perhaps the most dramatic evidence of former occupation comes at the turnaround point in the walk: A formerly paved road that once led to the village of North Dana disappears beneath the waters of the reservoir.

▼

Displays of photographs taken of the old towns and charts showing the changing water level over the years can be found at the Quabbin Visitor Center and Metropolitan District Commission headquarters near the Windsor Dam. Then head for the lookout tower on Quabbin Hill and savor both the most expansive view of the reservoir possible from the ground and, in the far distance to the north, mighty Mount Monadnock (*see* Experience 19).

GETTING THERE
By car:

Drive to Petersham, located on Rte. 32 in central Massachusetts, 27 mi. north of the Massachusetts Tpke. (I-90) exit 8 and 6 mi. south of Rte. 2. Take Rte. 32 north from the Tpke. and follow it (or connect to Alt. Rte. 32) to Petersham.

At the junction of Rtes. 32 and 122 in Petersham, drive 4.2 mi. north on Rte. 122 to the Petersham/New Salem boundary. Turn left at the "State Forest" sign and proceed into the Federated Woman's Clubs State Forest. (If you're driving from the north to Petersham, drive to the junction of Routes 202 and 122 and then follow Rte. 122 3.5 mi. to the state forest entrance on the right.) From the entrance, proceed on a paved road for 1.7 mi. as it winds its way into the forest. Park in the parking area on the right, immediately before a T-junction.

Walk Directions

TIME: 2 hours
LEVEL: Easy to moderate
DISTANCE: 3.5 miles
ACCESS: By car

The trails are mostly old roads and lanes (some show remains of pavement). There are no markers or blazes, though in places a posted map will indicate your position. **During hot summer days, it may be best to avoid this walk because of mosquitoes and deer flies.** The

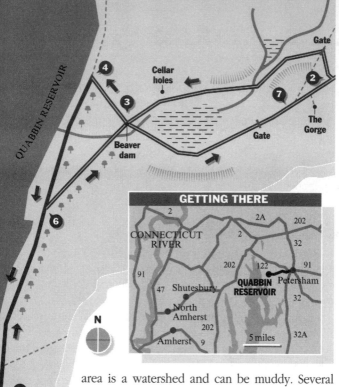

GETTING THERE

2

CONNECTICUT RIVER

2A   202

2   32

91   202   122   91

47   Shutesbury   **QUABBIN RESERVOIR**   Petersham

North Amherst   32

202

Amherst   9   5 miles   32A

N

area is a watershed and can be muddy. Several picnic tables are near the end of the walk, at Point 7. The Quabbin Reservoir area is isolated, so buy picnic provisions before you leave home.

TO BEGIN

Leave the parking area and walk to the T-junction. Turn right onto a gravel road and walk toward a gate.

1. Go through the gate and follow a wide lane past a stone water diversion and holding pond that was created as a source of water for fire fighting. Walk uphill through a clearing and under power lines. Continue straight, ignoring a road that's on your right.

2. At a Y-junction, where a boulder shows signs of once

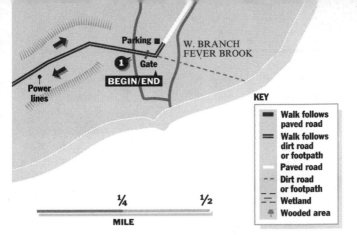

KEY

▬▬	**Walk follows paved road**
═══	**Walk follows dirt road or footpath**
	Paved road
- - -	**Dirt road or footpath**
═╤═	**Wetland**
♣	**Wooded area**

holding a plaque, turn right. Walk to a junction. Go straight ahead through gate 36 and follow the wide lane as it descends along the side of a hill. When the lane levels off, continue on, cross a brook, and then pass a large stone foundation. A sign indicates that you have entered the Quabbin Reservation. *On your left is a pond with evidence of beaver activity.* Continue to the far edge of the pond and ignore a path to the right.

3. At a junction a few steps ahead, turn right. Walk a short distance toward the reservoir and a former paved road.

4. At the road, turn left (you're heading south) and proceed parallel to the shore of the Quabbin Reservoir. Walk about 20 to 30 minutes on this road, while taking in the many vistas of the reservoir and its islands off to your right. *Evidence of former habitation is all around. In late summer, you may find ripe grapes that grow wild in the brambles on each side of the lane.*

5. Reach the end of the road—*it leads off into the water to the drowned village of North Dana.* Retrace your steps for about 10 to 15 minutes to a pine-forested area about halfway back to Point 4.

6. Turn right onto a grass and dirt lane that forks off the

▼

main road. *If it's too muddy, continue straight and then turn right at Point 4. You soon arrive at Point 3, the beaver pond.* If the lane isn't muddy, walk seven minutes and arrive at Point 3. Turn right onto a narrow path at the edge of the beaver pond and cross a beaver dam that's been built up with sand **but may also be wet.** Follow the path past rock walls. The path heads uphill and soon becomes a lane. It climbs gradually, passing a boundary sign and then a gate. Go straight and head downhill.

7. Arrive at campgrounds, a clearing, and picnic areas. At picnic site 4, just past a pine grove, ignore a trail that leads off to the right to a small gorge and continue straight. Just a few feet further, you arrive at Point 2. Continue ahead on the road, down the hill and through the gate. Turn left to find your car.

OTHER PLACES NEARBY

■ **Quabbin Reservoir and Park.** Stop at the visitors center for a map and visit its historical museum. Drive over the dam to a traffic circle and turn right to Quabbin Hill—a great picnic spot with views of the reservoir and distant Mt. Monadnock. Go straight at the circle to Enfield Lookout, where bald eagles can be seen through binoculars. *P.O. Box 628, Belchertown, MA 01007; tel. 413-323-7221. Park open daily dawn-dusk. Visitors center open daily 9-4:30. From Petersham, follow Rte. 32 south for 16 mi., then Rte. 9 west for 7 mi.*

■ **Harvard Forest.** Pick up a trail map at this 3,000-acre tract used by Harvard University for study and research. The Fisher Museum has exhibits about forest ecology and land use. *Petersham, MA 01366-0068; tel. 978-724-3302, Open Mon.-Fri. 9-5, Sat.-Sun. 12-4. On Rte. 32, 3.5 mi. north of Petersham.*

DINING

■ **Jenkins Inn Restaurant** (moderate). A cozy dining room serves inn guests and others. The lunch menu includes baked crab cakes, a focaccia sandwich, and a real buffalo

▼

burger. Baked bay scallops, chicken *cordon bleu,* beef Wellington, and other entrées are on the menu. Daily specials—which sometimes include alligator—can be ordered. *Rtes. 122 and 32, Barre Common, 7 West St., Barre, MA 01005; tel. 978-355-6444. Open Wed.-Sat. for lunch and dinner, Sun. for dinner.*

■ **Harding Allen Estate** (moderate) Treat yourself to lunch in an exquisite mansion or its walled garden. Expect such fare as Mediterranean tuna melt, ginger beef, French bread pudding, and ice cream truffles. *P.O. Box 933, Rte. 122, 59 Allen Dr., Barre, MA 01005; tel. 978-355-4920. Open Wed.-Fri. for lunch year-round; open Sun. for breakfast and Thu.-Sun. (Sun. noon-6) for dinner Nov.-Apr. Call for days serving dinner May-Oct.*

■ **Colonel Isaac Barre** (moderate). Named for a patriot colonel, this is actually two restaurants: ground-level dining rooms and a pub with less expensive fare downstairs. In the dining areas, expect appetizers like seafood chowder or escargot in phyllo triangles. Entrées include angel hair pasta, steak, and swordfish. *On the Common, Barre, MA 01005; tel. 978-355-4629. Dining rooms open Wed.-Sun. for lunch and dinner. Pub open daily for lunch and dinner. On the village green.*

■ **Fox Run** (moderate). An old barn in the country, the Fox Run offers reasonably priced meals. Downstairs is the old stable that now houses a bar. Dining rooms are nearby and in a hayloft. For an appetizer, try the "seahorses"—scallops wrapped in bacon, then grilled. Entrées include steak, rack of lamb, veal Oscar, and many seafood items. *Ward Hill Rd., Phillipston, MA 01331; tel. 978-249-8267. Open Tue.-Sun. for dinner late Mar.-Nov. Open Tue.-Fri. for lunch May-Nov. The easiest way to find the restaurant is from Rte. 2A, just east of Athol, where signs direct you.*

LODGING

Lodging may also be found in the nearby Amherst area (*see* Experience 10, Mount Holyoke).

■ **Harding Allen Estate** (expensive) This newly renovated elegant mansion is one of New England's classiest lodgings. Choose between five guest rooms, three with private bath. Request the Master Bedroom with its king-size four-poster canopy bed. A full breakfast is served. *P.O. Box 933, Rte. 122, 59 Allen Dr., Barre, MA 01005; tel. 978-355-4920.*

■ **The Jenkins Inn** (moderate). Five guest rooms, including the Sunrise Suite, are upstairs in this 160-year-old inn located on the edge of the large village green. Three include a private bath, two have balconies, and one features a working fireplace. A full breakfast is served. *Rte. 122/32, Barre Common, 7 West St., Barre, MA 01005; tel. 978-355-6444, 800-378-7373.*

■ **Winterwood** (moderate). Just off the Petersham village green, this inn offers six upstairs guest rooms with private baths, including five with working fireplaces. The house is an 1842 Greek-Revival summer home with a library, a dining room, a living room, and several porches. A continental breakfast is served. *19 North Main St., Petersham, MA 01366; tel. 978-724-8885.*

FOR MORE INFORMATION
Tourist Offices:

■ **Quabbin Visitor Center.** *P.O. Box 628, Belchertown, MA 01007; tel. 413-323-7221. Open daily 9-4:30. From Petersham, go 16 mi. south on Rte. 32, then 7 mi. west on Rte. 9.*

■ **North Quabbin Chamber of Commerce.** *P.O. Box 157, 521 Main St., Athol, MA 01331; tel. 978-249-3849. Open Mon.-Fri. 8-5.*

■ **The Trustees of Reservations.** *572 Essex St., Beverly, MA 01915; tel. 978-921-1944.*

For Serious Walkers:

The Quabbin is too large to explore in just a few days. Stop at the visitors center for maps and information. Excellent walks can be found in the Brooks Woodland Preserve, the North Common Meadow, and the Swift River Reservation, all Trustees of Reservations properties.

An Oasis in Suburbia

EXPERIENCE 12: WORLD'S END

Boston became the largest city in New England, in part, because of its good harbor. Numerous islands and necks of land scattered about Boston Harbor, Quincy Bay, and Hingham Bay shelter the mainland from the force of the open seas. Over the course of Boston's long history,

The Highlights: Views of Hingham Bay from gentle lanes that wind through pasture and past rocky shoreline.

Other Places Nearby: Historic houses on Boston's South Shore, a forest, a state park.

many of these islands—including the one on this walking tour—have been enlarged with fill and connected with others, or with the mainland. In this way, the size of Boston has grown.

All around Boston nearly every speck of land has become a pedestal for houses and roads. The town of Hull, located well out to sea, is connected to the mainland by an unbroken chain of buildings. South of Boston, along what is called the South Shore, is the town of Hingham, once a major port. In this vicinity were once two large islands; today they are joined and fully connected with the mainland by a road but, remarkably, remain undeveloped. Both are drumlins, created from debris carried along by the glacial ice sheet that was dumped

▼

and shaped into mounds by moving ice.

The outermost of the two islands has been called World's End for so long that no one knows where the name came from. The reference, though, seems obvious: World's End is the last of a string of four hills and abruptly terminates into Hingham Bay. Closest to the mainland, the first island, comprised of Pine Hill and Planter's Hill, was actually only an island at high tide. Two dams were created long ago on each side of what is now a marsh to block the rising sea and maintain constant access to its valuable farmland. A rocky neck of bedrock, called exactly that, Rocky Neck, extends eastward, jutting out toward Hull. The connection between the two islands is a narrow strip of land called the "bar." Here the waters almost meet, and there is just enough room for a single lane of traffic to reach World's End.

These four hills are now part of a reservation that is open to the public and maintained by the Trustees of Reservations, the oldest land conservation organization in Massachusetts. Not much is known about World's End's earliest settlers. A man named Abraham Martin lived here as early as 1635. The small cove that is located just before the entrance to the reservation, as well as the road that leads to it, is named after him.

In 1855, John R. Brewer of Boston began to acquire property in the area. Brewer and his wife Caroline created a "noble estate" that consisted of a number of buildings erected just to the south of World's End, where they raised prize-winning sheep and cattle.

Caroline Brewer's diary has survived and says much about how people related to animals during that time. Horses were considered pets and often were allowed to retire peacefully. They were named according to a 26-year alphabetical cycle—beginning with "A" during the first year, "B" in the second, and so on. Oxen, however, were repeatedly given the same

▼

names—"Buck" and "Bright"—and were eventually fattened and killed. Sheep were kept on World's End in an open sheep-fold, the only building ever erected on the land.

In 1886, John R. Brewer thought about subdividing World's End into house lots. For the general layout of roads and land-scaping before building could commence, he hired the best—Frederick Law Olmsted. In this book, we again encounter Olmsted's work at Vermont's Shelburne Farms (see Experience 18). But World's End and Shelburne Farms were minor jobs for the man who has come to be known as a father of American landscape architecture.

Olmsted was from Connecticut, born in Hartford in 1822 and a student for a time at Yale. In his early twenties, he sailed around the world, but then decided to become a farmer—an occupation that he took very seriously. By his late twenties, he had studied agriculture with many experts and acquired some practical experience, farming in Guilford, Connecticut, and Staten Island, New York. Olmsted then entered a most interesting part of his life.

In 1850, he traveled to Europe and later published an account of his four-week walking tour of Britain called, "Walks and Talks of an American Farmer in England." In Europe, he visited parks and gardens and met and talked with the leading agriculturalists. Back in the States, he took a horseback tour of the South and wrote about his impressions of slavery and the economy. Then Olmsted journeyed from New Orleans to Texas. His fame as a writer and unbiased thinker grew, and so did his connections with well-placed individuals. In 1857, he was appointed superintendent of New York City's Central Park project and entered the competition for its design. His worldly experience made him fully qualified for the job, which was awarded to him and his English partner, Calvert Vaux.

During the Civil War, Olmsted went to California where he designed landscapes in the San Francisco region, including the

▼

grounds of the University of California at Berkeley. Returning to New York, he and Vaux established a firm that designed many famous parks, including Prospect Park in Brooklyn, New York; Chicago's South Park, and Franklin Park in Boston. During his last six years as a professional, Olmsted designed the Biltmore estate for George Vanderbilt in Asheville, North Carolina, and Chicago's World's Fair.

Olmsted's talents as both farmer and thinker, combined with extensive trips away from home that showed how the rest of the world treated the outdoor urban landscape, quickly moved him to a leading position in the newly emerging field of landscape architecture. On World's End, there's an opportunity to see his ideas about how the landscape could be improved, without the clutter of buildings. The result is a wonderful park where tree-lined lanes hug the contours of the four barely forested hills. Olmsted's work was called the "natural" style—sculpting the land without destroying it.

Fortunately, Brewer never completed his development plan for World's End. It remained unchanged even after the death of his last surviving child in 1936. The estate was kept up by trustees who allowed visitors to use it for picnicking, camping, and even fox hunting. In 1945, World's End was proposed as the site of the United Nations, but that was not to be. During the 1950s and 1960s, developers from Boston made inquiries, and in 1965, it was considered as a site for a nuclear power plant. Plymouth, to the south, was chosen instead. Finally, in 1967, the tract was acquired by the Trustees of Reservations, the nation's oldest private conservation trust.

As you walk the lanes of World's End, look at the highly developed islands that surround it and contemplate what good fortune this small bit of land in Hingham Bay has had.

GETTING THERE

By car:

From Rte. 3 south of Boston, take exit 14 and follow Rte. 228

▼

north to Rte. 3A, where you turn left. Drive 1.2 mi. to the rotary. Enter the rotary and take the first right. Go a half mile and turn left onto Martin's Ln. Continue for 7/10 mi. until you see the entrance to World's End Reservation. There is an entrance fee of $4 per person. Several parking areas are to your right.

Walk Directions

TIME: 2 hours
LEVEL: Easy
DISTANCE: 4 miles
ACCESS: By car

The walk is mostly on wide carriage lanes. No trails are marked. The Rocky Neck section can be confusing in places since many small footpaths meander off the main route.

TO BEGIN

Walk to the end of the parking area (away from the toll booth), where there is a gate and a directory. Go straight on a rocky gravel lane into the woods. *To the right, residences in the town of Hull are visible across the bay.*

1. Just past a small inlet, you immediately reach a grassy triangular junction. Make a right off the wide path and walk up a narrow footpath under cedars to Rocky Neck. Ignore a path to the left and follow the footpath to the right. Where the lane meets the water, it turns to the left and becomes a narrower footpath. Follow the footpath as it passes a rock outcrop on your right and continue on as it turns to the left away from the water. Stay on the footpath as it loops around the perimeter of Rocky Neck.

2. You reach the highest point on the trail. *If it hadn't been preserved, World's End might look like the overpopulated islands across the waters.* Follow the trail as it descends and bear right at a

▼

junction. In less than a minute, turn left at the next junction. Within seconds, turn right and follow a path downhill through the trees. Continue through a grass meadow **that may be muddy.**

3. At a junction in the meadow, turn right. You immediately reach another junction. Turn right again and follow a maple-lined lane as it rises alongside Planter's Hill. The lane descends and then approaches another junction.

4. At this junction, bear right and cross a sandbar that connects World's End to the main peninsula. After crossing, bear right at the first junction, staying on the wider path, and go uphill.

5.. After 50 yards, you reach a junction. Go straight up a hill. At the next junction, bear right, You quickly arrive at another junction where you turn right. *Throughout this section of the walk, you'll pass many World's End overlooks where you can rest.* At the next major junction, turn right and follow a wide path uphill with the water to your right, At the next junction, bear right. Pass a bench and at the next junction (Point 5), turn right. Cross the sandbar and arrive at Point 4. Ignore dirt paths to the left and right and go between them through a field, up a path that leads to the top of Planter's Hill. At the top, turn left.

6. At a junction (there's a bench on your left), continue straight. *To your right is the stone memorial to F. Arthur Edwards, who worked as a farmhand at World's End for 40 years.* Continue down the lane and keep left at the next junction. Walk on a dirt-and-gravel road and continue on (ignoring paths that lead off) to the directory and then the toll booth. Turn left and head back to your car.

OTHER PLACES NEARBY

Boston's South Shore, as this area is called, was settled early on—Hingham in 1635 and Cohasset not much later. Visitors

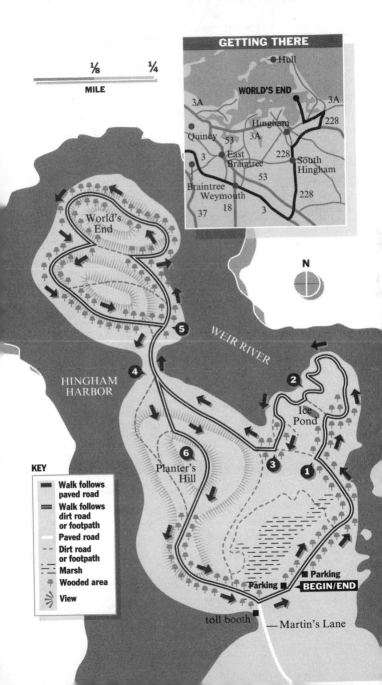

Hull

WORLD'S END

3A · 3A · 228

Hingham · 3A

Quincy · 53

East Braintree · 228 · South Hingham

3 · 53

Braintree Weymouth · 228

37 · 18 · 3

N

⅛ · ¼
MILE

World's End

WEIR RIVER

⑤

④

②

HINGHAM HARBOR

Ice Pond

③ · ①

⑥

Planter's Hill

KEY

▬ Walk follows paved road

═ Walk follows dirt road or footpath

── Paved road

- - - Dirt road or footpath

Marsh

Wooded area

View

Parking

Parking
BEGIN/END

toll booth

Martin's Lane

▼

will find many historic houses, particularly in Hingham, where Main Street is lined with 18th- and 19th-century dwellings. Old Ship Church in Hingham (1681) is the oldest continuously used church in America. West of Hingham is Quincy, home of two presidents, John Adams and John Quincy Adams.

DINING

■ **The Barker Tavern** (expensive). This is the second-oldest house standing in America, built in 1634. Along with its rich history, the restaurant offers fine dining. Lamb, lobster, pheasant, and venison are served, and the 16-ounce, center-cut broiled swordfish is a house specialty. Many appetizers are Greek or Middle Eastern, although smoked salmon and escargot are also on the menu. *21 Barker Rd., Scituate, MA 02066. Open Tue.-Sun. for dinner (Sun. dinner begins at 1). Off Rte. 3A.*

■ **Tosca** (expensive). Named for Puccini's opera, this stylish restaurant serves regional Italian cuisine in a brick industrial building with high ceilings and beams. The open grills and brick oven make the room warm and cozy. Popular menu items are wood-grilled pizzas and fried calamari. Entrées include grilled eggplant-wrapped swordfish with onion confit, carrot purée and smoky lentils. *14 North St., Hingham, MA 02043; tel. 617-740-0080. Open daily for dinner (including Sun. beginning at 2). Just west of the rotary on Rte. 3A.*

■ **Mount Blue** (moderate). Aerosmith's Steven Tyler and Joe Perry, along with three partners, own this eclectic, hip country cafe. The menu is fun and diverse, featuring such items as slow-roasted Cuban pork, jerk shrimp, grilled leg of lamb, and macaroni and cheese with country ham and sweet peas. Don't miss the banana bread pudding sundae. Local musicians, usually playing blues or acoustic rock, add even more flavor. An affiliated pizza parlor, with a unique assortment of pies, is next door. Ever hear of prosciutto and fig? How about lamb sausage pizza with dollops of garlic mashed potatoes? You can also stick with the traditional kind (but with

▼

three cheeses) or get a spicy kick from tequila-grilled chicken pizza with jalapenos, red onions, and cilantro. *707 Main St., Norwell, MA 02061; tel. 781-659-2999. Open daily for dinner; pizza parlor open daily for lunch and dinner. On Rte. 123, south of Hingham.*

■ **Stars** (inexpensive). This place may remind you of a diner—you can get just about anything you want at a good price. As at most diners, breakfast is a big attraction, but so is lunch. The beer list is long, and wine is also available. Stars is very popular locally, and often there's a wait on weekends for breakfast and dinner. *Rte. 3A, Hingham, MA 02043; tel. 617-740-3200. Open daily for breakfast, lunch, and dinner. Just west of the rotary on Rte. 3A.*

LODGING

Besides the lodgings listed below, there are very few inns and B&Bs in the area near World's End. If you're not looking to completely escape from the bustle of the city, Boston's numerous lodging choices are nearby. Pick up a *Fodor's* guidebook for Boston or, if you don't mind paying a little more, book a place through an agency. Contact A Bed & Breakfast Agency of Boston (617-720-3540, 800-248-9262), B&B Cambridge & Greater Boston (617-720-1492, 800-888-0178), or Bed and Breakfast Associates Bay Colony (781-449-5302, 800-347-5088).

■ **The Allen House** (expensive). Overlooking the harbor and a comfortable distance away from the main street of the small town of Scituate, this B&B has six tasteful guest rooms with private baths, decorated in late Victorian style with eclectic touches. Five rooms have a queen- or a king-size bed. Guests may enjoy the parlor, living room, and screened porch, where breakfast is served in summer. *18 Allen Pl., Scituate, MA 02066; tel. 781-545-8821. On the coast, southeast of World's End.*

■ **1810 House** (moderate). This half cape with three guest rooms has original beamed ceilings, wide pine floors, and stenciled walls. Book the downstairs room for its private bath and

▼

queen-size canopy bed. A full breakfast, often featuring quiche or eggs Benedict, is served on a screened porch or next to a fireplace in the country kitchen. *147 Old Oaken Bucket Rd., Norwell, MA 02061; tel. 781-659-1810. Off Rte. 3A.*

■ **Windy Bluffs** (inexpensive). With lodging choices so limited, this modern New England house on a quiet residential street may come in handy. The ocean can be seen from the sitting room. Room 3 is the largest of three rooms (two with private baths). The decor may be too cute, but the small home is very well kept, the owners are friendly, and the price is right. A continental breakfast is served. *44 Chickatawbut Ave., Marshfield, MA 02050; tel. 781-834-8309. Off Rte. 139 east. About 20 mi. southeast of World's End.*

FOR MORE INFORMATION

Tourist Office:

■ **South Shore Chamber of Commerce.** *36 Miller Stile Rd., Quincy, MA 02169; tel. 617-479-1111. Open Mon.-Fri. 8-4 May-Oct.; 8:45-5 Nov.-Apr.*

For Serious Walkers:

Walkers should visit Whitney and Thayer Woods, another Trustees of Reservations property. This 800-acre forest of pine, hardwoods, rhododendron, and huge boulders is laced with 12 miles of trails. Next door is the 3,500-acre Wompatuck State Park, which offers car camping.

■ **Whitney and Thayer Woods.** *Rte. 3A, Cohasset and Hingham. From its junction with Rte. 228, follow Rte. 3A for 2 mi. east. The entrance is on the right, opposite Sohier St.*

The Cape's Last Great Expanse

EXPERIENCE 13:
THE PUNKHORN PARKLANDS

The Highlights: Pine woods, expansive lake views, cranberry bogs, glacial ponds.

Other Places Nearby: Fabulous beaches, a natural history museum, excellent B&Bs and inns.

The population of Cape Cod has been growing at an alarming rate. During the 1980s, development fever was epidemic, and even now open space is shrinking fast as houses go up virtually everywhere. It's ironic that the untamed beauty of the Cape—the scenic country roads, cranberry bogs and, most of all, the Cape Cod National Seashore—is what drew people in the first place.

In Brewster, far-sighted conservationists drew a line in the sand, and during the 1980s the town acquired almost 800 acres of the Cape's last great expanse of woods and ponds. The tract, which is the site of this walking tour, was known as the Punkhorns.

The origin of the term Punkhorn is unclear. Some say it may have been an old English word meaning "a place of spongy or rotten wood." Others claim the term is a corruption of a Native American word that is correctly pronounced "spunkhorn." During the latter part of the 18th century, the area

▼

was known as Brewster Woods and used as a common sheep-grazing pasture by residents of northern Harwich. Today, the tract is called the Punkhorn Parklands and is under the direction of the Brewster Conservation Commission. People from the area are still sometimes referred to as "Punkhorners," a term signifying those who live far from town.

Aspects of Cape Cod's geology are well-illustrated in the Punkhorn Parklands. The Cape is a product of the Wisconsin period of the Ice Age, comprised of glacial till—clay, sand, rocks, and even boulders—dragged from the north by the glacial ice sheet. Many of these large boulders, called glacial erratics (so named because they were carried far from their place of origin), were actually mined in the Punkhorns, then dynamited and used to construct jetties.

Also formed by the glaciers were the many kettles of Punkhorn Parklands. These freshwater ponds were created as large blocks of ice broke off from the glacier and eventually melted.

Upper Millpond in the Punkhorns is a vast pond that drains into Cape Cod Bay. Every spring—from early April to mid-May—a small fish called the alewife leaves the bay and fights its way upstream, via Stony Brook, to this and other freshwater ponds where they spawn. After hatching, the baby fish live in the kettle for about six months and then migrate to the bay. The small fish, related to shad and herring, were once a part of the diet of Native Americans who lived in the area. They were also used as fertilizer.

For many years, Upper Millpond was used for duck hunting. A number of private duck hunting camps were located in the Punkhorns along the ponds, and old blinds can still be found between Walkers Pond and Upper Millpond. Here the sweet pepperbush was abundant and made good cover; hunters would do a little pruning and settle in with their guns. Around the turn of the century, ducks were so "thick" that they

▼

were harvested commercially.

The Punkhorn Parkland is partially wetland, making it perfect for cranberry cultivation. For many years, cranberries, which were used as a source of vitamin C by sailors, were grown in cleared bogs and low areas that could be flooded in the Punkhorns. At harvest, water was drained out of the ponds and into the cranberry bogs using pumps driven by auto engines. You can still find some rusty relics from this period.

Forest dominates a large part of the Punkhorn Parkland. Beech groves flourish in the northern section, oaks in the middle, and pitch pines in the southern part. During the 19th century, trees from the Punkhorns were cut to fire the glassworks in Sandwich. And, until relatively recently, the Punkhorn forests were subject to regular burns. But with fire towers, the number of fires has lessened, allowing the forest to grow. The trees are so big that the undergrowth has a hard time existing, and the open fields have practically disappeared.

GETTING THERE
By car:

Drive to Brewster, MA, by way of Rtes. 6 and 6A. From Rte. 6A, 1 mi. west of Brewster center, turn left at the blinking light onto Stony Brook Rd. Go 6/10 mi. and turn left onto Run Hill Rd. Proceed 1.2 mi. to the Punkhorn Parklands parking area ahead on the left, where you can get maps.

Walk Directions

TIME: 2 1/2 hours
LEVEL: Moderate
DISTANCE: 4 miles
ACCESS: By car

The paths and lanes through Punkhorn Parklands are surprisingly numerous. Three routes (that utilize a combination of paths and roads) in the preserve are designated with plastic markers and numbered trailposts. The walk described below fol-

▼

lows portions of these trails, along with some well-used sand roads and a section of paved road. Careful attention to directions should keep you on track.

During July and the first part of August, the Punkhorns are beseiged with biting flies. The best seasons for walking are late spring and autumn, although experienced walkers will find the woods interesting throughout the year. Expect to encounter other walkers, horses and even cars on some of the lanes. Swimming is permitted in Upper Millpond.

TO BEGIN

From the parking area, turn left onto unpaved Run Hill Rd. and walk to a junction of sand roads. To your right is a lane that leads to a boat launch on Upper Millpond.

1. Enter the woods on a path that is found between the road directly ahead of you and the road to the pond on your right. A sign indicates that this is the Eagle Point Trail, marked occasionally with blue plastic markers. After passing a bog, you reach the edge of the pond (trail post No. 2). *Notice the ruins of an old pump house (be careful of poison ivy here).* Ignore all side trails and continue ahead, keeping the pond to your right. A short climb brings you to Eagle Point. *Eagle Point offers a good vista over Upper Millpond and is a great place for lunch or a rest. If you descend to the water's edge, you will find the remnants of a duck blind.*

2. From Eagle Point, the trail swings to the left and passes a dedication plaque. Near trail post No. 5, leave the wider lane and bear right, following one of the two parallel footpaths high above the pond. *The one to the right offers better views.* Blue markers occur more frequently in the section ahead. At a junction, turn left, then bear right at the next fork.

3. On reaching a sand road (trail post No. 7), turn left. This road is called Eagle Cartway.

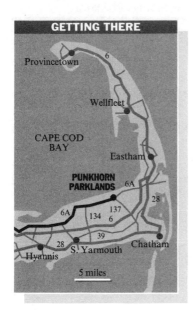

GETTING THERE

Provincetown

Wellfleet

CAPE COD BAY

Eastham

PUNKHORN PARKLANDS

6A

6A

134

137
6

39

28

Hyannis   S. Yarmouth

Chatham

5 miles

KEY

- ▬ Walk follows paved road
- ═ Walk follows dirt road or footpath
- Paved road
- ---- Dirt road or footpath
- ─ Bog
- 🌲 Wooded area
- 🔆 View

⅛   ¼

MILE

N

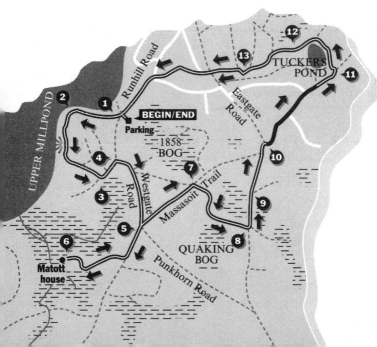

Runhill Road

TUCKERS POND

12

13

11

UPPER MILLPOND

2

1

BEGIN/END

Parking

1858 BOG

Eastgate Road

4

7

10

3

Westgate Road

Massasoit Trail

5

9

6

8

Matott house

QUAKING BOG

Punkhorn Road

▼

4. After a minute or two of walking, you reach Westgate Rd. Turn right (there is a cutoff lane that will shorten the turn) and begin a gradual uphill walk. Ignore two lanes on the left, one with blue markers.

5. After 5 minutes of walking, the road descends a bit, and you will reach Massasoit Rd., the first of two lanes that meet West Gate Rd. at nearly the same point. The other lane is Punkhorn Rd. *You may turn sharply left here, if you wish to skip the Matott house. If you do, follow Massasoit Rd. to the first intersection, which is Point 7.*

Otherwise, continue on Westgate Rd. for a few more minutes, passing two lanes leading off to the right. Turn right onto a third road that leads through a gate, downhill, and then right and uphill.

6. Arrive at the Matott house, which is slated to be an environmental center. *There is a partial view over bogs from the back of the house.* Return to Point 5. Proceed down Massasoit Rd. for about six minutes toward the first intersection.

7. Turn right onto a trail indicated by blue markers. This path will lead past (on the right) an abandoned cranberry bog still supporting cranberry bushes.

8. Arrive at a 4-way junction with a sand road (an old car body is just off the road in front of you) and turn left, leaving the blue markers.

9. Take the left fork at the next intersection (Eastgate Rd.) and walk past a residence toward a paved road in a suburban neighborhood.

10. Bear left onto the paved road (Pond St.) and follow it for 5 minutes, passing paved roads on the right and left.

▼

Continue on Pond St. until the pavement ends and the road becomes an unpaved lane.

11. Only 200 yards beyond the end of the pavement, turn left onto an unmarked footpath that leads downhill toward Tuckers Pond. At the pond, turn right and follow the unmarked paths around the perimeter of the pond, keeping left at the junctions.

12. At trail post No. 8, bear right, leaving the pond. Blue markers will indicate the trail from here. After passing near a bog (keep left at the fork), the trail swings back on itself at trail post No. 7. After trail posts No. 10 and No. 11, the trail goes by a residence and brings you to a T-junction, where you turn left and walk out toward a clearing and junction at the edge of a neighborhood.

13. At the junction, with a paved road visible to your left, turn right and immediately take the left fork. A post marks the trail. Make a left at the next post and keep to the left at the clearing. Turn right at the fence, pass trail post No. 1, and come to Run Hill Rd. Turn left and walk back to your car, just a few minutes away.

OTHER PLACES NEARBY

■ **Cape Cod Museum of Natural History.** Cape Cod's nature is on display, and both adults and children will find it interesting. Besides the museum, there are the grounds, on which the John Wing Trail is located. Call about special programs and field walks. *Rte. 6A, P.O. Box 1710, Brewster, MA 02631; tel. 508-896-3867, 800-479-3867. Open Mon.-Sat. 9:30-4:30, Sun. 11:00-4:30. Admission. Located 1.5 mi. east of Brewster center.*

■ **Moby Dick Farm.** One of the best ways to explore the Punkhorns is on horseback with a knowledgeable guide like

▼

Nick Rodday. At his farm, horses for individuals and groups are available, as are guided tours. *179 Great Field Rd., Brewster, MA 02631; tel. 508-896-3544.*

■ **Nickerson State Park.** This popular 1,955-acre state park has many campsites and some big ponds for swimming. There are a few walking trails and a section of the Cape Cod Rail Trail. *Rte. 6A, Brewster, MA 02631; tel. 508-896-3491. Admission.*

DINING

■ **Chillingsworth** (expensive). There are two restaurants here, one very expensive, offering a seven-course *table d'hote* menu, and a moderate to expensive bistro. Lunch and bistro fare are served in the greenhouse lounge, dinner in the formal dining room. The French-influenced menu changes daily; some favorite selections have been grilled swordfish with garlic mashed potatoes, sugarsnap peas with caper butter sauce, and fried pumpkin sweetbreads. There's an outstanding wine cellar. *2449 Main St., Rte. 6A, Brewster, MA 02631; tel. 508-896-3640. Open for lunch and dinner Tue.-Sun. in summer, Thu.-Sun. off season.*

■ **High Brewster** (expensive). Because it's not on Main Street, High Brewster is not listed in many guidebooks. Locally, however, it's regarded by some as the best on the Cape. The restaurant is part of a three-room, four-cottage guest house on a wonderful property with pond views. Classic American cuisine is served in cozy dining rooms with low, beamed ceilings, ladderback chairs, and candlelight. The seasonal *prix-fixe* menu has featured such items as pumpkin and sage bisque and tenderloin medallions with chives and cheese glaze. *964 Satucket Rd., Brewster, MA 02631; tel. 508-896-3636. Open for dinner only; call for reservations and times. From the center of Brewster, go 1 mi. south on 6A. Turn left at a flashing light onto Stony Brook Rd., left onto Satucket Rd.*

■ **The Bramble Inn & Restaurant** (expensive). Besides being an excellent inn that uses three historic houses located

▼

near each other in the center of Brewster, the first floor of the main building is an award-winning restaurant. Four-course *prix-fixe* dinners feature some very creative seafood, veal, lamb, and beef entrées. Roast rack of lamb with juniper red wine glacé and maple- glazed carrots julienne with Vermont cheddar red bliss potatoes is a signature dish. The several dining rooms are small and intimate. *Rte. 6A, 2019 Main St. P.O. Box 807, Brewster, MA 02631; tel. 508-896-7644. Open daily for dinner Apr.-Dec.*

■ **The Brewster Fish House Restaurant** (moderate). This small, nondescript restaurant (with a bar) has a great local reputation—in a town where every restaurant serves seafood. Aside from the single red meat special, you'll find only seafood here. Grilled tuna steaks, or baked cod with fresh herb stuffing, are favorites. *Rte. 6A, P.O. Box 71, Brewster, MA 508-896-7867. Open daily for lunch and dinner. East of Brewster center.*

■ **Longfellow's Pub** (inexpensive). Here's your basic pub—bar, TV, simple decor, and a varied menu with plenty of sandwiches. Prices are what you'd expect at a pub but seafood—as is the case everywhere—costs more. On Mondays during summer you can often get a lobster dinner for $7! *2377 Rte. 6A, 2208 Main St. Brewster, MA 02631; tel. 508-896-5413. Open daily for lunch and dinner. 1.5 mi. east of Brewster.*

LODGING

Brewster is a town where, many years ago, wealthy sea captains built their homes. Today, many of these mansions have become B&Bs and inns, each with an interesting history. Brewster is a very popular place to stay, so reservations for lodging should be made well in advance.

■ **The Brewster Farmhouse Inn** (expensive). Two miles south of the town center, but close to a natural area and walking trail, this wonderful B&B has five differently decorated guest rooms, each with a large private bath (bathrobes provided). The Shaker Room features a beautiful Shaker bed. A deck extends from the house to a hot tub and swimming pool;

▼

beyond is a large backyard. Full breakfast is served. Bicycles are provided for guests. *716 Main St. (Rte. 6A), Brewster, MA 02631; tel. 508-896-3910, 800-892-3910; fax 508-896-4232.*

■ **The Captain Freeman Inn** (expensive). Although its address is not on Route 6A, this inn faces the small oval that is the town green and is, therefore, in the center of things. There's much to recommend at this elegant rather than quaint inn— guest rooms tastefully decorated in updated Victorian fashion, and breakfast on the balcony. Third-floor rooms are small and share a bath. Bicycles are provided for guests. Reservations are required. *15 Breakwater Rd., Brewster, MA 02631; tel. 508-896-7481, 800-843-4664.*

■ **Candleberry Inn** (moderate). This nicely restored 1800 Federal-style home in Brewster center has six guest rooms, each with private bath, two common rooms, and a big backyard with several lawn swings. Three rooms have gas fireplaces, and there's a wood stove in a common room. You'll find antiques and wide pine plank floors throughout the house. A hearty continental breakfast (hot or cold cereals, muffins, coffee cakes) is served. *1882 Main St., Rte. 6A, Brewster, MA 02631; tel. 800-573-4769.*

■ **Isaiah Clark House** (moderate). Another historic sea captain's house, this B&B was built in the 1780s and is decorated in Colonial style. There are seven guest rooms with private baths and AC. A full breakfast is served inside or on the deck overlooking the gardens in the backyard. Nature trails are nearby. *1187 Old King's Hwy., Rte. 6A, Brewster, MA 02631; tel. 508-896-2223, 800-822-4001.*

■ **Old Sea Pines Inn** (moderate). Formerly a girls school, this turn-of-the-century inn has many large guest rooms (with private baths) decorated in a 1920s style. Smaller rooms with shared baths are a bargain. A full breakfast is served on a bright, cheerful, enclosed porch. A back cottage offers more modern amenities. The atmosphere is very casual here, unlike the more formal inns. *2553 Main St., Rte. 6A, P.O. Box 1070, Brewster, MA 02631; tel. 508-896-6114. Closed Dec. 21 through mid-Mar.*

▼

■ **The Old Manse Inn** (moderate). Captain Winslow Lewis Knowles was the sea captain who, in the early 1800s, built this mansion. Today, it's a nine-room inn that also offers gourmet, candlelit dinners in its two dining rooms. All guest rooms have private baths. The Old Manse has a good location, and is well run—17 years under the same management. *1861 Main St., Brewster, MA 02631; tel. 508-896-3149. Closed Jan.-Mar.*

FOR MORE INFORMATION

Tourist Offices:

■ **Brewster Chamber of Commerce/Board of Trade.** *P.O. Box 910, Brewster, MA 02631; tel. 508-896-3500. A summer visitors center, operated by the Brewster Board of Trade and the Chamber of Commerce, is located in the Annex Building at Town Hall. It's open daily from 9-3.*

For Serious Walkers:

Brewster offers some fine walking opportunities. The John Wing Trail, accessed from the Cape Cod Natural History Museum, explores woods, marsh, and beach. It was the Brewster Conservation Commission's first acquisition. Nickerson State Park has trails traversing pine woods and ponds. The Cape Cod Rail Trail runs through Brewster, and provides some excellent walking and bicycling possibilities. Walkers should be aware that ticks carrying Lyme disease are found throughout Cape Cod, and precautions should be taken.

Island-Hopping on the Cape

EXPERIENCE 14: GREAT ISLAND

Cape Cod's shape is constantly changing. This peninsula is really a pile of sand, gravel, and rock that was dumped well out to sea by the glacial ice sheet. Ocean currents batter and shift the debris into the swirls, points, and curves that we see when we examine a map of Cape Cod.

The Highlights: Glistening bays, picturesque seascapes, isolated pine forests and dunes, the site of a whaling tavern.

Other Places Nearby: Cape Cod National Seashore, excellent beaches, site of the first transatlantic broadcast.

On this walk, you visit Great Island, an island until the 1830s, when the southward drifting sand closed the gap between it and the mainland. At Great Beach Hill, the same thing happened; geologists call it a tombolo, or a sand bar that connects islands to the mainland, or each other.

The narrow connection between the mainland and Great Island is locally called "The Gut." A similar sand bar lies between Great Island and Great Beech Hill; another sits beyond that, and then, finally, the last patch of grassy land disappears under the high tide.

Your walk from the mainland to Great Island and beyond

▼

is a trek over a chain of diminishing islands, all linked by a narrow beach. A look at a topographic map reveals that north of Great Island are two more links in the chain, now well-cemented to the mainland. These are Bound Brook Island and Griffin Island, separated only by the flow of the Herring River.

Before the migration of sand linked the islands, they stood alone, guardians of Wellfleet Harbor. During the 17th century, the shore whalers of Wellfleet built lookout towers on Great Island to better sight their prey. Once they spotted a whale, they'd rush out into the water, surround, and beach their victim for its valuable meat, oil, and bones. In the latter part of the century, a tavern was erected there—to cater to these sailors far from the diasapproving stares of the Puritans on the mainland—and it operated until about 1740. All that is left are some boulders and artifacts collected and stored during an archaeological dig that took place in 1969 and 1970. These artifacts, though few in number, tell an interesting story.

Before the dig, the history of the Great Island site was unknown. Some thought it had been a 17th-century Dutch trading outpost, others a tavern run by a man named Samuel Smith. An accounting of the artifacts that were discovered at the site revealed a disproportionately high number of eating and drinking utensils and clay pipes—very suggestive of a tavern.

One of the ways that the site was dated was by measuring the diameter of the pipestem bores. Apparently, the pipestem bores (the smoking equivalent of tree-ring dating) found there were consistent with those in general use between 1710 and 1740. The abandonment date of the site was determined in part by this, and also by the lack of white salt-glazed pottery that was very prevalent by the mid-1700s. Comparisons with other known tavern sites and farm sites were used to confirm this interpretation.

Pieces of glass wine bottles, buttons and buckles, gunflints, a harpoon, ladies' fans, pig and sheep bones, and earthenware from Holland, Germany, and England were also

▼

unearthed at the site. Even more suggestive is an old ditty that local tradition has kept alive: "Samuel Smith, he has good flip (a frothy, spiced ale), good toddy (hot rum toddy) if you please, the way is near and very clear, 'tis just beyond the trees." An 1893 letter found around the time of the dig mentioned an early 18th century inn holder named Samuel Smith. One can imagine whalers and sailors drinking ale and rum out on Great Island, far from the main harbor. A roasted pig for dinner, served on white plates, tobacco smoked in a clay pipe, and friendly ladies for company.

As you have no doubt gathered, very little is known about Smith's Tavern. Seeing the site will make you wonder how anything at all is known.

As shore whaling declined, most likely due to overfishing, the tavern business did, too. Around 1770, the Wellfleet oyster beds, one of the town's chief assets, were exhausted. Nothing much happened on the island in the way of human history from this time on. Great Island's forest provided wood for building and charcoal. Farm animals were set to pasture on the island, which was an ideal location because little, if any, fencing was needed. By 1800, the forest had been cut down and the island stood out as a bare lump of grass-covered sand. A little later a cranberry farm was started but didn't amount to much. In the 1830s, with the land washing away due to the lack of trees, pitch pines were planted to stop sand and soil from filling the bay.

The wife of the last landowner on the island, Priscilla Alden Bartlett, lived here until 1962, and you will pass a monument to her along the walk. You will also come across a monument to a Native American who was discovered (and then reinterred) when a road was excavated.

GETTING THERE

By car:

Drive on Rte. 6 toward Wellfleet, MA, located south of Provincetown on Cape Cod. Go left at a traffic light where a

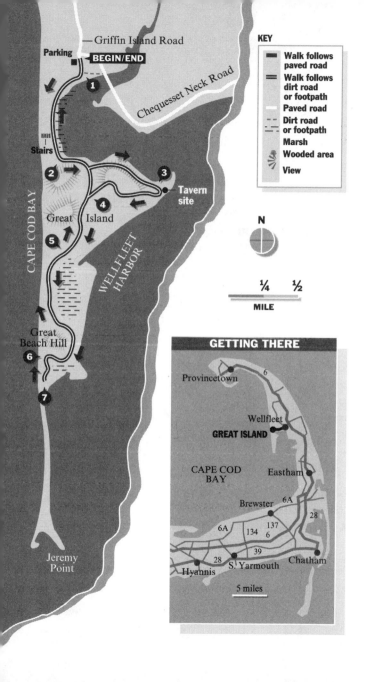

KEY

Walk follows paved road
Walk follows dirt road or footpath
Paved road
Dirt road or footpath
Marsh
Wooded area
View

Griffin Island Road
Parking
BEGIN/END
Chequesset Neck Road

Stairs

CAPE COD BAY

Great Island

Tavern site

Wellfleet Harbor

Great Beach Hill

Jeremy Point

N

¼   ½
MILE

GETTING THERE

Provincetown

Wellfleet
GREAT ISLAND

CAPE COD BAY

Eastham

Brewster   6A
6A   137
134   6   28
39
Hyannis   S. Yarmouth   Chatham
28

5 miles

▼

sign points to Wellfleet town center. Follow Main St. for 1/3 mi. and then turn left onto Commercial St. This road follows the beach to the right, becoming first Kendrick Ave. and then Chequesett Neck Rd. After crossing the mouth of the Herring River, drive another 1/3 mi. and turn left into the parking area for Great Island.

Walk Directions

TIME: 1 to 5 hours
LEVEL: Easy to difficult
DISTANCE: 1 1/2 to 6 miles
ACCESS: By car

Portions of this walk are on loose sand, which can prove tiring. This factor, along with the uphill sections on Great Island and Big Beech Hill and the length of the walk, make it difficult. But you don't have to do the complete walk, and can make it easy or moderate by walking to Point 2, 3, 4, or 5 and then turning back to your car. **Expect flies during the hotter months in summer, especially when there is no breeze.** If you are walking during fly season, take along a head net or strong insect repellent. **Jeremy Point, the land at the end of the walk, is submerged at high tide—don't get caught there.** Give yourself plenty of time, carry water, and enjoy some of the most beautiful scenery on Cape Cod.

TO BEGIN

From the east side of the parking area, follow the Great Island Trail downhill through the pines to the tidal flat. You will pass a monument marking the reinternment of a Native American woman.

1. Turn right and walk along the sandy path that follows the edge of the marsh. *This tidal flat is called "The Gut." Dunes are to your right, and Great Island is ahead of you.*

▼

2. When you reach Great Island, continue following the trail, which swings to the left, heading southeast but still paralleling the shore. Do not take the path uphill (this will be your return route). Continue on the trail as it gradually rises, bringing you into the pines, and then to a point where there are views of Wellfleet. *On sunny days, this forest will provide welcome shade.*

3. As you reach the old tavern site, marked by only a few boulders, a side trail leads to the cliff overlooking Wellfleet Harbor. *Enjoy the view.* Continue following the main trail through pitch pine forest, which is level ground. There's a drop in elevation before you reach the next junction.

4. Turn left at this junction and follow the wide lane that passes a field on the left where locals used to drill for water and then a monument to Priscilla Alden Bartlett.

5. When you reach "The Gut" between Great Island and Great Beach Hill, continue walking south with the marsh on your left and dunes on your right. Follow the path as it ascends Great Beach Hill on soft sand. Keep left at the fork in the path, and head downhill through the forest.

6. At the next "gut," follow the path southward, with marsh on your left and dunes on your right. **Be aware of the tides; portions of this area, especially Jeremy Point, are underwater during high tide.**

7. When you reach the last major patch of vegetation, return the way you came (except bear left at Point 4, bypassing the tavern site). *As an alternative from Point 7, you might follow the coastline northward. Then, after passing Great Island, climb over the dunes using the boardwalk and stairs, and turn left on the path along "The Gut."*

▼

OTHER PLACES NEARBY

■ **Cape Cod National Seashore.** These 27,700 acres preserved in their natural state allow visitors to see what the Cape was like before development. The historic Marconi site is where radio pioneer Guglielmo Marconi sent the first transatlantic message to England in 1903. The Salt Pond Visitor Center provides information on swimming areas, parking fees, nature trails, and bikepaths. *Rte. 6, Eastham, MA; 02642; tel. 508-255-3421, 508-349-3785.*

DINING

■ **Aesop's Tables** (expensive). In contrast to Wellfleet's typically casual restaurants, Aesop's Tables offers a more sophisticated dining experience. Located in an 1805 house overlooking Main Street, the restaurant has an upstairs bar, several dining areas, and tables on the terrace. The new American menu includes items like the wild vegetarian, filo dough torte with layers of sweet vegetables, mushrooms, and raisins; and uptown duck, marinated in spiced wine, roasted, and served with orange demi-glace. *316 Main St., Wellfleet, MA 02667 tel. 508-349-6450. Open Mothers Day-Columbus Day, daily for lunch and dinner mid-Jun.-mid-Sep. In the center of Wellfleet next to the Town Hall.*

■ **Bookstore and Restaurant** (moderate). The views over Wellfleet Bay to Great Island, which are best from the balcony, make this a good stop after the walk—for food or drinks. Seafood, of course, rules the menu, but there are some pasta and vegetarian dishes. There is a used bookstore in back, and next door is a playground for kids. *Kendrick Ave., Wellfleet, MA 02667; tel. 508-349-3154. Open daily for breakfast, lunch, and dinner. From Rte. 6, take Main St., and turn left on Commercial, then right on Kendrick.*

■ **Finely JP's** (moderate). J.P., the chef-owner of this very modest high-quality restaurant, was getting tired of cooking for other owners. Finally, he got his own place and named it accord-

▼

ingly. No reservations, no frills—just locally acclaimed entrées including J.P.'s *cataplana* with Cajun andouille sausage, Wellfleet paella, and sautéed medallions of pork with apples and goat cheese. *Rte. 6, P.O. Box 1360, South Wellfleet, MA; tel. 508-349-7500. Open daily for dinner mid-Jun.-Labor Day; Wed.-Sun. mid-May-mid-Jun. and Sep.-mid-Nov.; Thu.-Sun. mid-Nov.-mid-May.*

■ **Flying Fish Cafe** (moderate). Here's a simple cafe/bakery that offers a very interesting menu: Mexican mussels, jerk chicken Caribe, shrimp stir fry—and some vegetarian dishes, too. Sample the breads and pastries. *Briar Ln., Wellfleet, MA 02667; tel. 508-349-3100. Open daily from early spring-Oct. for breakfast, lunch, and dinner. Closed winter. Just off Main St.*

■ **Painter's Food and Drink** (moderate). This restaurant is the upscale offspring of a snack bar along the bay. The scene is funky, but the emphasis is on food, with creative preparations of seafood, pork, lamb, poultry, and pasta. Upstairs is a tavern with live music most summer nights until 12:30. *50 Main St., Wellfleet, MA 02667; tel. 508-349-3003. Open daily for breakfast and lunch. Open daily for dinner except in winter.*

LODGING

Wellfleet has limited lodging, but Brewster and Chatham are reasonably close by, and both have many inns and B&Bs.

■ **Aunt Sukie's Bayside B&B** (expensive). This is a real find—excellent location, tasteful (eclectic, mostly contemporary) rooms, and privacy. From the decks and balconies, you look over the tidal flats to the bay and Great Island. A boardwalk takes you down to a private sandy beach. Each unit has a private bath and a queen-size bed; two guest rooms have balconies. There's a ground floor suite. *525 Chequessett Neck Rd., Wellfleet, MA 02667; tel. 508-349-2804, 800-420-9999. On the road to Great Island, marked with a house number.*

■ **Cahoon Hollow B&B** (moderate). This small and private B&B, built in 1842 for a sea captain, is two miles out of town. Two suites—each with private bath and sitting room—are avail-

▼

able at a very reasonable price. Full gourmet breakfast is served. You can use bicycles without a charge. *Cahoon Hollow Rd., P.O. Box 383, Wellfleet, MA 02667; tel. 508-349-6372. Just off Rte. 6.*

■ **The Inn at Duck Creeke** (moderate). This four-building inn is situated on a duck pond and a salt marsh, although the calm is marred by adjacent Rte. 6. The 27 guest rooms are simple and functional; some have shared baths. Sweet Seasons, the inn's restaurant, serves fine cuisine (expensive), and the Tavern Room Restaurant and Lounge is a good place to hear live music. *Main St., Wellfleet, MA; tel. 508-349-9333. Closed Nov.-Apr.*

■ **The Holden Inn** (inexpensive). This inn has little charm but good value with 27 basic rooms in three buildings— an old sea captains home, a cottage, and a lodge. About half have shared baths. The lodge has good views, but it's on a busy road. No breakfast is served. *140 Commercial St., P.O. Box 816, Wellfleet, MA 02667; tel. 508-349-3450. Closed Nov.-mid-Apr. On Commercial St.*

FOR MORE INFORMATION

Tourist Office:

■ **Wellfleet Chamber of Commerce.** *P.O. Box 571, Wellfleet, MA 02667-2510; tel. 508-349-2510. Information booth off Rte. 6 in South Wellfleet; 24-hour information line.*

For Serious Walkers:

The Cape Cod National Seashore, which includes Great Island, has many other walking opportunities ranging from beach walks to footpaths in forests. The Nauset Marsh Trail, from the Salt Pond Visitor Center to Coast Guard Beach and back, is an excellent walk. The Atlantic White Cedar Trail, accessed from the Marconi Station site, goes through a cedar forest, on footpath and boardwalk.

The Hoot, Toot & Whistle Railroad

EXPERIENCE 15: HARRIMAN DAM

Around the time of the Civil War, Holyoke, Massachusetts, was one of the leading manufacturing cities in the country. Paper was one of its products, and the mills were hungry for wood

> **The Highlights:** A dam and a reservoir, a walk along an old rail line through a beautiful forest of evergreens, white birches, and ferns.
>
> **Other Places Nearby:** White-water rafting and canoeing in a rugged gorge, tall mountains, great B&Bs, a winery, great skiing.

pulp. To continue making profits, businessmen realized that wood from outside the local area must be found and transported cheaply. In nearby southern Vermont were deep forests where large tracts of virgin timber stood ready to fuel the Industrial Revolution. The best transport in those days was the railroad and an existing line came within a few miles of the Vermont border. Through the mountainous valley of the Deerfield River ran the tracks of the Fitchburg Railroad, passing through the five-mile-long Hoosac Tunnel toward the Vermont forests.

In 1884, four business-minded brothers from Holyoke formed a corporation called the Deerfield Valley Railroad. The

▼

very next year tracks were laid from the Hoosac Tunnel to Readsboro, Vermont, just over the Massachusetts border. In 1886, the corporation's name was changed to the Hoosac Tunnel & Wilmington Railroad Company, or HT&W (Hoot, Toot & Whistle). Isolated communities in southern Vermont were enthusiastic about the railroad's arrival. The town of Wilmington, whose name was part of the new corporation's name, pushed for an extension which came about in 1891. In November of that year, the official first run on the completed line began in Wilmington. Several hundred people and the town band jammed onto the train as it rolled south to the Hoosac Tunnel, though the mountain and on to North Adams in northwestern Massachusetts.

The HT&W line was not easy to build or to maintain. It hugged cliffs and spanned ravines on trestles. It climbed steep grades—800 feet in 24 miles—as it wound along the course of the Deerfield River. Eventually, manufacturers realized that it was easier to make pulp where the trees grew. The river was dammed near Wilmington, and a mill complex was built on the reservoir that resulted. This industrial area, which once had about 300 residents, became known as Mountain Mills. The once-thriving community, including a three-story building, is now submerged beneath the Harriman Reservoir. Portions become visible only in time of low water.

Lumbering in southern Vermont was controlled by the Deerfield Lumber Company. To bring out the timber, they built narrow gauge railroads well into the upper Deerfield Valley. In 1904, the company bought the HT&W. This was the peak of the harvesting of southern Vermont's virgin forests. By 1915, about 40 miles of track had been laid and more than 25 logging camps operated in the forests.

Then a new player entered the scene. The New England Power Company (NEPCo) began its eventual takeover of the area with the building of the Somerset Dam northwest of

▼

Wilmington. In 1920, they bought the HT&W, along with most of the land within the Deerfield Valley. Now with near total control of the area, NEPCo began to construct the Harriman Dam, a 200-foot high monster which, at the time, was the largest in the world. Water flowed from the reservoir through an enormous drain (the Glory Hole) to the power station three miles downstream in an underground pipe. The waters of the Harriman Reservoir flooded acres of farmland and covered all of Mountain Mills. This flooding required the relocation of the HT&W track higher up the hillside.

The relocation of the line was fraught with problems and NEPCo attempted to sell the people of Wilmington on the idea of a ferry that would carry railroad cars down to the end of the dam where the line would end. Wilmington didn't like the idea and forced the company to restore rail service to the town. To accomplish this, the company built switchbacks to bring the trains to the top of the Harriman Dam. Other major obstacles appeared later. It wasn't a simple job.

Meanwhile, logging was in decline, and few of the narrow-gauge lines were being used. NEPCo wasn't really interested in running a railroad, and in 1926 it sold most of its stock. The very next year flooding and mudslides ruined parts of the line, including a long trestle. By the time repairs were made, bus service had been established between Wilmington and the Hoosac Tunnel. The railroad was no longer needed to carry passengers, and from then on, the HT&W handled only freight. In 1936, a big spring runoff washed out the trestle again. The line's owners had enough. The railroad was sold, the line short-ened to Readsboro, and the line north to Wilmington was abandoned. Service continued on the remaining 11 miles until 1971.

Today, the Harriman Reservoir, also known as Lake Whitingham, is popular among boaters, fishermen, picnickers, and swimmers (there's even a nude beach). The relocated HT&W bed, now called the Harriman Trail, can still be walked from end to end, although the middle section uses woods roads. This route is also a part of the Catamont Trail, a 280-mile cross-country ski trail, marked with blue diamonds with a cat-print, that spans the length of Vermont.

The Harriman Trail is not heavily used and if you walk early in the day, you may be alone. In summer, you may occasionally hear motor boats on the nearby reservoir.

GETTING THERE
By car:

Drive to Wilmington in south-central Vermont near the Massachusetts border. The town is reached by taking I-91 to Rte. 9 east. In Wilmington, go east on Rte. 9 to Rte. 100 south. Travel seven miles to Jacksonville. Stay on Rte. 100, which will make two right turns. In another 4 mi., you come to Whitingham and Brown's General Store. Continue for another mile on Rte. 100 and then turn right onto Harriman Rd. Drive nearly 2 mi. on Harriman Rd. to a hairpin turn. Just beyond, look for a parking area in front of a gate to Harriman Dam.

Walk Directions

TIME: 3 1/2 hours
LEVEL: Moderate
DISTANCE: 7 miles
ACCESS: By car

Although the full length of this walk seems long to inexperienced walkers, it has few serious ups and downs and allows you to go just a short distance to enjoy views and a nice place to picnic.

TO BEGIN

From the parking area, find the gate to the Harriman Dam. About 50 feet left of the gate, between a large white birch and a maple tree, find an opening that allows a person, but not a motor vehicle, access to the dam. A smaller gateway to the right of the main gate sometimes is open as well. Pass through the

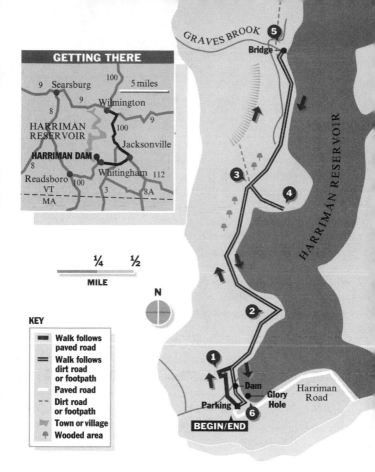

GETTING THERE

9 Searsburg
100
5 miles
9
8
Wilmington
HARRIMAN
RESERVOIR
100
9
Jacksonville
HARRIMAN DAM
8
Whitingham 112
Readsboro
VT
100
3
8A
MA

¼   ½

MILE

N

KEY

▬ Walk follows
paved road

═ Walk follows
dirt road
or footpath

▭ Paved road

-- Dirt road
or footpath

🌲 Town or village

🌲 Wooded area

GRAVES BROOK ⑤
Bridge

③

④

HARRIMAN RESERVOIR

②

①

Dam
Glory
Hole
Harriman
Road
Parking
⑥
BEGIN/END

gate and follow the paved path as it proceeds beneath the dam.

1. At a hairpin turn near power lines at the end of the dam, turn right, still on the pavement, and walk to the top of the dam. Face the reservoir. Continue straight ahead onto the unpaved railroad bed that follows the western shore of the reservoir. On a tree, you may see a marker for the Catamont Trail, which is used for cross-country skiing.

2. Pass through a narrow rock cut. In wet periods, there may be large puddles in this area.

▼

3. After a short descent to a brook, you arrive at a four-way junction. Turn right and follow the path downhill past a stone wall and a secluded picnic table.

4. Arrive at the edge of the reservoir. *This is a good area for resting or eating.* To resume walking, return to Point 3, turn right, and continue north on the Harriman Trail. *For a shorter walk, retrace your steps to the parking area.*

5. After another 30 to 45 minutes, bear right at a fork and descend to the bridge over Graves Brook. *This is a convenient terminus for the walk and also a place to relax and enjoy the scenery. Good views of the Harriman Reservoir are near the mouth of the brook, which is close to the bridge.* To return, retrace your steps to Point 1. Instead of descending the dam, turn left onto the paved road atop the dam and walk along it.

6. Stand next to the unique spillway known as the Glory Hole. *Notice how the water level in the reservoir can be changed by placing boards along the spillway rim. The cone is 160 feet wide and tapers to 22 feet at its base. Water drops 170 feet from the spillway to the bottom of the dam. When high water rushes over its lip, the spillway looks like a morning glory.* Your car is directly below. Follow a path down to it.

OTHER PLACES NEARBY

■ **Gallery at the White Church.** The beautiful glasswork of Kathleen Young and Christopher Constantin, as well as artwork and jewelry, are on display inside an 1840's church converted into a stylish art gallery. Notice the impressive original stained-glass windows and the tin ceiling. *10 S. Main St., Wilmington, VT 05363; tel. 802-464-2515. Open daily 10-5.*

■ **Green Mountain Flagship Co. Ltd.** This company operates a large cruise boat and rents canoes, kayaks, and sailboats for use on the Harriman Reservoir. The 1 1/2-hour cruise

▼

includes a historical description of sites by the captain. *389 Rte. 9 West, Wilmington, VT 05363; tel. 802-464-2975. Open daily May-Oct. On Rte. 9, west of the Wilmington traffic light.*

■ **North River Winery.** This riverside winery, which produces 11 apple wines, offers free tours and tastings in an old farmhouse and barn. *Rte. 112, Jacksonville, VT 05342; tel. 802-368-7557. Open daily 10-5 for tasting and sales. Tours late May-Dec.*

DINING

■ **The Inn at Sawmill Farm** (very expensive). Savor the country elegance inside the beautiful dining room of this renowned Relais & Chateaux inn serving five-course dinners. Expect appetizers such as shrimp in beer batter with pungent fruit sauce and salmon mousse with black caviar. Entrées include grilled marinated duck breast, Indonesian curried chicken breasts, poached halibut, and grilled veal chop. The wine cellar boasts 36,000 bottles and 900 selections. A jacket is requested. *Rte. 100, P.O. Box 367, West Dover, VT 05356; tel. 802-464-8131, 800-493-1133.*

■ **Le Petit Chef** (expensive). In an old farmhouse, you can casually enjoy the area's finest restaurant, serving creative French-influenced dishes. Look for such appetizers as bird's nest—a potato basket with shiitake mushroom cream sauce—and tomato, basil, and goat cheese tart. Stellar entrées include roast duckling, which has a slight Oriental touch, and rack of lamb with a vegetable bouquet. *Rte. 100, Wilmington, VT 05363; tel. 802-464-8437. Open daily except Tue. for dinner.*

■ **The Deerhill Inn & Restaurant** (expensive). The elegant dining room offers a magnificent vista overlooking West Dover and Mt. Snow. The eclectic Italian-influenced menu includes veal with wild mushrooms and lemon cream sauce, scallops, peppered sirloin steak, and such specials as striped bass sautéed in cream sauce. *Valley View Rd., West Dover, VT 05356; tel. 802-464-3100. Open daily except Wed. (open Wed. during holiday weeks) for dinner. 1/10 mi. west of Rte. 100.*

■ **Julie's Cafe** (moderate). The eclectic menu at this road-

▼

side bistro features Southwest steak tips with black bean salsa, pasta with asparagus and roasted red peppers in a gorgonzola cream sauce, and grilled baby back ribs. There's also a long list of pizzas made over a wood fire. Lunch items include pesto grilled chicken wrap and grilled vegetables with provolone cheese on a focaccia roll. *Rte. 100, West Dover, VT 05356; tel. 802-464-2078. Open daily except Wed. for lunch and dinner.*

■ **Maple Leaf Malt & Brewing** (inexpensive). The beer is first-rate in this new brew pub—a welcome addition to the small downtown area. The menu is very limited and the dining area small, but it's a good place to socialize or to grab a quick lunch. The menu includes chicken with vegetables in puff pastry and three variations of a half loaf of sour dough bread and melted cheddar. *3 N. Main St., Wilmington, VT 05363; tel. 802-464-9900. Open daily for lunch and dinner.*

■ **The Perfect Cup** (inexpensive). Here's the place to find a special cup of coffee to start the day. You'll also find fresh-squeezed orange juice, bagels, and tasty muffins. Lunch consists of bagel sandwiches, vegetarian chili, and homemade soups. *Rte. 100, P.O. Box 1684, West Dover, VT 05356; tel. 802-464-8606. Open daily for breakfast and lunch.*

LODGING

■ **The Inn at Sawmill Farm** (very expensive). Though it's a world-class property in the Green Mountain foothills, "we think of our inn as unpretentious but curiously sophisticated," the innkeepers say. The inn is a recreation of an old barn, with hand-hewn posts, beams, and weathered boards. The elegant rooms have no televisions or telephones. The room rate includes breakfast and dinner. *Rte. 100, P.O. Box 367, West Dover, VT 05356; tel. 802-464-8131, 800-493-1133.*

■ **The Hermitage** (very expensive). The Hermitage is a world unto itself. There's the main building with its expansive dining room displaying Delacroix prints and decoys, a carriage house, and, up the road, the Brookbound Inn. The

▼

many acres of grounds are nice, and game birds are raised on site. The wine cellar houses an incredible collection—more than 40,000 bottles and 2,000 labels. The rooms are okay, but, considering the rate, many should be more elegant. There are no queen-size beds; three king-size beds are in less desirable rooms. Attractions include a swimming pool, a clay tennis court, a hunting preserve, and cross-country ski trails. Dinner and a full breakfast are included. *Coldbrook Rd., Box 457, Wilmington, VT 05363; tel. 802-464-3511.*

■ **The White House of Wilmington** (expensive). Sitting high above the road, this 16-room inn (a former Victorian mansion) and restaurant is a powerful sight. The views from the rooms are equally impressive, especially rooms with balconies. All rooms have private baths, including nine with fireplaces. Seven extra rooms are available in a guest house. There's also a pool, a great patio/lounge, and, in winter, a ski touring center. *Rte. 9, Wilmington, VT 05363; tel. 802-464-2135, 800-541-2135. Near the junction of Rtes. 9 and 100.*

■ **Whitingham Farm** (expensive). On 50 acres with great views of the New Hamsphire mountains 60 miles away, this Greek Revival B&B offers three guest rooms with private baths, antique furniture, and handmade quilts. The parlor room has a baby grand piano. Ask the owners for horse-drawn carriage or sleigh rides, which are free with a three-night stay. *RR1, Box 89D, Abbie Morse Rd., Whitingham, VT 05361; tel. 802-368-2620, 800-310-2010. Call for directions.*

■ **Nutmeg Inn** (expensive). The 14 rooms, including four suites, are in a former 18th-century farmhouse. It's a cozy and friendly place, with a full gourmet breakfast and a BYOB bar. The rooms are somewhat small but charming and newly renovated. Each has a private bath, a four-poster bed, and a quilt bed cover, and most have wood-burning fireplaces. The inn is next to a main road just outside the town center, but it's quiet inside. *Rte. 9, Box 818, Wilmington, VT 05363; tel. 802-464-3351. 3/4 mi. west of Wilmington.*

▼

■ **Deerfield Valley Inn** (moderate). From the front of this freshly painted 1885 country house that sits next to a main road, there's a good view of Mt. Snow. Serving a full breakfast in an attractive dining room, the inn is a bargain for a popular ski area. Request Room 5 with its canopied queen-size bed and working fireplace. *P.O. Box 1834, West Dover, VT 05356; tel. 802-464-6333. On Rte. 100.*

■ **Candlelight B&B** (inexpensive). There are four guest rooms—each with a private bath and a fireplace—a family room, and a great front porch. Full breakfast is served. *3358 Rte. 100, Box 380, Whitingham, VT 05361; tel. 802-368-7826, 800-992-2635. Just outside Jacksonville.*

■ **Engel House** (inexpensive). A well-groomed bargain, this B&B offers three modern, nicely decorated rooms that share two baths and an attractive common room. Families are welcome. *River Rd., Jacksonville, VT 05342; tel. 800-331-3757. On Rte. 112 across from the North River Winery.*

FOR MORE INFORMATION

Tourist Office:
■ **Mt. Snow/Harriman Region Chamber of Commerce.** The visitors center will make lodging reservations. *Box 3, Wilmington, VT 05363; tel. 802-464-8092. Visitors center located on West Main St. Open daily 10-5 Memorial Day-Oct.*

For Serious Walkers:
The lift at Mt. Snow brings walkers to mountaintop trails, and nearby Mt. Haystack is well worth a climb. Many top-notch trails are found on Kelly Stand Road, northwest of West Dover. For hiking information, go to Mt. Snow's Merrell Hiking Center, which offers tours, maps, and backpack and boot rentals. *Merrell Hiking Center, Mt. Snow Resort, Mt. Snow, VT 05356; tel. 802-464-4130. Open daily 8:30-5 late Jun.-mid-Oct.*

A Walk on the Wild Side

EXPERIENCE 16: LITTLE ROCK POND

Hidden behind the wall of mountains running parallel to Route 7 in southern Vermont is Little Rock Pond, a small gem in Green Mountain National Forest's White Rocks Recreation Area. Walking is easy at Little Rock Pond because the road leading to it, Forest Road 10,

The Highlights: An easy walk through forest to a beautiful, spring-fed pond edged by a mountain ridge, historic charcoal kilns.

Other Places Nearby: The town of Manchester and its outlet shopping, great walking and skiing trails, a summit you can drive to.

takes you to nearly the same elevation as the pond. Though this makes the area very popular with outdoors enthusiasts, the pond and its environs are spotless, mostly because of the Green Mountain Club.

In the late 19th century, clubs dedicated to building and maintaining hiking trails became popular in the Northeast. The Appalachian Mountain Club, founded in 1876, was one the nation's first major hiking clubs (*see* Experience 21, Zealand Notch) dedicated to walking and trail building. Its focus was primarily on the White Mountains of New Hampshire. Around the same time, smaller clubs formed to

▼

build trail systems in other mountainous areas, including the Adirondacks and the Catskills.

The movement didn't reach Vermont until 1910. The catalyst was a teacher, James Taylor, who believed that education was incomplete without hiking. He came up with the idea of a trail that would link all of Vermont's major mountains. In order to realize this vision, Taylor first needed a club. He promoted his concept vigorously throughout Vermont and then called a meeting of 18 prominent citizens to form the Green Mountain Club. Taylor was a masterful publicist and ran his project as if it were a political campaign. He gave speeches, wrote letters, and befriended the governor. A 30-mile section of the Long Trail near Mount Mansfield was built within a year or two. Taylor didn't find the actual work of building the trail very interesting. It took other dedicated supporters who were willing to do the physical work of building to make his dream come true.

Work on the trail in southern Vermont began in 1915, and the section between Manchester and Killington was mostly complete by 1920. The Appalachian Trail, which now shares its route with the Long Trail, was only conceived in 1920, so there's little doubt Taylor was visionary.

Today, the Green Mountain Club sponsors a caretaker who lives in a tent at Little Rock Pond during the summer. The caretaker collects a small fee from campers who use the area, keeps watch of what's going on, and is always willing to answer walkers' questions.

Before the coming of the Long Trail, the vast forests in the vicinity of Little Rock Pond were lumbered, mostly by Silas L. Griffith, Vermont's first millionaire. Griffith was born in Danby, Vermont, in 1837 and became a clerk in the general store. During the financial panic of 1857, he became a logger in Buffalo, New York, but he returned to Danby when he was able to borrow funds and set up his own store. Griffth's store was a success,

▼

and he rapidly became one of the town's leading businessmen.

About ten years later he acquired some timberland as payment for a debt and got involved in the lumber business. After a few false starts, he made a deal with an iron-making company in Lime Rock, Connecticut, to supply them with charcoal. Wood was becoming scarce in Connecticut (see Experience 1, Bear Mountain), so it had become economically viable to ship charcoal made in Vermont to fire the furnaces. Griffith was now set. He had a buyer, he owned acres of forest, and a rail line already existed in Danby.

The charcoal was made by stacking cut wood in piles, covering it with dirt except for a small opening at the top, and setting it on fire. The fire was left smoldering inside the mound for a week or two, and then the top hole was covered to extinguish the fire. Some old charcoal kilns are located near the beginning of the walk to Little Rock Pond, along a blackened section of trail.

For several years, Griffith ran the largest individually owned business in Vermont. He owned more than 50,000 acres of land, nine sawmills, and six general stores. Besides making charcoal, he sold lumber, manufactured boxes, and even found a market for the sawdust. Griffith used his wealth to build a large and interesting house in Danby which is now the Silas Griffith Inn. He also built a summer home on Griffith Lake, south of Little Rock Pond.

In 1930, the forests around Little Rock Pond were acquired by the National Forest Service, and in 1984, they were designated a wilderness and a part of the White Rocks National Recreation Area.

GETTING THERE

By car:

Drive to the southwestern corner of Vermont, near the New York border. From the junction of Rtes. 7 and 7A near Manchester Center, drive 12.5 mi. north on Rte. 7. Turn right at the hamlet of Mt. Tabor (a lumber depot helps mark the spot).

Cross the railroad tracks and drive 2.9 mi. on Forest Rd. 10 to the Appalachian/Long Trails parking area, which is on your right. The parking area is past Big Branch picnic area, which offers a vista over a ravine created by Big Branch Brook. The parking area for the Appalachian/Long Trails is large, but at peak times may fill up with day-hikers and backpackers. Additional parking may be found along Forest Rd. 10.

Walk Directions

TIME: 2 1/2 hours
LEVEL: Easy to moderate
DISTANCE: 4 1/2 miles
ACCESS: By car

While the walk has no major climbs, the last section is rocky. Be sure to wear sturdy shoes. Proceed carefully on the wooden boardwalks, particularly when they're wet.

TO BEGIN

From the parking area, walk across Forest Rd. 10 and enter the woods near a wooden signboard to the left of Big Black Brook. The white blazes of the Long Trail and Appalachian Trail mark the route. Follow the trail as it rises and then swings away from the brook.

1. Where the footpath becomes black, *look around for old charcoal mounds. One of them is right next to the trail.* Continue up the white-blazed trail for about 10 minutes.

2. Cross over Little Black Brook on a steel beam. Follow along the left bank of the brook for a few minutes before crossing it again, this time on rocks. **Be very careful when rocks are wet.** Turn left and follow the trail on the brook's east side as it passes a few wet areas on boardwalks and becomes rockier. Continue for a long stretch, walking on numerous boardwalks.

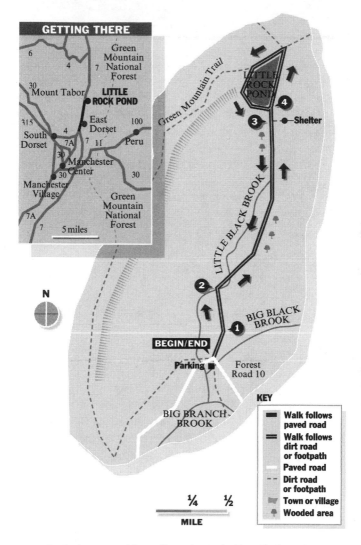

Green
Mountain
National
Forest

6

4

7

30
Mount Tabor

**LITTLE
ROCK POND**

315

30

South
Dorset

4

7A

East
Dorset

7

11

100

Peru

Manchester
Center

30

Manchester
Village

30

7A

7

Green
Mountain
National
Forest

5 miles

Green Mountain Trail

LITTLE
ROCK
POND

4

3

Shelter

LITTLE BLACK BROOK

2

BIG BLACK
BROOK

1

BEGIN/END

Parking

Forest
Road 10

KEY

BIG BRANCH
BROOK

- **Walk follows
  paved road**
- **Walk follows
  dirt road
  or footpath**
- **Paved road**
- **Dirt road
  or footpath**
- **Town or village**
- **Wooded area**

N

¼   ½

MILE

3. Arrive at a side trail to the Lula Tye Shelter. Ignore it and continue on.

4. Arrive at the south end of Little Rock Pond, where there is a trail junction. Retrace your steps to your car. *To the right is*

▼

*a camp area and the summer residence (a tent) of the Green
Mountain Club caretaker. A number of resting areas can be
found at the pond.*

*If you're not quite ready to return, follow the trail to the
right around the pond. You can explore the paths that encircle
the pond. Those on the west shore are narrow and rocky in
places. A walk around the pond adds at least 30 minutes to your
trip. Green Mtn., which towers over the western side of the pond,
offers a steep climb over ledges to a vista overlooking the pond
and the mountains beyond. The trail head is at the northern
end of the pond. The ledges are about a 30-minute walk away.*

OTHER PLACES NEARBY

Manchester is known by most tourists as either a summer
retreat for the wealthy or a place to shop at brand-name outlets. It's also become a trendy place for skiers who flock to the
Stratton or Bromley ski resorts. Visitors should expect crowds in
peak seasons.

■ **Merck Forest & Farmland Center.** Nearly 3,000 acres
of farm, forest, and mountain were a gift from George Merck
(of Merck Pharmaceuticals). This is a community-supported
conservation area that offers excellent walking opportunities,
educational programs, camping, farm animals, organic gardens,
and more. *Box 86, Rte. 315, Rupert, VT 05768; tel. 802-394-
7836. Open daily for hiking and cross-country skiing. Office
open Mon.-Fri. 9-5.*

DINING

As with lodging, the choice of restaurants in this part of
Vermont is seemingly endless. Here are just a few. Many of the
restaurants listed below don't use street numbers, but the towns
are tiny and the restaurants are easy to find.

■ **Chantecleer** (expensive). This former dairy barn has
been converted into a restaurant with elegant dining rooms and
a massive fireplace. The continental cuisine prepared by the

▼

Swiss chef-owner is highly rated. A menu that includes whole Dover sole, frog's legs in garlic butter, quail, pheasant, Wiener schnitzel, rack of lamb, and veal sweetbreads should give you an idea of what to expect. *Rte. 7A, East Dorset, VT 05739 ; tel. 802-362-1616. Open Wed.-Sun. (closed Tue. in summer) for dinner. 5 mi. north of Manchester.*

■ **Danby Village Restaurant** (moderate). A friendly establishment, this intimate eatery offers such appetizers as steamed mussels and pita pizza with spinach, roasted red peppers, and mozzarella. For the main course, you'll find a few Greek dishes, including moussaka and shish kabob souvlaki, and maybe such specials as crab cakes, chilled poached salmon, and garlic and spinach ravioli in a light pesto sauce. In warm weather, there's an outdoor eating area. *Main St., Danby, VT 05739; tel. 802-293-6003. Open daily except Wed. for lunch (Sun. brunch) and dinner. A block away from Rte. 7.*

■ **The Black Swan** (moderate). There's a special, romantic ambience and a friendly staff working inside this former farmhouse. Start dinner with country paté, fried calamari, or portabello mushroom stuffed with spinach and asiago cheese. For the main course, the chef cooks an excellent rack of lamb with lingonberry-mint sauce and garlic mashed potatoes, and zesty Maine crabcakes with avocado-pepper mayonnaise. *Rte. 7A, Manchester, VT 05254; tel. 802-362-3807. Open daily except Wed. for dinner Jun.-Oct. Open Tue. and Wed. for dinner late Nov.-May. Closed first three weeks in Nov.*

■ **Sirloin Saloon** (moderate). It seems that every guest house owner reports that their guests like this place and its sister restaurant in Shelburne (*see* Experience 18, Shelburne Farms). The western decor is authentic, the meat is all top-quality western beef, and the salad bar is extraordinary. *Rtes. 11 and 30, Manchester Center, VT 05255; tel. 802-362-2600. Open daily for dinner. Just off Main St.*

■ **The White Dog Tavern** (moderate). An English-style pub in a restored 1812 farmhouse, the White Dog offers a good

▼

selection of seafood and meats, including prime rib, and a full bar. The pub atmosphere is great, and on the outside deck, you gaze up at the Green Mountains. *Rte. 7, Danby, VT 05739; tel. 802-293-5477. Open daily except Mon. for dinner. 2 mi. north of Danby on Rte. 7.*

■ **The Quality Restaurant** (inexpensive). The restaurant has been around since 1920 and was actually the setting for Norman Rockwell's *War News*. A casual family-style restaurant, the menu includes any standard restaurant item you might want for breakfast, lunch, or dinner. *4940 Main St., Manchester Center, VT 05255; tel. 802-362-9839. Open daily for breakfast, lunch, and dinner.*

LODGING

Tourism in the Manchester area is heavy most of the year (summer vacations, fall foliage, winter skiing), so there are many places to choose from. Some lodgings below were chosen on the basis of their proximity to the walk.

■ **The Inn at Manchester** (expensive). This restored 1880 Victorian inn offers 14 rooms and four suites, each named for a flower or herb. All rooms have private baths and AC, and some have fireplaces. There's a relaxed atmosphere, and walkers will find host Stan Rosenberg very knowledgeable about hiking and outdoor activities in the area. A three-course breakfast is served, as well as afternoon tea. The motto is "peace, pancakes, and pampering." *Rte. 7A, Box 41, Manchester, VT 05254; tel. 802-362-1793, 800-273-1793. Just south of Manchester.*

■ **Silas Griffith Inn** (moderate). This inn, a mansion built in 1891 by Silas Griffith, has much to offer. The main house and the carriage house have been attractively restored and offer 17 rooms, most with a queen bed and a private bath. Off the large living room is a set of Jules Verne-style circular wooden doors that Griffith built. Friendly innkeeper Lois Dansereau is knowledgeable about trails in the area. A full breakfast is served, and dinner (open to the public) is prepared on weekends. *178 Main*

▼

St., Danby, VT 05739; tel. 802-293-5567, 800-545-1509. From Rte. 7, enter Danby and turn left onto Main St.

■ **White Rocks Inn** (moderate). In a scenic location between towns, a nicely restored historic farmhouse includes five rooms with private baths and large canopy beds. In summer, breakfast may be served on the veranda overlooking a farm. A cottage with a loft bedroom, a kitchen, and a whirlpool bath is also available. The location is excellent for exploring the White Rocks area. *Rte. 7, Box 297, Wallingford, VT 05773; tel. 802-446-2077. 10 mi. north of Danby.*

■ **Barnstead Innstead** (moderate). This is surely a country lodging—12 rooms built into a restored hay barn. The grounds are quiet, the rooms rustic but comfortable, and the location (for town visits) very good. *Bonnet St., Box 988, Manchester Center, VT 05255; tel. 802-362-1619, 800-331-1619. A short walk from town.*

■ **Sutton's Place** (inexpensive). Frank Sutton runs this conveniently located lodging house (no breakfast, but town restaurants are only a block away). There are three guest rooms with a shared bath and one room (containing a queen and twin beds) with a private bath. Hikers often stay here, and Frank will drive them to trail heads for a $1 fee. *School St., Manchester Center, VT 05255; tel. 802-362-1165. A block west of Main St.*

■ **The Quail's Nest** (inexpensive). This small, comfortable, country guest house is in the middle of the village of Danby. The six rooms, four with private baths, have quilt-covered beds. Full breakfast and afternoon tea are served. *Main St., P.O. Box 221, Danby, VT 05739; tel. 802-293-5099.*

FOR MORE INFORMATION
Tourist Office:

■ **Manchester and the Mountains Chamber of Commerce.** *5046 Main St., Ste. 1, Manchester Center, VT 05255; tel. 802-362-2100. Open Mon.-Sat. 9-5 year-round, Sun. 9-5 May-Nov.*

▼

For Serious Walkers:

The Danby and Manchester area has much to offer trail walkers. The Merck Forest and Farmland Center has 28 miles of lanes and paths. In Green Mountain National Forest are outstanding destinations such as Griffith Lake, Baker Peak, and White Rocks. Even Mount Equinox has a hiking trail to its summit, though most people drive there. From the walk described above, there's a three-mile extension that serious hikers may find interesting. It continues from the pond for another three miles on the Green Mountain Trail back to Forest Rd. 10. A left turn onto the road and an uphill walk will bring you back to your car in 1/2 mile. This route is steep and difficult in sections.

■ **Green Mountain National Forest.** The Forest Service manages the forest for all users. It produces some free fliers that describe hikes and walks on its land. *2538 Depot St., Rtes. 11 and 30, Manchester Center, VT 05255; tel. 802-362-2307. Office open Mon.-Fri. 8-4:30.*

■ **The Green Mountain Club, Inc.** The group, which publishes the *Guide Book of the Long Trail, Day-Hiker's Guide to Vermont, Long Trail End-to-End Maps,* and other books, maintains trails for walkers and hikers. *4711 Waterbury-Stowe Rd., Waterbury Center, VT 05677; tel. 802-244-7037. Office open Mon.-Fri. 9-5.*

A Monument for Billings

EXPERIENCE 17: WOODSTOCK

The town of Woodstock, Vermont, beautifully framed from this walk's vista on Mount Tom, has long been a home to the notable. Since the mid 18th century, scholars, clergy men, attorneys, and others have stamped their influence on the town. Among them was Frederick Billings. Born in 1823 in Royalton, his family moved when he was young to Woodstock, a place he would leave and return to many times in the course of this life.

The Highlights: A covered bridge, a unique set of switchbacks on the trail to Mount Tom, wide-ranging views of town, country, and distant mountains from the summit.

Other Places Nearby: Excellent shops and restaurants, a farm and museum, great trails for walking and cross-country skiing.

Billings studied law at Vermont's state university. After graduation, he was drawn west by the California gold rush. There were few lawyers and much lawyering to be done in California's booming, get-rich-quick economy, so Billings found his fortune not in the gold fields, but the courtroom. Within a short period of time, he was part of San Francisco's leading law firm, a position that allowed him to meet many well-placed

▼

people. By 1864, at the age of 41, poor health prompted Billings to return to Vermont. He purchased the Marsh house, the home of a prominent Woodstock family, and built it into a large estate. By 1866, a recuperated Billings was out west again. He bought a one-twelfth interest in the Northern Pacific Railway and became deeply involved in its operation. When the economic panic of 1873 hit, it was Billings who came up with a feasible reorganization plan—a move that later made him president of the company. The town of Billings, Montana, was named for him as a result of his influence.

But Billings was more than just a businessman. One of the leading conservationists of his time, he was an advocate, along with Starr King (*see* Experience 22, Mount Starr King) of the protection of Yosemite in California. He was a friend of Frederick Law Olmsted (*see* Experience 12, World's End), and he initiated tree-planting projects along the Northern Pacific rail line. He was also interested in protecting historical sites along the route.

Billings was an admirer of George Perkins Marsh, a distinguished scientist, statesman, and an early advocate of conservation. Marsh's 1864 book on ecology, *Man and Nature,* deeply influenced Billings' thinking. Like Billings, Marsh had lived in Woodstock and even summered in a house Billings owned.

Back in Woodstock after his experiences with the Northern Pacific, Billings settled into his estate. He expanded the acreage from an original 270 to 2,000 acres. In his later years, Billings spent much time and money on forestry and agriculture, turning his estate into a sort of research center. He experimented with different types of trees that might be useful in restoring deforested areas of Vermont. He also was one of a number of wealthy late-19th-century Vermonters who were attracted to experimental farming. A generous man, he made substantial gifts to educational institutions and churches, including the purchase of Marsh's library for the University of Vermont.

▼

On the slopes of his vast acreage on Mount Tom, Billings built a series of carriage roads, as was the fashion at the time. These wide paths, that he declared were "to be his monument," allowed him to travel by horse and carriage throughout his estate. He made frequent use of them right up to his death in 1890. Along these roads Billings planted many nonnative species of trees, including larch and Norway spruce. One of the carriage roads you follow on this walking tour extends to an overlook on Mount Tom. From this lower summit, the entire town of Woodstock can be seen 500 feet below, with the steeple of the Congregational Church appearing prominently. The Billings farm can be seen off to the left, Mount Peg straight ahead, and other mountains, including Ascutney, in the distance. The horse-hitching posts along the wide lane that circles the summit, and the stone watering troughs at carriage road junctions, are further reminders of the Billings era, when industry and nature were not yet enemies.

GETTING THERE

By car:

Drive on Rte. 4 to Woodstock, 11 mi. west of exit 1 on I-89. Park at the village green on the western end of downtown, where you will find limited parking. If you are staying at one of the guest houses, you may be able to walk to the village green and the beginning of the walking tour. You can also drive to Faulker Park (Point 1) and park your car along Mountain Ave.

Walk Directions

TIME: 2 to 3 hours
LEVEL: Moderate to difficult
DISTANCE: 2 1/2 to 4 1/2 miles
ACCESS: By car

The walk described below requires a climb of about 500 feet, accomplished by way of an interesting series of switchbacks. Most of the walk is on wide lanes and shouldn't pre-

▼

sent any problems. But if you're fainthearted, you may wish to retrace your steps after you reach the impressive views of Point 3. For a short stretch after Point 3, you encounter steep terrain that requires use of handrails. Point 3 makes a scenic picnic spot.

TO BEGIN

From the northern side of the village green, walk through the covered bridge. *The bridge was built in 1969 using 19th-century techniques and tools, including wooden pegs and ox-power. Its construction marked the first time in this century that such techniques were used.* Cross River St. and continue following Mountain Ave. as it swings left. After a few more minutes of walking you approach un-marked Faulkner Park on your right.

1. When you reach the park and a stone wall, go right, then take the paved path to your left uphill toward the southwestern side of the park. When the paved trail veers to the left, turn right to enter the woods. You will see a large boulder. At this point, you are at the first switchback of the Faulkner Trail. The original trail actually begins near the northeastern side of the park, but it's simpler to start here.

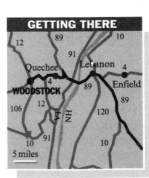
GETTING THERE

▼

2. Follow the graded trail uphill in a northerly direction to a short switchback. The path rights itself before coming to a major switchback which then goes gradually uphill in a south-westerly direction. The path has about ten more large switch-backs. There are many shortcuts between the switchbacks you may choose to take. Ignore the two yellow-marked footpaths that lead away from the main path. Higher up, the switchbacks are shorter and the climb steeper.

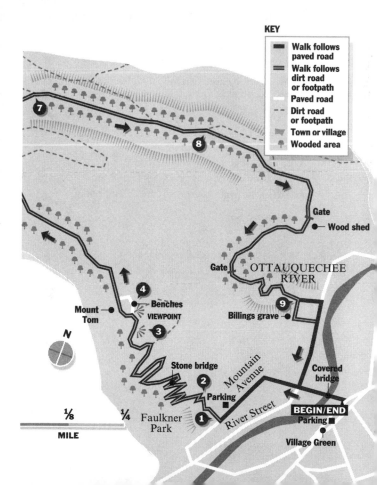

KEY

■■■	Walk follows paved road
═══	Walk follows dirt road or footpath
—	Paved road
- - -	Dirt road or footpath
🛖	Town or village
🌲	Wooded area

▼

The switchbacks provide an easy 1.5 mi. ascent of Mt. Tom. *This trail was built in 1938, patterned after the Cardiac Trail at the German spa at Baden-Baden.*

3. Arrive at a tree-framed vista overlooking Woodstock. Notice that the continuation of the trail requires a minor descent and then a climb along ledges toward the summit. **Wire cables provide handholds along the ledges. This section of the trail is steep and narrow, and may not be pleasant for the fainthearted. However, it is quite safe.** *If you wish to return at this point, simply retrace your steps, making sure you take the same trail you came up on.*

4. Arrive at the cleared summit with its wooden benches and antique hitching posts. *With a commanding view over Woodstock below, you see views to the horizon in several directions—east toward New Hampshire, south to Mount Ascutney, and west to the spine of the Green Mountains.*

To continue, walk to the left around the summit area in a clockwise direction on the nearly circular lane, and then follow the broad road away and down from the summit area.

5. After a short distance, you see where the road is shored up by a stone causeway. Continue ahead on the lane, ignoring side trails. After another ten minutes or so, the lane passes near some old European larch and under white pine and Norway spruce, *all planted in 1887.* Immediately thereafter, the lane passes through open meadows, where you'll find a bench.

6. Make a sharp right just beyond the meadow at a crossroads where there is a stone watering trough used to water horses since the Billings era. *A left turn leads to the Pogue, a quaking bog that was dammed in 1895 to create a pond. The name is believed to be a corruption of the word bog.* Pass through another pasture on your left where cattle graze.

▼

7. Pass a second watering trough and keep right. *A left here and an immediate right just after a brook crossing will lead you to a log cabin shelter used by picnickers and cross-country skiers.* Continue along the trail by walking downhill on the lane.

8. Keep right at a fork. Continue the descent, ignoring side trails. Turn right just after a first gate, then keep left after a second gate. The last section of the descent has a few switchbacks.

9. Arrive at the River Street Cemetery, *where Billings is buried.* Turn right on a path through the cemetery to see the Billings grave, then go left to River St., where you go right. Or, walk down to River St. and make a right toward Mountain Ave. Turn left, walk through the covered bridge and back to the village green. If you parked at Faulkner Park, turn right on Mountain Ave. and return to the park.

OTHER PLACES NEARBY
■ **Billings Farm and Museum.** Billings established this farm for the scientific breeding of Jersey cows. This is a living farm museum maintained as a national park, with gardens, livestock, and daily farm activities. *Rte. 12 and River Rd., P.O. Box 489, Woodstock, VT 05091; tel. 802-457-2355. Open daily 10-5 May-Oct. Admission. On Rte. 12, just north of Woodstock.*

DINING
■ **Simon Pearce Restaurant** (expensive). This is elegant dining with a striking view overlooking the Ottauquechee River falls. The glassware is made in a shop just below the restaurant. Entrées may include chili-cured roast tenderloin of pork with grilled corn salsa or horseradish-crusted cod with crispy leeks and herb mashed potatoes. The wine list is long. *The Mill, Quechee, VT 05059; tel. 802-295-1470. Open daily for lunch and dinner. East of Woodstock.*

▼

■ **The Prince and the Pauper** (expensive). Near the river's edge you'll find what is probably Woodstock's finest restaurant. The price is fixed at $30, and the cuisine is nouvelle French with a Vermont accent. Colonial decor and candlelight make this restaurant a great escape. *24 Elm St., Woodstock, VT 05091; tel. 802-457-1818. Open daily for dinner. Closed Sun.-Mon. Apr., May, and Nov.*

■ **Kedron Valley Inn** (expensive). The chefs here bring a creative flare to such traditional dishes as oven-roasted rack of New Zealand lamb and grilled black Angus porterhouse steak, and the setting makes for a special country escape. *Rte. 106, So. Woodstock, VT 05071; tel. 802-457-1473. Open for dinner Thu.-Mon.; closed Apr. 5 mi. south of Woodstock.*

■ **Bentleys** (moderate). Located downtown, Bentleys is full of atmosphere with Victorian decor, a long bar, and live entertainment on weekends. There's also a menu that ranges from sandwiches to entrées like roast duckling or champagne trout. *3 Elm St., Woodstock, VT; tel. 802-457-3232. Open daily for lunch and dinner Mon.-Sat. (Sun. brunch).*

■ **Woodstock Inn & Resort** (moderate). The Woodstock Inn and Resort is enormous, including a restaurant with pleasant garden views and outdoor dining during summer. The menu includes a good selection of salads and sandwiches and gourmet pizza, as well as a few entrées for under $10. *14 The Green, Woodstock, VT 05091; tel. 802-457-1100. Open daily for lunch and dinner.*

■ **Mountain Creamery** (inexpensive). Here's a good place for a light lunch (sandwiches, bagels, salads) and the best ice cream in town. *33 Central St., Woodstock, VT; tel. 802-457-1715. Open Mon.-Fri. for breakfast and lunch.*

■ **Gettis & Co.** (inexpensive). Come here for gourmet picnic fixings, including hot and cold entrées. *Rte. 4, Woodstock, VT; tel. 802-457-1715. Open daily for lunch and dinner.*

▼

LODGING

■ **Woodstock Inn & Resort** (very expensive). This 147-room inn has everything. The location on the village green is excellent, and there are all the extras of a major hotel. Much of the best walking and hiking in Woodstock is on land owned by the inn. During winter, these trails turn into one of the finest cross-country ski centers in the East. *14 The Green, Woodstock, VT 05091; tel. 802-457-1100, 800-448-7900.*

■ **Kedron Valley Inn** (expensive). A visit to this award-winning inn takes you into another time. With a 50-horse stable nearby and a pond for swimming, you get the impression the Kedron hasn't quite made it into the 20th century. It is a self-contained world, with its country grounds, 27 guest rooms with private baths, a large living room with a bar, and an outstanding restaurant. Full breakfast is served. *Rte. 106, So. Woodstock, VT 05071; tel. 802-457-1473. Closed Apr. 5 mi. south of Woodstock.*

■ **The Charleston House** (expensive). A restored 1835 Greek Revival townhouse, the Charleston is furnished with quality antiques. A bonus: It's at the eastern edge of town near walking areas. All seven rooms include AC. Choose your breakfast: a full meal in the dining room or continental breakfast in bed. Bicycles are provided for guests upon request. *21 Pleasant St. (Rte. 4), Woodstock, VT 05091; tel. 802-457-3843.*

■ **The Maple Leaf Inn** (expensive). Located in the countryside, this exquisite retreat offers charm and comfort in absolute quiet. Most of the nine rooms are large and feature a king-size bed, sitting area, fireplace, and TV/VCR. A gourmet breakfast is served. *Rte. 12, Barnard, VT 05030; tel. 800-41-MAPLE. 9 mi. north of Woodstock.*

■ **The 1830 Shire Town Inn** (moderate). A restored farmhouse contains three tastefully decorated guest rooms. Each room is different (the Quechee Room has a private porch), and the living room beckons (VCR and fireplace). A country breakfast is served. The location of this B&B is great for walkers—

only a block from town and also near the trailhead for Mount Peg. *31 South St. (Rte. 106), Woodstock, VT 05091; tel. 802-457-1830. Just south of town.*

■ **The Barr House** (inexpensive). This small B&B (two rooms with a shared bath) is an inexpensive alternative to the generally high-priced guest houses in the area. Your hosts are Vermonters, and the location is good for walkers. A full breakfast is served. *55 South St., Woodstock, VT 05091; tel. 802-457-3334. Closed Jan. Two blocks south of town on Rte. 106.*

FOR MORE INFORMATION

Tourist Office:

Woodstock Area Chamber of Commerce. *18 Central St., P.O. Box 486, Woodstock, VT 05091; tel. 802-457-3555. An information booth (tel. 802-357-1042) on the green is open daily 10-4 May-mid-Oct. Other times of year open Tue.-Thu. 10-4.*

For Serious Walkers:

Both Mount Tom and Mount Peg are laced with miles of trails and carriage roads that are a delight for walkers. These areas, part of the Woodstock Inn and Rockefeller estate, have been earmarked to become a national park. The best map of the area is the Woodstock Ski Touring Center's trail map. The center is part of the Woodstock Inn (*see* Lodging). Southeast of Woodstock, Mount Ascutney offers excellent hiking. Try the Wethersfield Trail to the summit, or a loop using the Brownsville and Windsor trails.

A Millionaire's Dream Farm

EXPERIENCE 18:
SHELBURNE FARMS

During the 19th century, many rich people built summer homes in places such as Saratoga Springs, New York, and Newport, Rhode Island. Often, the homes were palaces. Members of this privileged class passed the time admiring nature and

> **The Highlights:** A five-story barn that resembles a castle, landscaping created by Frederick Law Olmsted, lake and mountain views.
>
> **Other Places Nearby:**
> A magnificent summer house from a bygone era, an impressive museum, the city of Burlington, good restaurants.

socializing with their friends. One wealthy couple chose instead to head north to Vermont, not just to build a vacation home, but to create a modern farm. The creation of Shelburne Farms, the site of this walking tour, is the story of a wealthy couple's dream and their descendants' efforts to preserve it.

Dr. W. Seward Webb, a physician turned businessman, worked for William Henry Vanderbilt of the famous railroad family. Webb earned his employer's trust by saving the Wagner Palace Car Company from economic disaster and was rewarded by being named the company's president. About the same time, in the 1880s, Webb was scouting for possible railroad

▼

takeovers, and, in the process, found himself in Burlington, Vermont. The area's scenic beauty sparked his imagination, and he knew he wanted to live there. Interestingly, Webb's grandfather had been deeded land in the same area many years before as a reward for his service in the Revolutionary War.

anderbilt, Webb's employer, had a daughter named Lila who spent some of her youth on the family farm in Staten Island, New York. Like other young women of high society, Lila was sent to a finishing school to be groomed for marriage; in 1881, she married Webb. The newlyweds decided to spend their summers in Vermont. They quickly built a relatively modest country house in Burlington that they called Oakledge. Not long afterward, Webb began buying shorefront property at Shelburne Point, a wide arm of land just south of Burlington that extends into Lake Champlain. In 1886, he used an inheritance from Lila's father to buy several farms in the area with the intention of creating a single estate for himself and his family. He even acquired his grandfather's original holdings, which included a high point along the shore named Lone Tree Hill. Oakledge was left behind, and a newly built two-story "cottage" measuring 128 feet by 50 feet served as the new summer home. This building was later enlarged and modified into a Queen Anne-style mansion (today, it is the Inn at Shelburne Farms).

Webb's acquired farms, pieced together into one huge estate, called for a master plan. He called on Frederick Law Olmsted, an old friend of Vanderbilt's who later became known as a father of American landscape architecture (*see* Experience 12, World's End). In July 1886, Olmsted submitted his plan for the estate. It called for distinctions between farm, forest, and park. Roads connected the sections. Although some of Olmsted's recommendations were abandoned, his main ideas were implemented, and Shelburne Farms (as it was now called) bore his imprint. Roads, shaded by trees in some sections, open to farm and lake views in others, wind through this world unto itself.

▼

In addition to Olmsted, Webb sought the services of Gifford Pinchot, a leading forestry expert and a pioneer environmentalist. At Shelburne Farms, Pinchot oversaw the planting of some trees and probably influenced Webb's vision of how the land was to be used.

What emerged over the years was a fantastic vision of a model agricultural operation, one that left the land healthy and beautiful. The scale of the Farm Barn, which is along the walk, is astounding. The Breeding Barn is even larger but is not on the walk and has not been completely restored.

In the Breeding Barn (which, until 1931, was the largest open-span structure in America), Webb raised Hackney horses that he believed were superior to the Vermont-bred Morgan horse. The breed never caught on, partly because Vermonters were slow to accept it. But, primarily, the timing was bad—the internal combustion engine had reduced the need for horses.

Webb died in 1926, and Lila ten years later. Their sons, Van and Seward, continued to summer at the house, but as the years went by, the house and farm began to deteriorate. Taxes on the property were high and maintenance was costly. In 1960, Van's son Derick, who had inherited the farm four years earlier, told family members they would have to sell some of the property. The response from his children was yet another vision: to save the farm by creating a nonprofit company. This was done, and today Shelburne Farms is intact, devoted to education and conservation, with the Webbs' descendants actively involved in its operations.

A walk through the farmland and forest of Shelburne Farms is unlike the more typical forest-and-footpath walking that is so common in New England. You will walk on wide swaths of cut grass, over lanes used by farm equipment, and up a gentle hill with 360-degree views overlooking farmland, a lake, and mountains. Unlike the majority of visitors, who ride in hay wagons and crowd the gift shop, you will discover the essence of a most special place.

▼

GETTING THERE

By car:

From exit 13 on I-89 in northwestern Vermont, drive 5 mi. south on Rte. 7 to the stoplight on Rte. 7 in the center of Shelburne. Turn right (west) and proceed about 1.5 mi. to the entrance of Shelburne Farms and the welcome center.

Walk Directions

TIME: 2 to 3 hours
LEVEL: Moderate
DISTANCE: 4 miles
ACCESS: By car

Using a combination of footpaths and farm lanes, the walk passes through the varied landscape of Shelburne Farms. The walking is not difficult, but you will want to give yourself plenty of time to visit the Farm Barn, where animals roam about and cheese makers work. Lone Tree Hill has excellent views and a grassy summit that is a popular spot for picnicking. There's another good picnic spot farther along the walk near the shore of Lake Champlain. Much of the walk is exposed to the sun, so you may want to bring along a hat and sunscreen.

An option is to omit the first segment of the walk, which leads from the visitors center to the Farm Barn, and ride on the hay wagon with a tour guide. If you do this, begin the walk at Point 3.

KEY

▬ Walk follows paved road
═ Walk follows dirt road or footpath
▭ Paved road
╌ Dirt road or footpath
🌿 Town or village
🌲 Wooded area

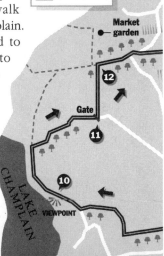

▼

TO BEGIN

Pay the admission at the booth and stop in at the visitors center to see an excellent slide show that tells the story of Shelburne Farms. Behind the visitors center, notice a mowed path leading west toward a row of trees. Follow this path, which is marked with signs, across the open field to the trees.

1. At the lane, turn left. Walk between the stately lines of huge poplar trees that provide cool shade on hot summer days.

2. Cross a road and find the continuation of the walking trail on the other side. You are now on a mowed path that runs alongside a hedge. *The Farm Barn is visible to your right.* The path par-

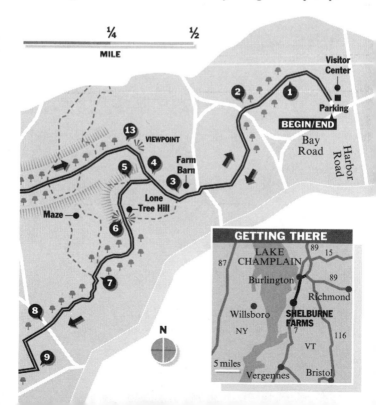

▼

allels the front of the Farm Barn before it swings right, crosses the road, and approaches the barn. *You should now be near the children's farmyard at the southern end of the Farm Barn.*

3. Arrive at the Farm Barn. From the rear of the children's farmyard at the south (left) end of the Farm Barn, go through a gate and walk up the lane past the donkey pen.

4. Following signs that direct you to Lone Tree Hill, turn left onto a lane that enters the woods. Walk a few minutes uphill.

5. Turn left again onto a path covered with wood chips. Follow this path uphill to the top of Lone Tree Hill. *There is a memorial to Derick Webb facing west just off the main path.* In an open field at the top of the hill, you approach a junction.

6. *If you wish to shorten the walk, turn left and follow signs back to the Farm Barn.* To continue, walk straight ahead, now descending the hill and entering a wooded area.

7. Arrive at a T-junction. Go straight. Upon reaching another field, bear to the right along the edge of the woods and arrive at a lane.

8. Cross the lane and follow the path, covered with wood chips, through a small wooded area. At the edge of a large wheat field, the path swings left toward the edge of another woods.

9. At the woods, follow the path as it swings to the right along a grassy boulevard now heading west toward Lake Champlain. At a barbed-wire fence, the path turns right for only 100 yards, then turns left following a mowed path. Continue following this mowed path toward the lake.

▼

10. When you arrive at the lake, *notice the cedar grove to your left and the small bluff to your right. Both provide excellent viewpoints over the water.* To continue the walk, follow the lane north, with the lake to your left. The walkway swings to the right (ignore the path straight ahead) and away from the lake, following the edge of woods and a field. You approach a gate.

11. Turn left through the gate and proceed directly ahead (do not turn right) onto a gravel road. The road takes you past beehives and the wood yard.

12. Arrive at a T-junction and turn right. Pass a lane on your left that leads to the market gardens that provide fresh vegetables for the inn. Pass through a junction with another lane near a small sugar house. Continue walking straight ahead and uphill.

13. At the top of the rise, there's an excellent vista to the left of Mt. Mansfield and the Green Mtns. The lane you have been following continues downhill past Point 4 and past the children's farmyard to Point 3. Cross the lane to the walking path by which you came, and retrace your steps.

OTHER PLACES NEARBY

■ **The Shelburne Museum.** This is a world-class collection of Americana and a major target for foreign tourists. The 37 buildings on 45 acres display art, crafts, tools, furniture, decoys, toys, and boats. There are also trains, a train station, a lighthouse, a covered bridge, and a Greek Revival mansion. You may need a two-day ticket to see it all. *Rte. 7, Shelburne, VT 05482; tel. 802-985-3344. Open daily 10-5 mid-May–mid-Oct. Off-season hours limited and by reservation. Admission.*

DINING

Besides the choices below, there are many fine restaurants in downtown Burlington. Most are within a few blocks of the

▼

Church Street Marketplace. In the marketplace are many sidewalk cafes that combine good food with excellent opportunities for people watching.

■ **Cafe Shelburne** (expensive). This French restaurant has an excellent reputation—thanks in large part to the efforts of chef-owner Patrick Grangien. The intimate dining rooms and patio go nicely with the cuisine. Recommended dishes include the escargot appetizer, filet of monkfish on a bed of spinach, and filet mignon. *Rte. 7, Shelburne, VT 05482; tel. 802-985-3939. Open Tue.-Sat. for dinner.*

■ **The Inn at Shelburne Farms** (expensive). The lakefront setting and the food are remarkable. The menu changes daily, but the fare typically includes dishes such as grilled scallops, shrimp, and calamari with sorrel sauce and lamb shank with succotash and sautéed greens. The kitchen creates excellent soups, including cheddar and ale and roasted sweet pepper and pumpkin with herb goat cheese. The vegetables are fresh from the farm's garden. *Shelburne Farms, Shelburne, VT 05482; tel. 802-985-8498. Open daily for dinner. Closed mid-Oct.-mid-May. Off Harbor Rd. Follow signs from the entrance to Shelburne Farms.*

■ **Pauline's** (moderate). Pauline's is really two restaurants. You can dine casually downstairs in the cafe at inexpensive prices, or upstairs where serious main courses are served. Lobster, duck, rack of lamb, and filet mignon are on the menu. "Healthy heart" options can be ordered. *1834 Shelburne Rd., South Burlington, VT 05403; tel. 802-862-1081. Open daily for lunch and dinner, Sunday for brunch. On Rte. 7.*

■ **The Sirloin Saloon** (moderate). This is one of six Sirloin Saloons in the Northeast. Burlington residents voted it their "favorite all-around restaurant," and innkeepers seem to agree. The restaurant uses only choice western beef, offers a wide selection of fresh seafood, and has a fabulous salad bar. Western-style art adorns the dining rooms. *Rte. 7, Shelburne, VT 05482; tel. 802-985-2200. Open daily for dinner. Between Shelburne and South Burlington.*

▼

■ **Chef Leu's House** (inexpensive). The dining areas, including an outdoor patio, are pleasant, the menu is varied, and the prices are very reasonable. What's unique is the variety of styles: Szechuan, Hunan, Mandarin, and Vietnamese. *3761 Shelburne Rd., Rte. 7, Shelburne, VT 05482; tel. 802-985-5258, 802-985-5259. Open daily for lunch and dinner. Between Shelburne and South Burlington.*

LODGING

B&Bs are scarce south of Burlington. Route 7, south of Burlington near the junction with I-89, is loaded with chain hotels and motels. The Econo Lodge is a good, inexpensive choice among these establishments. It's off the main road a bit and twice was picked as the chain's top motel.

■ **The Inn at Shelburne Farms** (expensive). The setting is outstanding, the service and dining are excellent, and the history is fascinating. The 24 rooms, including 17 with private baths, feature original furnishings. The common rooms are huge and contain books, paintings, antiques, and a grand piano. A game room (with a pool table and board games) opens onto a porch and the gardens that overlook the lake. The inn is not air-conditioned or heated. *Shelburne Farms, Shelburne, VT 05482; tel. 802-985-8498. Open mid-May-mid-Oct. From the stoplight at Shelburne center, take Harbor Rd. about 1.5 mi. to the Shelburne Farms entrance. Proceed 2 mi.*

■ **Heart of the Village Inn** (expensive). Standing next to the town green and a library, this romantic Queen Anne Victorian built in 1886 by successful merchant Cyrus Van Vliet is on the National Register of Historic Places. There are five guest rooms in the inn and four in a carriage barn. Each room contains a private bath and is tastefully furnished. The nicest— a two-room suite with a skylight over a queen-size bed and a whirlpool for two—is very expensive. A full breakfast is served. *P.O. Box 953, 5347 Shelburne Rd., Shelburne, VT 05482; tel. 802-985-2800.*

▼

■ **The Inn at Charlotte** (moderate). It seems like a motel at first, but it is a B&B with a pleasant innkeeper and comfortable common areas, including a living room, a pool, and a patio. All six rooms have private baths and entrances onto the patio/courtyard. A full breakfast is served in the dining room, and by prior arrangement, innkeeper Letty Ellinger will cook an Oriental dinner. Hiking on Mount Philo begins just down the street. *1188 State Park Rd., Charlotte, VT 05445; tel. 802-425-2934, 800-425-2934. 12 mi. south of Burlington on Rte. 7.*

FOR MORE INFORMATION

Tourist Office:

■ **Lake Champlain Regional Chamber of Commerce.** *60 Main St., Ste. 100, Burlington, VT 05401; tel. 802-863-3489. Open Mon.-Fri. 8:30-5 year-round and Sat.-Sun. 10-2 Memorial Day-Labor Day.*

For Serious Walkers:

The 220-mile Long Trail, located east of Shelburne Falls, leads to the top of 4,083-foot Camels Hump (south of I-89 in Mount Mansfield State Forest). Many trails can also be found in the Green Mountain National Forest, located southeast of Shelburne Falls.

Sacred Mountain of the East

EXPERIENCE 19: MOUNT MONADNOCK

To some, Mount Shasta in northern California is considered a sacred place. They say Shasta hides a UFO base, or that the Great White Brotherhood, a group of ancient masters who have transcended death, live deep inside the mountain. Aside from those fantastic notions, Shasta is a perfectly formed, snow-capped mountain whose majesty inspires a sense of the sublime. New England has its own sacred mountain—New Hampshire's Mount Monadnock, the site of this walking tour. In the mid 19th century, it served as a retreat for the Transcendentalists, a group that included Henry David Thoreau, Ralph Waldo Emerson, and other influential writers and thinkers.

In the language of the Abenaki, Native Americans who once lived in the region, Monadnock refers to a special type of mountain: one that is isolated, unique and, often, revered. Early European settlers adopted the word, but used it for any

The Highlights: A mountain adventure: forests, ledges, huge boulders, and a bare summit with views in all directions; sites of former mountain houses; an abandoned graphite mine.

Other Places Nearby: Pack Monadnock Mountain, Cathedral of the Pines.

▼

isolated summit. This mountain was referred to by the early settlers as Grand Monadnock. More than 3,100 feet above sea level, the mountain towers 2,000 feet above the land that surrounds it. Monadnock's bare, treeless summit is an inspiring sight—so striking that it has lured artists and thinkers to the area for more than a century.

Among them was Henry David Thoreau. Not only one of America's great thinkers, Thoreau was an avid walker who made several trips to Mount Monadnock. During one of them, in September 1852, Thoreau walked to the mountain from Peterboro. In June 1858, he returned and spent two nights on the mountain. In 1860, he camped near the summit with his friend, the poet William Ellery Channing. Thoreau loved Monadnock and has left us the details of his experiences there. Aside from his insights, his account gives us a glimpse of what walking, hiking, and backpacking were like in earlier times.

During the 1858 visit, Thoreau and a friend shouldered their knapsacks in Troy and walked several miles to the base of the mountain. According to Thoreau's journal, they followed a road to the mountain's shoulder, passed Fassett's Shanty (the ruins of which are on your walk), and camped in what Thoreau described as a "sunken yard in a rocky plateau." They covered the ground with spruce boughs for bedding and built a low wall and roof of spruce to keep out the wind. At dusk, Thoreau and his companion, identified only as Blake, left for the summit to watch the sun set, on the way stopping to look at the nest of a junco, or snowbird. Thoreau referred to the mountain as a temple and noted that other less-caring visitors to the summit had left litter. Others, who Thoreau described as "pretenders to fame," had inscribed their names on the rocks with chisels. On the way down, Thoreau lost the path but made it back to camp and prepared a dinner of boiled rice.

The next day they examined the summit in detail. Thoreau wrote

▼

about the smoothness of the rocks, their mineral composition and arrangement. He was fascinated by the bogs, where he found toad and frog eggs, tiny mosses, and alpine plants. He noticed that it was the lichens on the rocks that gave the mountain "that Ararat brown color of antiquity." Of his day on the summit, Thoreau wrote: "It is a very unique walk, and would be almost equally interesting to take though it were not elevated above the surrounding valleys. It often reminded me of my walks on the beach and suggested how much both depend for their sublimity on solitude and dreariness. In both cases we feel the presence of some vast, titanic power."

Emerson, who also found Monadnock fascinating, made the pilgrimage and wrote poetry from its "dark ledges over the spruce forest." Other poets of the time also found Monadnock a source of inspiration. Later, in the early 20th century, Mark Twain summered in nearby Dublin and wrote about the mountain's impressive appearance.

Grand Monadnock wasn't always bare at the summit. A two-week fire on the mountain sometime around 1800 destroyed the trees on the upper reaches of the mountain. The jumble of wood and stumps that was left on top was prime denning territory for wolves, who fed on the sheep of local farmers. The farmers endured it for a decade or so before becoming so frustrated that they torched the summit. The fire was so intense that it could be seen from Boston, and so hot that it completely burned any remaining organic material. Since then, the summit has been treeless.

Around the time of Thoreau's visits, an inn was opened in a level area part of the way up the mountain. It was called the Half Way House, a four-story hotel that could accommodate as many as 100 guests. Trails ran from the inn site to the summit and to other interesting spots, some of which are on your walk. Thanks to the owners of the inn, Monadnock became public land. When they claimed the summit, area residents pressured the New Hampshire Forestry Commission to acquire the land.

▼

From 1912 to 1948, a firetower and a warden's cabin stood on Mount Monadnock's summit, the remains of which can be seen today. The Half Way House was acquired by the state in 1945 and was run by the Association to Protect Mount Monadnock until it burned in 1954. The Old Toll Road remained open, and a refreshment stand existed until 1969, after which both were closed permanently.

Today, most visitors to the summit (dogs are banned) start their journey at the state park. Diane Eno, a modern dance artist, performs atop Mount Monadnock in late August and early September. Some of her pieces are based on Native American themes, but one of her pieces is called, of course, Transcendental Suite.

GETTING THERE

By car:

Drive to Jaffrey, NH, located east of I-91 and southeast of Keene, in southern New Hampshire. At the Jaffrey village green—at the junction of Rtes. 202, 124, and 137—turn west on Rte. 124. Pass the turnoff to Monadnock State Park on Dublin Rd. in about 2 mi., and, after 3 more miles, arrive at the Old Toll Rd. parking area. A modest parking fee is charged.

Walk Directions

TIME: 4 to 5 hours
LEVEL: Difficult
DISTANCE: 6 miles
ACCESS: By car

This Alpinelike walk is for the adventurous, not for the faint of heart, even though the mountain is climbed by tens of thousands of people each year. You need to wear sturdy shoes, preferably hiking boots. Portions of the walk are steep, and much of it is over exposed rock. In places, you will need to use your hands to steady yourself or pull yourself up onto a ledge. Exposed areas, including Bald Rock, the summit, and Monte Rosa, will be windier and colder than in the forest. Temperatures at the

▼

summit may be ten degrees cooler than at the trailhead, so bring along a windbreaker and carry extra clothing.

TO BEGIN

Leave the parking area and walk around the gate to the Old Toll Rd. To your right are portable toilets. Follow the wide gravel and dirt lane for about 20 minutes, passing a junction with the Parker Trail on the right, and then a residence near the end of the lane. When the road swings right toward the residence, turn left, following the remains of the Old Toll Rd., which is no longer maintained and is very rocky. Proceed about 200 yards toward a clearing, *the former site of the Half Way House.*

1. At the Half Way House site, turn right into the field. Find the trailhead for three trails: the Hello Rock, Point Surprise, and Thoreau Trail. From this trailhead, follow the path another 30 yards to another sign and bear left as indicated onto the Thoreau Trail. Here, you begin your climb through a spruce forest. The trail is lightly used, so keep your eye on the path, especially in those sections where the trail crosses large expanses of rock. After about 10 minutes of gentle climbing and meandering, the Thoreau Trail ends.

2. At a T junction, look to the right to find an overlook. *This vista is named Thoreau's Seat.* To continue the walk, turn left at the junction, now on the Cliff Walk Trail, which is marked with a white "C." Proceed on the trail another 10 minutes through similar terrain. The next vista, near Bald Rock, is called Emerson's Seat. At a wall, where the Do Drop Trail cuts off to the left, climb the ledge and bear to the left. The next section requires use of your hands. Continue following white C markers over rocks and ledges. At a fork, turn right. *A left turn brings you to the site of an old graphite mine.* Follow the trail as it emerges into the open and rises toward the summit of Bald Rock.

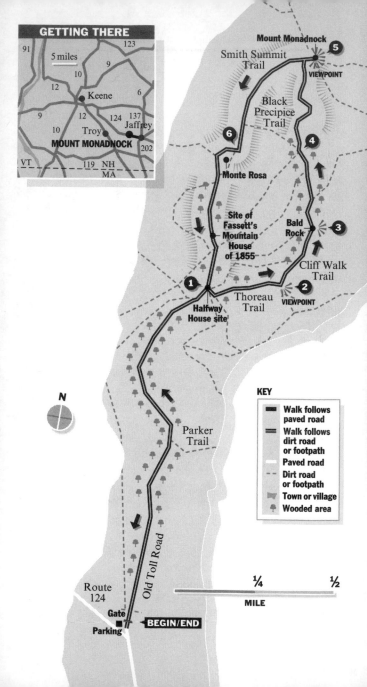

5 miles

91
123
9
10
12
Keene
6
9
12
124
137
Troy
Jaffrey
10
MOUNT MONADNOCK
202
VT
119 NH
MA

Mount Monadnock

Smith Summit
Trail

5
VIEWPOINT

Black
Precipice
Trail

6

4

Monte Rosa

Site of
Fassett's
Mountain
House
of 1855

Bald
Rock

3

Cliff Walk
Trail

1

2
VIEWPOINT

Halfway
House site

Thoreau
Trail

N

Parker
Trail

KEY

Walk follows
paved road

Walk follows
dirt road
or footpath

Paved road

Dirt road
or footpath

Town or village

Wooded area

Old Toll Road

Route
124

Gate

Parking

BEGIN/END

¼   ½

MILE

▼

3. From the top of Bald Rock (also called Kiasticuticus, after a cube-shaped monster from Greek mythology), look for yellow paint markers in the shape of an "S." Follow these markers down the rocks, toward the summit of Monadnock. *If you wish to end your walk here, take the Hedgehog Trail down to the Half Way House clearing, then follow the Old Toll Rd. back to your car.* To continue, proceed a short distance through woods. You arrive at a junction noted by signs and four dots. Keep left here, following signs to the Amphitheater Trail. Do not take the White Cross Trail. The trail you want to follow, now marked with yellow dots, will emerge from the woods onto rock slabs. **Pay careful attention to the route here, so you don't lose it.** Soon come to a junction with the Side Foot Trail. Continue straight ahead and, after picking your way through a jumble of rocks, approach the White Arrow Trail.

4. Turn right onto the well-traveled White Arrow Trail. Cross a wet area, and climb over huge boulders, exposed to the elements, toward the summit. Just before the summit is reached, you must use your hands to pull yourself up through a gully. After this last climb, the summit will be off to your right.

5. Arrive at the summit and enjoy breathtaking views in all directions. *Expect to find other hikers at the top of this popular place.* When you're ready to go, retrace your steps down over the rocks for a few hundred feet and look for the white dots of the Smith Summit Trail. Follow this trail (which makes a much easier descent than the White Arrow Trail) over rock slabs, being careful to stay with the white dots. At one point during the descent, the trail turns back on itself. Pass a junction, ignoring the Black Precipice Trail coming in on the left. As you descend, look for the small nub of rocks ahead of you that is Monte Rosa.

6. At a trail junction near a large overhanging boulder, turn right, following the cairns (small piles of stones) on the

▼

Monte Rosa Trail to the little summit of Monte Rosa. *From here, the summit of Monadnock looms ahead of you and Bald Peak is to the right.* Just before you reach a ledge topped by a metal post, follow the trail to the left. It becomes steep as you walk downhill, leaving Monte Rosa. At a junction, turn left on the Fairy Springs Trail, following the yellow markers. A steep descent brings you to Fairy Springs. *Water sometimes runs here.* Cross the spring and follow the path over rocks, alongside a stream, and then past the foundation of Fassett's Mountain House of 1855. After crossing another wet area and a pile of stones, reach the White Arrow Trail. Turn right and walk a short distance to Point 1, the Half Way House clearing. Retrace your steps on the Old Toll Rd. back to your car.

OTHER PLACES NEARBY

■ **Cathedral of the Pines.** This peaceful, outdoor all-faith cathedral stands as a memorial to those who died during this country's wars. The Women's Memorial Bell Tower is the first monument in the country commemorating the women who lost their lives in military service. Under tall pines, the Altar of the Nation looks out to Monadnock. *75 Cathedral Entrance, Rindge, NH 03461; tel. 603-899-3300. Open daily 9-5 May-Oct. Just off Rtes. 202 and 119, south of Jaffrey.*

■ **Monadnock State Park.** This state park is the starting point of the White Dot Trail, perhaps the most used trail on Mount Monadnock. The park has a large parking area, picnic areas, a visitors center, and a campground that is open all year. *P.O. Box 181, Jaffrey, NH 03452-0181; tel. 603-532-8862. Limited services from Nov.-Mar. Entrance is off Dublin Rd.*

■ **New England Marionettes.** In a plush theater, opera is performed with marionettes and recorded music. The costumes on the 32-inch figures, and the elaborate sets, suspend reality

▼

and draw you into the action. A fire recently destroyed the theater; call for information about future performances. *Main St., Peterborough, NH 03458; tel. 603-924-4333. Admission.*

DINING

■ **The Monadnock Inn** (expensive). Dinners at this traditional country inn feature lamb, pork, beef, and seafood. Try the mixed grill of beef tenders, breast of chicken, and Gulf shrimp. A popular appetizer is baked bel paese cheese. There's a nice old tavern room called Robert's Lounge where you might enjoy a drink. The inn also has 15 rooms, some with shared baths, that come with a continental breakfast. *442 Main St., Jaffrey, NH 03452; tel. 603-532-7001. Open daily for lunch and dinner, Sun. brunch.*

■ **Latacarta Restaurant** (moderate). Recently moved from its downtown location to its stunning setting in a high-ceilinged former mill on Noone Falls, this restaurant is one of best in the area. Master chef Hiroshi Hayashi, considered a pioneer in natural foods cooking, is the star of his restaurant. Fresh ingredients go into appetizers like shrimp tempura and gyoza (Japanese dumplings), or entrées like the Latacarta dinner (pan-grilled eggplant with oyster mushrooms in wine sauce plus minipumpkins filled with potatoes and cream cheese). *Noone Falls, Peterborough, NH 03458; tel. 603-924-6878. Open Tue.-Sun. for lunch and dinner; Sat.-Sun. for dinner.*

■ **Del Rossi's Trattoria** (moderate). A 1786 restored Colonial home is the setting of this creative Italian restaurant. Pasta is made daily, the wine list is extensive, and there's good entertainment on weekends. Affordable entrées include gnocci Bolognese (pasta dumplings made with potato and cheese) and northern-style scallops, sautéed and served with cheese-filled tortellini and fresh spinach in a Gorgonzola cheese sauce. *Rte. 137 North, Dublin, NH 03444; tel. 603-563-7195. Open daily for dinner. Just north of the junction with Rte. 101.*

▼

■ **Lilly's on the Pond** (moderate). The dining room looks out to a waterfall that spills from a small duck pond, providing a pleasant view to go along with the good food. Housed in a 1790 former sawmill, this restaurant is popular with locals. Along with standard entrées of beef, fresh seafood, and pasta, you'll find appetizers like Jamaican jerk pork and entrées like apple/brandy/walnut chicken and black bean pork. On Sunday, roast leg of lamb is served. *426 Rte. 202, Rindge, NH 03461; tel. 603-899-3322. Open Tue.-Sun. for lunch and dinner. About 1/4 mi. north of junction of Rte. 202 and Rte. 119.*

■ **Michaels' Jaffrey Manor** (moderate). This small family restaurant, located in an 18th century house, is a popular local eatery. Featuring such standard New England fare as fresh lobster, prime rib, and homemade clam chowder, the restaurant sometimes offers "all you can eat" specials. *E. Main St., Jaffrey, NH 03452; tel. 603-532-8555. Open daily for dinner and Sun. for brunch. Near the junctions of Rtes. 202 and 124.*

■ **Cafe Marquis** (moderate). Featuring traditional American cuisine with Asian influences, this restaurant occupies an historic community theater building. Inside, a contemporary atmosphere sets the mood for such offerings as Southern Comfort barbecued shrimp, Asian vegetable rolls, and grilled steaks. *6 School St., Peterborough, NH 03458; tel. 603-924-5000. Open Tue.-Sat. for lunch and dinner; Sun. for brunch.*

LODGING

■ **The Benjamin Prescott Inn** (moderate). There are 10 rooms in this Greek Revival country house, several of which can be arranged to accommodate groups. A suite on the top floor offers several beds and sleeping areas, AC, a sitting room with skylights, a wet bar, and a balcony overlooking the farmland that surrounds the house. Rooms are tastefully decorated and all have private baths. A full breakfast is served. You'll find walking opportunities nearby. *Rte.*

▼

124 East, Jaffrey, NH 03452; tel. 603-532-6637. About 2.5 mi. east of Jaffrey.

■ **Woodbound Inn** (moderate). This inn is really an old resort. There's a lake, golf, tennis, hiking, cross-country skiing, and a great view of Monadnock. Basic rooms, with breakfast, are found in the old inn. Twenty rooms have private baths. You can also rent cabins or motel-style rooms in the adjacent Edgewood building. Dinner is available as part of the lodging package every night during the summer and on weekends the rest of the year. *62 Woodbound Rd., Jaffrey, NH 03452; tel. 603-532-8341, 800-688-7770. Off Rte. 202, southeast of Jaffrey. Signs on Rte. 202 will get you there.*

■ **Apple Gate B&B** (inexpensive). One of our favorites in the area, this cozy B&B is surrounded by forest and apple orchard (visible from the Granny Smith room), and yet not far from town. There are four guest rooms, all with private baths, and a music room with piano and guitar. Full breakfast is served. Walking possibilities are right across the street. *199 Upland Farm Rd., Peterborough, NH 03458; tel. 603-924-6543. About 1.5 mi. south of Rte. 101 on Rte. 123.*

■ **Cathedral House Bed and Breakfast** (inexpensive). Five rooms, one with private bath, are available in the original home of the family that founded the Cathedral of the Pines. The house was built in 1850 and the rooms are decorated with a colonial flavor. Located on a quiet spot on the grounds of the Cathedral of the Pines. *63 Cathedral Entrance, Rindge, NH 03461; tel. 603-899-6790.*

FOR MORE INFORMATION
Tourist Office:

■ **Monadnock Travel Council.** *48 Central Sq., Keene, NH 03431; tel. 603-355-8155. Leave a message to get a brochure.*

▼

For Serious Walkers:

Serious walkers will find climbing Monadnock via the Pumpelly Trail from Dublin Lake a delight. Mount Monadnock links two long-distance trails: the 117-mile Metacomet-Monadnock Trail, and the 48-mile Monadnock-Sunapee Greenway that runs north to Mount Sunapee. To the east is the 21-mile Wapack Trail that links Watatic Mountain in Maine to Pack Monadnock Mountain in New Hampshire. Information on these trail systems is available from the Appalachian Mountain Club. *5 Joy St., Boston, MA 02108; tel. 617-523-0636. Open Mon.-Fri. 8:30-5:30.*

Greeley and the Ponds

EXPERIENCE 20: WATERVILLE VALLEY

Known primarily as one of New England's major ski resorts, Waterville Valley sits in the southwestern corner of the White Mountains. Owned by a large manage-

The Highlights: A woods walk following the Mad River to its source, two beautiful mountain ponds.

Other Places Nearby: A scenic region that includes several 4,000-foot peaks, waterfalls, and ledges with dramatic vistas.

ment company, the "town" is crammed with shops, restaurants, inns, and lodges. Walkers and hikers, on their way to trail heads, often find all the development confusing. But this is just the latest version of an old, long-standing resort area, near the site of this walking tour. Tourism began in Waterville Valley more than a century ago, when the mere existence of a cleared walking trail for visitors made a resort unique.

The resort lies at the head of a deep valley created by the Mad River. The first settlers came in the 1820s, about 50 years after the nearby towns Campton and Thornton had been established. The newcomers had it rough. The taming of this last wild valley—a total wilderness—required courage and hard work. Settlement began when most people looking for a new

▼

life were heading west in search of open land or to the big cities for factory jobs.

One of the earliest settlers in the valley was Nathaniel Greeley. He was born in Salisbury, New Hampshire, in 1802 and moved to the valley with his brother after their father gave them land. Greeley's brother took one look at the wilderness and left. But Nathaniel and his wife Nancy accepted the challenge and cleared 100 acres by cutting and burning. An orchard was planted, and they began to raise cattle and sell timber. Many neighboring settlers found the work and lifestyle too difficult, and Greeley bought their land.

In 1835, a man with lung trouble asked to spend a few weeks at Greeley's house, called the "little red cottage." The next year, he returned with his wife, and then fishermen and tourists asked to stay. A trend had begun. In 1853, the railroad was extended to Plymouth, about 20 miles away, and the tide of visitors increased. Greeley, now with 18 years of experience in the guest-house business, responded to this latest opportunity by building his own hotel. With his son Merril, he erected a new building measuring 40 by 100 feet and opened for business in the summer of 1860. Unfortunately, the hotel burned to the ground the next year. It took another seven years, but Greeley and his son managed to put up another building. This one was attached to their farmhouse and accommodated up to 60 guests. The facilities were crude by modern standards—candlelit bedrooms, oil lamps in the common rooms, no running water, and a row of privies in a shed. Probably, there was no bathtub. But Greeley's hotel appealed to an emerging middle class eager for recreation. While the wealthy vacationed in sumptuous hotels located in dramatic settings, Greeley's red cottage offered accommodations for the common man.

Greeley's guests were morally strict. In addition to the modest price of the rooms, Greeley provided the right atmosphere.

▼

The hotel served as a church on Sundays, and drinking and smoking were not allowed until after 1915.

Greeley's guests also liked to walk, so he constructed an extensive trail system. Although a few mountain trails for walkers already existed in other parts of the White Mountains in the mid 19th century, nowhere except in Waterville was there a system linking many trails together. Beginning as early as the 1850s, Greeley began to clear paths to the high summits that surrounded the valley. These were not short nature trails but full-fledged hiking paths. He and his men cleared paths to the source of the Mad River, two ponds that are now named for him. He also built bridle paths, including one that led to Crawford Notch. It is said one could ride from Waterville to the summit of Mount Washington, 30 miles away, in a day using Greeley's paths.

In 1883, Greeley sold the hotel to Silas Elliot and his wife Carrie. The railroad was extended to Campton, bringing in more guests, so the Elliots enlarged the building. After the Elliots died, their heirs decided to get out of the hotel business, a decision that drew a strong response from the other residents of Waterville. They joined with regular vacationers in 1919 to purchase the hotel as a group investment. Now run by the Waterville Valley Association's appointed manager, the hotel continued to draw visitors. Skiing began on Mount Tecumseh during the 1930s, and the inn began to operate in winter. In 1940, the hotel was leased to the Treadway Inn Company for a time, and some improvements were made, but by 1947 the company pulled out. In 1948, the inn was sold and the association was dissolved. Things started to change in the 1950s, when the Waterville Lift Corporation was formed and the hotel began to focus on skiing. In 1966, ski champion Tom Corcoran bought out the Lift Corporation and purchased additional land for the resort. Then, in 1967, the inn burned. An era had ended.

Since the burning of old Waterville Inn, a number of other lodges have been built, along with condos, stores, and services. Summer activities are promoted, including golf, hiking, and mountain biking. In 1994, the skiing operation, the conference center, central reservations, and a few other components of the town were acquired by SKI Inc., the corporation that owns the Killington, Mount Snow, and Sugarloaf USA ski areas. Today, Waterville Valley continues to attract skiers from all over the Northeast, but the beautiful walks built by Greeley remain.

GETTING THERE

By car:

From exit 28 on I-93 in central New Hampshire, drive east on Rte. 49 for about 11 mi. In Waterville Valley, the road turns left, passing a golf course. Turn right onto Valley Rd., drive about 1/2 mi., and then turn left at a library. Follow signs to Woodstock, Lincoln, and Tripoli Rd. Drive another 3/4 mi., pass over the Mad River and, just before a bridge, go right into the Livermore Rd. parking area.

An alternative way to the parking area is to drive 10 mi. from the exit on Rte. 49 and turn left onto Tripoli Rd. Drive 2 mi. on Tripoli Rd., keeping right where the paved road climbs up to the ski area. Turn right at a junction, cross a bridge, and bear left into the parking area.

Walk Directions

TIME: 4 hours
LEVEL: Moderate
DISTANCE: 6 3/4 miles
ACCESS: By car

The walk goes up to the source of the Mad River, the dynamic force that created the Waterville Valley. The ponds are a wonderful destination and are fairly easy to get to, so expect to find other walkers there as well. The ponds can also be reached from the Kancamagus Hwy. Most visitors who hike up to the ponds come from that direction, so you won't see many people until you get to the ponds.

▼

TO BEGIN

Leave the parking area and turn left onto the Livermore Trail, a wide lane used by both hikers and mountain bikers.

1. After walking for a few minutes, you reach a clearing called Depot Camp, *a former logging camp.* Just beyond the clearing, cross a bridge and turn left onto the Greeley Ponds Trail. Follow this trail, which is an old lane, past junctions with the Scaur Trail, the Goodrich Rock Trail, and the Timber Camp Trail.

2. After more than 30 minutes of walking, follow the Livermore Trail as it crosses the Mad River on Knight's Bridge. Further along, the trail passes a junction with the Flume Trail and then crosses Flume Brook. The trail is more of a footpath now.

3. After 2.5 miles (about 2 hours), you arrive at a sign indicating that you are entering the Greeley Ponds Scenic Area. After another crossing of the Mad River, the trail reaches the western side of lower Greeley Pond. *The pond is shallow, much like a beaver pond.*

4. From lower Greeley Pond, continue heading north on the trail.

5. In about 15 minutes or so, you reach upper Greeley Pond. *This pond, surrounded by old-growth timber, has a dramatic view of the cliffs of East Osceola from its eastern shore, reached via an unmarked trail that circles the pond.* Retrace your steps to return to your car.

OTHER PLACES NEARBY

Waterville Valley is a self-contained settlement in a mountainous cul-de-sac. If you leave the valley and head north to Lincoln and Woodstock along Interstate 93, you will find many

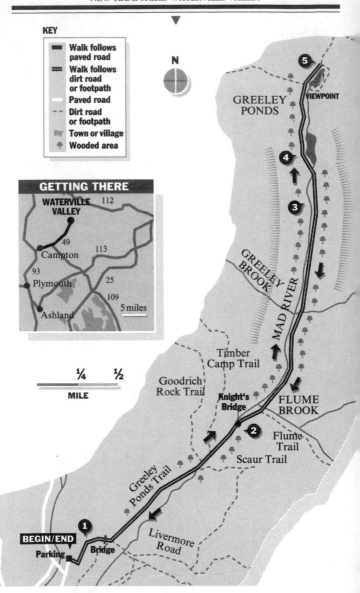

KEY

Walk follows paved road
Walk follows dirt road or footpath
Paved road
Dirt road or footpath
Town or village
Wooded area

N

GREELEY PONDS

VIEWPOINT

5

4

3

GREELEY BROOK

MAD RIVER

GETTING THERE

WATERVILLE VALLEY 112

49
Campton 113

93
Plymouth 25

109
Ashland

5 miles

¼   ½
MILE

Timber Camp Trail

Goodrich Rock Trail

Knight's Bridge

2

FLUME BROOK

Flume Trail

Scaur Trail

Greeley Ponds Trail

BEGIN/END
Parking   Bridge

1

Livermore Road

more shops and tourist attractions, as well as some of the main scenic areas of the White Mountains.

DINING

■ **Bridge House Inn** (moderate). Besides being a three-room B&B, this inn has a popular pub and a restaurant that serves a variety of dishes prepared Bermuda style (the owner used to live there), including Bermuda fish chowder, veal Susanne, and fresh haddock Bermudiana. You'll also find vegetarian offerings. *Rte. 49 East, Thornton, NH 03223; tel. 603-726-9853. Open Wed.-Sun. for dinner, Fri.-Sat. for breakfast (Sun. brunch). At Hill Rd. junction.*

■ **Campton Village Cafe & Pub** (moderate). Antiques and a lounge fireplace add character to this restaurant, a nice place for a relaxed meal. With a wide assortment of choices, the menu is geared to please every taste. The Village Platter dinner appetizer, for example, consists of pierogies, Oriental barbecue shrimp, and barbecue ribs. Some other dishes are roast turkey, quesadillas, trout almondine, and sautéed chicken with roasted red peppers, spinach, and mushrooms on linguini. The inexpensive lunch menu includes a tasty Reuben sandwich. Musicians entertain on Saturday evenings. *P.O. Box 776, Campton, NH 03223; tel. 603-726-4904. Open daily except Wed. for breakfast, lunch (Sun. brunch), and dinner. At the intersection of Rtes. 49 and 175.*

■ **Mad River Tavern** (moderate). This comfortable, casual restaurant/bar offers a wide variety of dishes. Frequent customers like the deep-fried Buffalo chicken wings. Main courses include seafood Alfredo, made with lobster chunks and jumbo shrimp, and baked swordfish with dill butter, Locals come on Friday and Saturday nights for the prime-rib special. Sandwiches are a bargain. *Rte. 49, Campton, NH 03223; tel. 603-726-4290. Open daily except. Tue. for lunch and dinner.*

■ **The William Tell** (moderate). You'll find Swiss and German specialties, fresh seafood, and even venison in this restaurant, which is highly regarded by locals. In summer, you can dine outside on a patio overlooking a fish pond. *Waterville Valley Rd., Rte. 49, Thornton, NH 03223; tel. 603-726-3618. Open daily except Wed. for dinner and Sun. for brunch.*

LODGING

Today's town of Waterville Valley is a huge ski resort with a number of typical lodging options. The Golden Eagle Lodge is a grand hotel, the Snowy Owl Inn is more personal, the Valley Inn includes its own restaurant, and the Black Bear Lodge offers only suites. Call 800-468-2553 for more information. The inns below are in nearby Campton, about ten miles southwest of Waterville Valley.

■ **The Mountain-Fare Inn** (moderate). In winter, this inn is a ski lodge, but it's a B&B in other seasons. There are six guest rooms in the main house—a large, white 1830s farmhouse—and three more in a carriage house. All rooms have private baths. A big backyard that includes a soccer field and a game room in the carriage house make this a good choice for families with children. *Mad River Rd., Box 553, Campton, NH 03223; tel. 603-726-4283. From Rte. 49, go north on Rte. 175, then right onto Mad River Rd.*

■ **Osgood Inn** (inexpensive). The two large guest rooms in the main house (one has a king-size bed) share a bath. An annex has a two-bedroom suite with a kitchen and a sitting room. There is a large common room with a fireplace, a back porch, and a dining room where a full breakfast is served. Families are welcome. No smoking is permitted. *Box 419, Campton, NH 03223; tel. 603-726-3543. From Rte. 49, go north on Rte. 175 and turn right onto Osgood Rd.*

■ **The Campton Inn** (inexpensive). The gabled house includes five guest rooms, one of which has a private bath. Rooms have antique beds and wide-board floors. In the living room, guests can take advantage of a piano and a wood-stove. A full breakfast is served. *Main and Owl Sts., Campton*

▼

Village, NH 03223; tel. 603-726-4449. From I-93, drive 1 mi. on Rte. 49, turn left at the lights (Rte. 175). The inn is 1/4 mi. ahead on the left.

FOR MORE INFORMATION

Tourist Office:

■ **Waterville Valley Central Reservations.** *Waterville Valley, NH, 03215; tel. 603-236-8311, 800-468-2553. Open Mon.-Fri. 8 a.m.-9 p.m., Sat.-Sun. 9 a.m.-9 p.m. Open daily in Feb. 8 a.m.-8 p.m.*

For Serious Walkers:

Hiking was popular in the Waterville Valley 100 years before skiing became the main attraction. Welch and Dickey mountains are low but offer fine views. Mount Osceola has a good trail to its high summit ledge overlooking the valley. For the adventurous, the north slide of Mount Tripyramid offers a challenging rock climb. For maps and other information, call or write the Waterville Valley Central Reservations (*see* Tourist Office).

The Healing
Power of Nature

EXPERIENCE 21:
ZEALAND NOTCH

During the Ice Age, the glacial sheet invaded the White Mountains, pushing south through the steep north-south river valleys. Thousands of years of abrasion and scraping left these valleys with rounded, U-shaped

The Highlights: Brooks, beaver ponds, waterfalls, mountain vistas, a back-packer's B&B.
Other Places Nearby: New Hampshire's tallest peaks, spectacular national forest lands.

walls. European settlers called the long valleys "notches," and used them as major transportation routes. Of the four major notches in the White Mountains (Pinkham, Crawford, Franconia, and Zealand), only Zealand, the location of this walking tour, remains roadless.

It wasn't always that way. During the late 19th century, lumber barons entered the White Mountains, cut lumber, and shipped it out using railroads that extended into remote areas. From 1884 to 1897, the Zealand Valley Railroad operated in the Zealand Notch, controlled by the greatest local lumber baron, James Everell Henry. Your walk follows this long-defunct railroad's route into the notch.

Like many of the financial giants of the late 19th century,

▼

Henry was tough, intensely individualistic, and motivated by the notion that he could control his own destiny through hard work and a forceful personality. Born into a poor family in 1831, he spent the first 40 years of his life working hard. He drove freight wagons, moved for a few years to Minnesota and eventually returned to New Hampshire and entered the lumber business. Like the other local lumber barons, he benefited from New Hampshire's decision in 1867 to sell all of its wild lands for a pittance. Soon he acquired much land in the Zealand area and beyond.

The Zealand Valley Railroad started in Zealand near the present-day Route 302, where it connected with the Boston, Concord & Montreal Railroad. The village was a mill town—a busy place with a post office, shops, a store, and a school. The Zealand line left the village and pushed into the notch along a steep, crooked route. Changes in the course of the Zealand River have obliterated parts of this original route. The line eventually ran for about ten miles, along the side of Whitewall Mountain and out to Shoal and Ethan ponds. Along the line six lumber camps were established. Nowadays, it's difficult to tell just where they were. However, you'll pass one probable site along this walk, near the junction of the A-Z Trail and the Zealand Trail.

At first, Henry lumbered with some restraint. Trees that were ten inches in diameter or smaller were left standing for harvest in future years. But Henry's policy changed after 1886, when a wildfire swept over 12,000 acres of his land. Fueled by slash—limbs, stumps, and other debris left on the ground by loggers—the flames destroyed virtually all vegetation in the area. In some places, nothing was left but scorched rock. A second major fire occurred in 1903. The bare evidence of these fires can be seen in Zealand Notch about 1.3 miles into the notch from Point 3 on your walk. Here rockslides from unstable mountainside covered the railroad grade, preventing the return

▼

of the forest. Henry's response to the fires was to adopt a clear-cut method of logging—a practice that was so appalling to some that he was called names like "Wood Butcher" and "Mutilator of Nature."

The logging of the White Mountains, dominated by Henry, continued into the 20th century. But public concern about the forests grew. Affluent conservation-minded tourists summering at the mountain hotels were disturbed by the destruction of the forests. Concern turned into outrage, and, in 1901, activists created the Society for the Protection of New Hampshire Forests. The society lobbied for laws to protect the forest and helped persuade Congress in 1911 to pass the Weeks Act, which created the White Mountain National Forest. Since then, logging in the White Mountains has been regulated by the federal government.

Today, the forest has returned in many areas. Only a few signs of the once-thriving logging industry remain. There are the barely discernible parallel lines, seen on mountainsides, that mark the location of old logging lanes, and a few areas where rockslides have prevented trees from growing.

One organization whose presence in the White Mountains rivals that of the Forest Service is the Appalachian Mountain Club (AMC). This outdoor hiking club was founded in Boston in 1875 and may be the oldest continuously operating club of its kind in the country. (The Sierra Club, formed in 1892, was modeled after the Appalachian Mountain Club.) Besides building and maintaining much of the trail system in the White Mountains, the AMC also established huts, actually rough inns, along the trails. You'll see one of them along your walk.

In 1888, the club built its first mountain shelter, the Madison Springs Hut, above tree line between Mount Madison and Mount Adams. It was a high-altitude base for mountain hiking, modeled, to some extent, after Swiss mountain huts. By 1916, second and third huts were built in Carter Notch and on Mount Washington. Around 1930, more were built, creating a

▼

chain of seven shelters that spanned the White Mountains from west to east. An eighth hut opened in 1965. Each had men's and women's bunkrooms, a kitchen, a dining room, and crew quarters. The staff (known as the "croo") were mostly students from Dartmouth University who prided themselves on carrying heavy loads of supplies up long trails leading to the isolated huts. The croo established other traditions, including comedy routines for the guests that explained the rules of the huts.

Today, the hut system remains popular, and reservations must be made in advance. The huts are about a day's walk apart, and arrangements can be made to stay in more than one if you want to continue a walk over a period of several days. As you'll see at the Zealand Hut on your walk, the accommodations are Spartan. You get a croo-cooked breakfast and dinner, a bunk, and a blanket (you can bring your own sleeping bag). There's a dining room, a porch, and, of course, the beautiful outdoors as common areas. Spectacular sunrises and sunsets are reason enough to spend the night.

GETTING THERE
By car:
Drive to the White Mountain National Forest, off I-93 in north-central New Hampshire. I-93 connects to Rte. 302. From Rte. 302, about 2.5 mi. east of Twin Mountain Village, turn south at Zealand Campground onto Zealand Rd., also known as Forest Rd. 16. (The road is closed between November and May.) Drive 3.5 mi. to the last parking area, passing a campground along the way. During summer, and especially on three-day weekends, the parking area at the end of the road may be full. Get an early start, or park at the trailhead for the Hale Brook Trail, about 2.5 mi. down Zealand Rd. Parking there adds 2 mi. to the walk, although it may be a convenient choice if a return over Mt. Hale is planned.

▼

Walk Directions

TIME: 3 to 4 hours
LEVEL: Moderate
DISTANCE: 5.6 miles
ACCESS: By car

The walk to Zealand Notch follows remnants of a railroad bed, rocky footpaths, and a boardwalk through wetlands. Only the climb to the hut is difficult. Still, this is not a manicured trail, and it leads into the heart of the most rugged mountains of the Northeast. Walkers should wear sturdy shoes and carry warm clothing in case of a turn in the weather.

TO BEGIN

Walk to the south end of the parking area. Pass a directory and go over a brook toward the end of a road.

1. At the end of the road, keep left, following the railroad grade. *The Zealand River is off to your left.* Much of the trail is on the railroad grade, but in some sections it leaves the grade and follows a rougher, rockier pathway.

The original railroad route through this part of the notch was full of curves. This was considered an asset because the curves slowed the train as it came down out of the notch with its heavy load of logs.

2. Cross a brook, the first of several crossings, about 30 minutes after you begin the walk. You enter an area where beavers are active. A boardwalk carries you over the wet areas.

3. About 15 minutes later, you arrive at a junction with the A-Z Trail, which enters from the left. Cross the outlet of Zealand Pond and walk along its east shore. *Zealand Pond has two drainages, the Zealand River to the north and*

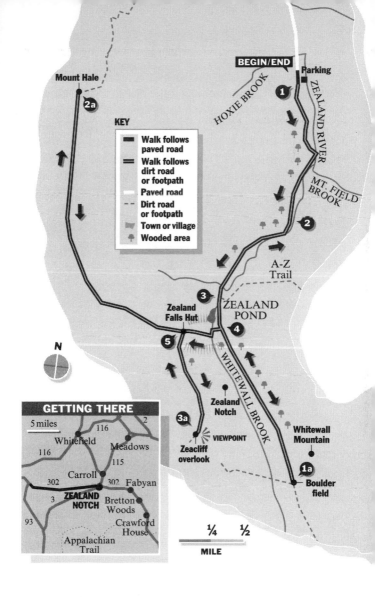

KEY

- Walk follows paved road
- Walk follows dirt road or footpath
- Paved road
- Dirt road or footpath
- Town or village
- Wooded area

BEGIN/END

Parking

HOXIE BROOK

ZEALAND RIVER

MT. FIELD BROOK

A-Z Trail

Mount Hale

ZEALAND POND

Zealand Falls Hut

Zealand Notch

WHITEWALL BROOK

Whitewall Mountain

VIEWPOINT

Zeacliff overlook

Boulder field

N

GETTING THERE

5 miles

Whitefield
116
116
2
Meadows
115
Carroll
302
302
Fabyan
3
ZEALAND NOTCH
Bretton Woods
93
Crawford House
Appalachian Trail

¼   ½

MILE

▼

Whitewall Brook to the south.

4. After a few minutes, you reach the south end of the pond, where there is a trail junction. Turn right, following the white markers of the Appalachian Trail/Twinway. You ignore the Ethan Pond Trail, which continues straight ahead. Cross over a wet area and begin a steady climb on stone steps.

5. Arrive at the Zealand Falls Hut in about 15 minutes. *The falls are next to the hut. Experienced hikers may choose an option below to extend the walk.* ***Be careful. Some areas, including those in Option 3, are very steep.*** Otherwise, return to Point 4. Turn left and retrace your steps.

Optional Extensions

Option 1: Go back to Point 4 and turn right. Continue straight ahead to follow the Ethan Pond Trail, which is the old railroad bed. This will take you—after 30 minutes or more—to the fire-scarred boulder field of Whitewall Mountain at Point 1a. *This is a stunning open area that not only illustrates the extent of fire damage, but shows the return of life.* Return to Point 3, then retrace your steps to the parking area.

Option 2: From Point 5, turn right onto the Lend-a-Hand Trail, which climbs to the summit of 4,000-foot Mt. Hale in 2.7 mi. From the summit (Point 2a), follow the Hale Brook Trail for about 1 1/2 hours (2.2 mi.) to Zealand Rd., and then turn right back to your starting point. This loop totals 8.5 mi.

Option 3: From Point 5, follow the white Appalachian Trail/Twinway markers steeply uphill for 1.2 mi. to the Zeacliff overlook (on a side path off the main trail). *The vista from the ledges over Zealand Notch is stunning.* Return to Point 4, then walk back the way you came.

▼

OTHER PLACES NEARBY

■ **Mount Washington.** Everyone flocks to the summit of the tallest mountain in the Northeast, which can be reached by auto, cog railway, or foot. *Mt. Washington Auto Road; tel. 603-466-3988. Open mid-May-late Oct. Admission. Cog railway; tel. 603-846-5404, 800-922-8825, ext. 7. Open Sat.-Sun. 8:30-4:30 in May and daily 8:30-4:30 Jun.-Oct., weather permitting. Admission.*

■ **Old Man of the Mountains.** This unique rock formation, a side of Cannon Mountain, juts out over Franconia Notch. Viewed from the visitors parking area, yup, it does look like an old guy up there. *On Rte. 93, north of North Woodstock.*

■ **Ski resorts.** Excellent slopes abound throughout the area. Pick from one of many resorts, including Cannon (603-823-5563), Loon (603-745-8111), Waterville Valley (603-236-8311), Wildcat (603-466-3326), and Bretton Woods (603-278-5000).

DINING

■ **Lloyd Hills** (moderate). This popular restaurant in the center of town serves a late breakfast (until 2 p.m.), lunch, and dinner. Look for a variety of omelets for breakfast, salads and sandwiches for lunch, and entrées like an excellent vegetarian lasagna for dinner. Many daily specials expand the possibilities. The atmosphere is very pleasant inside; on the outside, a deck overlooks the street. *Main St., Bethlehem, NH 03574; tel. 603-869-2141. Open daily for breakfast, lunch, and dinner.*

■ **Riverview Restaurant** (moderate). This restaurant is generally regarded as the place to go for quality dining in the area. The river view from the dining room is striking, and chef-owner Victor Hofmann has won culinary awards. The menu offers a wide selection of meats, seafood, poultry, and Swiss specialties. *Rte. 302 at Pierce Bridge, Box 480, Bethlehem, NH 03574; tel. 603-869-3364. Open Tue.-Sun. for dinner only in summer; Thu.-Sun. in winter. East of Bethlehem at the Wayside Inn.*

■ **Rosa Flamingo's** (moderate). You'll find a large menu

▼

that includes classic Italian entrées, as well as other meat and poultry options. You can also choose gourmet pizza, steak, and scampi. Stop in at the downstairs pub. *Main St., Bethlehem, NH 03574; tel. 603-869-3111.. Open Fri.-Sun. for lunch and daily for dinner.*

■ **Fabyan's Station Restaurant** (inexpensive). This pub-like restaurant with a railroad theme is part of the Mount Washington Hotel enterprises. It's the place for nachos, chili, sandwiches, burgers, and beer—and also some entrées like baby back ribs and broiled haddock. *Rte. 302, Bretton Woods, NH 03575; tel. 603-278-2222. Open daily for lunch and dinner. Located just before the entrance to the Mount Washington Hotel.*

LODGING

■ **The Bretton Arms Country Inn** (expensive). An 1896 inn tucked off to the side of the Mount Washington Hotel, the 34-room Bretton Arms is elegant and quiet, with its own dining room and lounge. *Rte. 302, Bretton Woods, NH 03575; tel. 603-278-1000, 800-258-0330. Near the Mount Washington Hotel*

■ **The Mulburn Inn** (moderate). This seven-room B&B offers spacious rooms with private baths, many with king- or queen-size beds. The house, a mansion built in 1908, has a wraparound front porch, a hot tub, and three acres of land, including a playground. *2370 Main St., Bethlehem, NH 03574-9717; tel. 603-869-3389, 800-457-9440. On Rte. 302.*

■ **Fieldstone Country Inn** (moderate). Located close to the mountains, this friendly B&B features seven guest rooms, three with a private bath. The rooms are filled with antiques, and there's a wood-burning stove in the common room. A full hot breakfast is served. *Fieldstone Ln., Box 456, Twin Mountain, NH 03595; tel. 603-846-5646. On Rte. 302, near the junction with Rte. 3.*

■ **Northern Zermatt** (inexpensive). You have many options here. The main building is an eight-room inn that offers inexpensive B&B guest rooms, each with private bath (shower).

▼

There are motellike rooms in another building and two cottage suites. Children under age 16 stay free. *Rte. 3, Box 83, Twin Mountain, NH 03595; tel. 603-846-5533, 800-535-3214. Just north of the junction for Rtes. 3 and 302.*

■ **Zealand Hut** (inexpensive). If you don't mind primitive lodging (a bunk and no showers) and can share a room with many others, it's unique, friendly, and in the mountains. "The croo" prepares and serves your meals with theatrical flair. *Box 298, Gorham, NH 03581; tel. 603-466-2727. Full service May-Oct. Open in winter (no services, unheated bunk rooms). Walk directions will lead you.*

FOR MORE INFORMATION
Tourist Offices:

■ **Northern White Mountains Chamber of Commerce.** *164 Main St., Box 298, Berlin, NH 03570; tel. 603-752-6060, 800-992-7480. Open Mon.-Fri. 8:30-4:30. During summer months, the chamber operates an information booth on the common in Gorham at the junction of Rtes. 16 and 2.*

■ **Mt. Washington Valley Visitors Bureau.** *Box 2300, North Conway, NH 03860; tel. 603-356-5701, 800-367-3364.*

For Serious Walkers:

Look to nearby Crawford Notch for excellent trails. A hike up Mount Avalon offers great views, as does the Webster Cliff Trail on the other side of the notch. Get information from the Appalachian Mountain Club in Gorham (603-466-2721).

The Reverend's View of the Heights

EXPERIENCE 22: MOUNT STARR KING

I n 1859, Thomas Starr King wrote the first major guide to New Hampshire's White Mountains, *The White Hills: Their Legends, Landscape, and Poetry*. This was the height of the Romantic period in America; the Hudson River School of painting was well

> **The Highlights:** A graded trail to a high summit, an excellent vista taking in most of the Presidential Range.
>
> **Other Places Nearby:** The high peaks of the Presidential Range, Mount Washington's auto road and cog railway, Crawford Notch State Park, outstanding golf courses.

established, and mountain tourism was booming. Nature had become a source of inspiration, and mountains, nature's largest creations, had become the focus of painters, art lovers, and wealthy tourists. Americans began to view rugged places as the finest work of the Creator, rather than as an impediment to transportation. Starr King's book, very much in step with the times, touted the White Mountains as sublime, a range with all the grandeur of the Alps and a powerful source of spiritual inspiration. The book was a big hit.

Starr King was born in 1824 in New York, the son of a Universalist minister. When he was very young, his family

▼

moved to Maine, then to Charlestown, Massachusetts. Starr King (Starr was his mother's maiden name) was an exceptionally bright boy and, in spite of very little schooling, became an assistant teacher at age 16. He absorbed everything he read, attended lectures, and debated with his friends. He learned to read in several languages and was regarded by many as a man who "captivated all who met him." With this combination of learning and personal charisma, it is no surprise that he became one of the leading clergymen of his time.

Between 1848 and 1869, Starr King preached at a Unitarian church in Boston. He also traveled, drawing large audiences. His love of the outdoors and the mountains of New Hampshire led to the writing and publication of *The White Hills*, a book which brought him even more fame. Ironically, he left the East Coast the year it was published.

The White Hills is not at all like the mountain guidebooks of today. It's more a piece of art and a prayer to nature. Long poems appear on every other page, and shaded sketches depict dramatic mountain scenes. Along with all the flowery prose and poetry, Starr King includes many interesting tales of the White Mountains. The story of the first explorers of the region and the first ascent of Mount Washington by Darby Field is told—interspersed with poetry, of course.

As a guidebook, *The White Hills* is organized according to drainage. The reader is directed to the four main river valleys of the White Mountain region that were accessible by train and carriage in those days. These include the Androscoggin Valley, which leads to the easternmost base of Mount Washington (at Gorham and Pinkham Notch); the Saco Valley, which leads to the westernmost base of Mount Washington (at Crawford Notch); the Pemigewasset Valley (at Franconia Notch), and the Connecticut Valley, the region of this walking tour. Starr King raves about the views of the mountains from this location. Of

▼

this region's village of Bethlehem, he wrote, "No village commands so grand a panoramic view." Of the nearby town of Jefferson, he wrote that it had "the very grandest view of the White Mountain range, and of Mount Lafayette...Here Mount Washington towers, in satisfactory majesty, above the whole curving line of the confederate summits."

Starr King loved to write about Jefferson. "And now let us take a ride towards the village of Jefferson. Can anything be more fascinating than those ripples of shadow that flow down the twin peaks of Madison and Adams, chased by flushes of sunshine, which again are followed by thin waves of gloom?" Jefferson Hill, he said, "may without exaggeration be called the *ultima thule* of grandeur in an artist's pilgrimage among the New Hampshire mountains, for at no other point can he see the White Hills themselves in such array and force."

As you admire the views on this walk, you might think of Starr King's words. "But the most surprising beauty awaits us as we ride opposite the great ravine of Mount Adams, and look far up to the cascades, with which the rains have enlivened its cliffs and slides. Now for a display of mountain jewelry, such as is rarely seen. A long, narrow, leaping stream gleams aloft, a chain of diamonds dropped from the neck down the bosom of the mountain. The sun looks full upon it, while the wings of the ravine are in deep shadow, and you see a broad wrapper adorned from the collar downwards with flashing gems. They blaze like lumps of sunshine, like the diamonds on the crown of the skeleton in the pass."

Starr King wrote about many interesting aspects of the White Mountains, including the naming of the summits. He lamented the loss of their Native American names and the "wretched jumble" of names that have nothing to do with the mountains. The name "White Mountains" is even inappropriate, he complained, because they are only white when covered with snow in winter. The bare shoulders and Alpine summits of the Presidential Range are really dim green. Starr King preferred the name given by the early explor-

▼

ers of these mountains, the "Crystal Hills," which was suggested by the small chunks of mica that glisten in the rocks. He argued that it would have be richer to retain the original Native American name, "Waumbek-Methna," which means "Mountains with snowy foreheads." (Although the name was not retained in Starr King's day, it is now the name of a 4,000-foot peak connected to, appropriately, Mount Starr King.)

In 1860, Starr King moved to San Francisco, where he helped to more securely establish the struggling Unitarian church. He achieved great success, raising money for a new church and in the process winning great popularity as a speaker and preacher. During the Civil War, many in California considered joining the Confederacy; Starr King, through his influence, helped prevent that from happening. He continued to hike and, through a series of letters to the *Boston Transcript,* described the wonders of the West's natural areas to eastern readers.

At the age of 40, Starr King died from diphtheria and pneumonia. California government offices closed for three days, and the state legislature adjourned in tribute. Poets commemorated him in poems, and a monument was erected in Golden Gate Park. A peak in Yosemite also was named for him, as were a ravine (King Ravine on Mount Adams) and a mountain in the White Hills. Fittingly, the vista from the summit of Mount Starr King, located high above Jefferson, looks at the White Mountains in a direction that was one of his favorites.

GETTING THERE

By car:

Drive to Jefferson, northeast of I-93 in northern New Hampshire. From the junction of Rte. 116 and Rte. 2 in Jefferson, drive 7/10 mi. east on Rte. 2 and turn left onto a gravel road marked with a sign for a trail. This gravel road is 3.6 mi. northwest of the junction of Rte. 2 and Rte. 115, and 2/10 mi. east of the junction of Rte. 2 and Rte. 115A. Once on the road, keep left and proceed about 1/4 mi. to a parking

▼

area at the trail head. If parking is a problem, park at the lot for the Jefferson Village swimming pool, just east of Rte. 2 and Rte. 115A.

Walk Directions

TIME: 4 to 6 hours
LEVEL: Moderate to difficult
DISTANCE: 5.2 to 7.2 miles
ACCESS: By car

The trail to the summit of Mt. Starr King uses old logging roads and is quite an easy walk when compared with other White Mountain trails. But this is relative, and some may find the walk quite strenuous. The trail climbs steadily from the trail head, but nowhere does it get steep or require the use of your hands. On the summit, walkers have the option of extending the walk by making a short descent and then a climb to the 4,000-foot summit of neighboring Mt. Waumbek.

TO BEGIN

Find a footpath located at the north end of the parking area. Follow the footpath as it swings left and upward to join an old logging road. The path climbs at a steady pace alongside, but well above, a brook to your left.

1. Pass the remains of an old circular springhouse on the right. A short while later, the trail veers sharply to the right away from the stream.

2. After 40 minutes, follow the path to the left, where it begins a long steady climb along the southwest ridge of the mountain. *In this section you enter the boreal zone, an evergreen forest of spruce and fir.*

3. Pass a spring on the left below the trail. *There is usually*

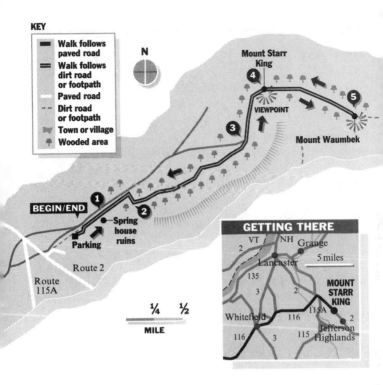

KEY

■ Walk follows paved road

= Walk follows dirt road or footpath

Paved road

-- Dirt road or footpath

🚩 Town or village

🌲 Wooded area

N

Mount Starr King

4

VIEWPOINT

3

Mount Waumbek

5

BEGIN/END

1

2

Spring house ruins

Parking

Route 2

Route 115A

¼ ½

MILE

GETTING THERE

VT NH Grange

2

Lancaster 5 miles

135

3 2 **MOUNT STARR KING**

Whitefield 116 115A

116 2

116 3 115 Jefferson Highlands

water here, even during dry periods.

4. After the trail swings around to the right, you arrive at the summit, which is marked by a brass survey marker on an outcrop. *The elevation of Mt. Starr King is 3,907 feet.* Continue on 200 feet to reach a vista that overlooks the Presidential Range. In summer, the vista may be overgrown with vegetation. *Just below this lookout is a small clearing where a cabin once stood. If you don't want to proceed another mile to the summit of Mt. Waumbek, retrace your steps back to the parking area.* Otherwise, follow the trail down across the shelter site and descend to the pass between Mt. Starr King and Mt. Waumbek.

5. After a climb of about 200 feet, you reach the 4,006-foot

▼

summit of Mt. Waumbek. *The vista from this summit is similar to, though not as open as, the one on Mt. Starr King.* Return to Mt. Starr King, Point 4, the way you came, and retrace your steps to your car.

OTHER PLACES NEARBY

See Chapter 21, Zealand Notch.

DINING

Fine dining is hard to come by this far north in the White Mountains. *See* Experience 21, Zealand Notch.

■ **Seasonings** (moderate). Your basic family restaurant offers a little of everything: burgers, sandwiches, spaghetti, chicken, steak, fish, etc. You'll find a breakfast buffet, a children's menu, and a full bar. *Rte. 2, Jefferson, NH 03583; tel. 603-586-7133. Open daily for breakfast, lunch and dinner Jun.-Columbus Day. Next to Santa's Village.*

■ **The Inn at Whitefield** (moderate). One of the nicer dining rooms in the Jefferson/Whitefield area, this inn's restaurant has a varied menu, including pasta, chicken, veal, and seafood. Next door is the Weathervane Theatre. A lounge with an old bar and live jazz add a touch not seen elsewhere in this area. Rooms are also available. *Rte. 3 North, Whitefield, NH 03598; tel. 603-837-2760, fax 603-837-3049. Open Mon.-Sat. for dinner Jun.-Oct., Tue.-Sat. for dinner Nov.-May.*

■ **Barbara's Little Restaurant** (moderate). A variety of sandwiches and entrées (including shrimp scampi and fettuccine Alfredo) are on the menu in this simple family restaurant. It's popular with the locals for its good home cooking. *Rte. 3 North, Whitefield, NH 03598; tel. 603-837-3161. Open daily for breakfast, lunch, and dinner. North of Whitefield.*

■ **Double S Restaurant & Lounge** (inexpensive). This small Chinese restaurant offers a fairly standard menu. It's also a nightclub that's open until 1 a.m.. *70 Main St., Lancaster, NH 03584; tel. 603-788-4444. Open daily for lunch and dinner. On Rte. 2/3.*

▼

LODGING

Here, in the northern section of the White Mountains, you won't find as many tourists as nearby Conway, Jackson, Lincoln, or Woodstock. You won't find as many options for lodging either, but those you do find will generally cost less. *See* Experience 21, Zealand Notch, for other options.

■ **The Jefferson Inn** (moderate). Only a short walk to the Mount Starr King trail head, this 1896 Victorian offers great mountain views from the upstairs front rooms, especially the Tower Room. There are 13 rooms with private baths, two of which are family suites. Cozy common rooms, a wraparound porch with sunset views, a gourmet breakfast, and an afternoon tea contribute to the relaxed and friendly atmosphere. *Rte. 2, Jefferson, NH 03583; tel. 603-586-7998, 800-729-7908; fax 603-586-7808. At the junction of Rtes. 2 and 115A.*

■ **Applebrook B&B** (inexpensive). This Victorian farmhouse bed-and-breakfast has 14 guest rooms, some with a private bath. Dormitory rooms are available and can handle large groups. A hearty breakfast is served on a long table, and there's a hot tub in back open to the sky. Applebrook draws many hikers and bicyclists, and the living room, with its goldfish pool, is where guests gather to talk about the day's activities. *Rte. 115A, Jefferson, NH 03583; tel. 603-586-7713, 800-545-6504. On Rte. 115A between Rtes. 2 and 115.*

■ **The Little House B&B** (inexpensive). This house off the main road has two large guest rooms with private baths and a sitting-room suite that sleeps four. A full breakfast is served. Next door is a lodge with room for eight, a fireplace, and a kitchen. There's a pool and a hot tub. Families and dogs are welcome. *Black Velvet Rd., Jefferson, NH 03583; tel. 603-586-4373. From the junction of Rtes. 2 and 115, take Rte. 2 east for 1/2 mi., turn onto a Methodist church driveway and bear left.*

▼

FOR MORE INFORMATION

Tourist Offices:

■ **Northern White Mountains Chamber of Commerce.** *P.O. Box 298, 164 Main St., Berlin, NH 03570; tel. 603-752-6060, 800-992-7480. During summer, an information booth is open on the Gorham Common (at the junction of Rtes. 16 and 2) Mon.-Fri. 8:30-4:30.*

■ **Mount Washington Valley Visitors Bureau.** *P.O. Box 2300, North Conway, NH 03860; tel. 603-356-5701, 800-367-3364.*

For Serious Walkers:

Hikers will find the Jefferson area an excellent base for exploring the Presidential Range, Crawford Notch, and the Twin Range. Trail maps and information may be obtained from the Appalachian Mountain Club. Closer to Jefferson are a number of lower summits, including Cherry Mountain and Randolph Mountain, that offer fine walking opportunities.

■ **Appalachian Mountain Club.** Run by the club, the Pinkham Notch Visitors Center offers valuable information about hiking in the White Mountains. It has a store stocked with guidebooks and maps and offers lodging and food. *P.O. Box 298, Gorham, NH 03581; tel. 603-466-2721, 603-466-2725. On Rte. 16, 11 mi. south of Gorham, 20 mi. north of Conway.*

The Land Between Waters

EXPERIENCE 23:
WOLF NECK WOODS

East of Freeport, a narrow piece of land called Wolf Neck extends south into Casco Bay. It's not named for an animal (although wolves certainly must have lived here at one time) but for an early settler, Henry Wolf, who married the daughter of Thomas

> **The Highlights:** Pine forest, river and bay views, wildlife.
>
> **Other Places Nearby:** Great dining, lodging, and shopping in Freeport, L.L. Bean, an Audubon sanctuary, a maritime museum.

and Anne Shepherd. Before this marriage the land was called Shepherd's Point, after Wolf's in-laws, who had originally settled the land in the late 17th century. Before that, the Indians called the area Harraseeket. It seems the buck stopped at Wolf. Then again, there is long-standing controversy about the spelling: Some say it's Wolfes Neck, others Wolfs Neck; many more say there should be an apostrophe before the "*s.*"

During the past 300 years, Wolf Neck was used mainly for farming, but today it's part farmland and part woodland preserved as a state park. Its location near the water, which keeps the temperatures milder, and its general flatness make it desirable for agricultural pursuits. From the nearby sea, farmers car-

▼

ried seaweed to spread on the fields, greatly increasing the soil's productivity. The salt marshes along the neck were good sources of hay for cattle. As you drive to Wolf Neck Woods State Park for this walking tour, you'll pass active farmland before you reach the wooded part of this "neck" that extends from the Harraseeket River to Casco Bay.

The origins of Wolf Neck Woods State Park are tied to farming and Philadelphia. Lawrence M. C. "Sam" Smith and his wife, Eleanor Houston Smith, bought a farm on Wolf Neck in 1946 as a summer retreat. Smith, a lawyer and entrepreneur, owned, among other things, a radio station in Philadelphia. However, it was in their role as conservationists and land philanthropists that the Smiths made their major contribution to Maine.

The Smiths were passionately concerned about the preservation of open space, as well as the conservation of natural resources through environmentally sound practices. They expressed these values through numerous projects; at Wolfe's Neck Farm (yes, that's how *they* spelled it), they practiced alternative farming. They raised Black Angus cattle using organic methods, beginning in 1959—decades ahead of both the environmental and the health-food movements.

The Smiths also believed strongly that the public should have access to open space, particularly to the coast. In 1969, Smith and his wife donated the original 219 acres of Wolf Neck Woods to the state of Maine. The Smiths previously had been instrumental in the creation of Popham Beach State Park and donated the Mast Landing Sanctuary (*see* For Serious Walkers) to the Maine Audubon Society. In 1984, Mrs. Smith donated Wolfe's Neck Farm to the University of Southern Maine to be operated as an educational model of alternative farming; the farm includes the waterfront Recompence Shore Campground, which is still open to the public.

A walk through Wolf Neck Woods becomes a peaceful ram-

▼

ble through a forest of old hemlock and white pine—some trees are as much as 100 years old. On the high bank overlooking the Harraseeket River, you will see the boats in South Freeport harbor. You may even see the top of the old stone Casco Castle tower, all that remains of a resort hotel that burned around 1913.

On the Casco Bay side of the neck sits Googins Island, a home to osprey for almost 100 years. Osprey mate for life. They establish a permanent nesting site to which they return every year after wintering in South America. Googins Island has been set aside as a sanctuary for these birds, which are easily disturbed by visitors.

Wolf Neck Woods is a part of the Harraseeket Historic District, which includes Mast Landing, Porters Landing, and South Freeport. The Harraseeket River is actually a tidal estuary where fresh water from streams mixes with salt water from Casco Bay. The first settlers in this area came during the late 17th century, but Indian wars kept the population very low. Serious settlement began after 1713, when hostilities ceased, and in 1789 Freeport was established as a town—in the Commonwealth of Massachusetts. (It was not until 1820 that Maine entered the Union as a separate state.)

Mast Landing, one of the earliest settlements in the Harraseeket District, derived its name from the cutting and shipping of local, large white pines to be used for ships' masts. In the early 1800s, Mast Landing, known then as Harraseeket Landing, was a small but busy place with a school, shops, a mill, and other commercial enterprises. Today, Mast Landing is no longer active. Walkers can experience the trails of the Maine Audubon Society sanctuary now located there, where they can explore the remains of the mill and the cellar holes of former houses.

Porter's Landing, another village within the town of Freeport, was named after the Porter family who built ships there during the early 19th century. The most noteworthy ship built there was the *Dash,* famous in the War of 1812 for outrun-

▼

ning the English. Beyond Porter's Landing is South Freeport, another village centered around shipbuilding until the decline of that industry, when its residents turned to fishing and canning. Today South Freeport, with two marinas, provides a harbor for hundreds of boats, mostly for pleasure, though some are still used for fishing. These you will see from the Harraseeket Trail.

Notice that downtown Freeport is not directly on the water. This settlement grew because of its location at a crossroads, where the roads to the harbors and the old King's Highway—the early route along the Maine coast—met. With the arrival of the railroad, Freeport became a manufacturing center and entered a period of rapid growth. In the 20th century, the Old King's highway route became Route 1 (more or less), keeping Freeport connected with the rest of the world by automobile. Summer visitors came, and an amusement park was built in South Freeport in 1903. In 1912, L.L. Bean began a mail-order business that has grown so big that now L.L. Bean, Freeport, and "shopping" are (alas) spoken of in the same breath. Walkers will be glad to find Wolf Neck Woods, a true escape from the acquisitive pursuits of the modern world.

GETTING THERE

By car:

Take I-95 north of Portland, ME, and get off at Freeport. Follow Rte. 1 into the center of Freeport. Opposite the L.L. Bean retail store, turn onto Bow St. and go east for 2.4 mi. Turn right onto Wolf Neck Rd. The entrance to Wolf Neck Woods State Park is reached after another 2.2 mi. During the summer season, turn left into the park, pay the fee at the gate house, and enter a large parking area. The trailhead is at the far end of this lot, to the right of the information directory (do not take the trail that reads "to picnic tables").

If you arrive during the off-season, turn around and park along the side of the road. Now on foot, return to the park

▼

entrance and walk past the gate and then the gate house. At a
fork in the road, keep right and enter the large parking area
described above.

Walk Directions

TIME: 2 hours
LEVEL: Easy
DISTANCE: 2 1/2 miles
ACCESS: By car

Walking in Wolf Neck Woods
involves very little climbing, but
walkers should be warned of the
many rocks and roots along the
trails. Trail junctions are common,
although close attention to the
directions should keep you on
course. Also, the park is small enough so that getting lost for
more than a few minutes would be difficult.

TO BEGIN

At the end of the parking area, follow a footpath that leads
into the forest to the right of a large, wooden trail guide.

1. In only a few hundred feet, turn right onto the
Harraseeket Trail (ignore the Casco Bay Trail that's straight
ahead), which is marked by a sign. The trail immediately climbs
up a few feet over roots and rocks. Pass a junction with a dirt
lane, then continue straight ahead over log bridges through a
wet area. After a short climb, cross a power line, then pass the
junction with the Hemlock Ridge Trail on the left. *In this section
of forest are some of the oldest trees in the park.*

2. Cross Wolf Neck Rd., which is not paved here, and re-
enter the forest. Follow the trail through a mature hemlock forest downhill toward the river.

3. Next to the water, follow the trail as it swings to the left
and then parallels the water's edge (though high above it).

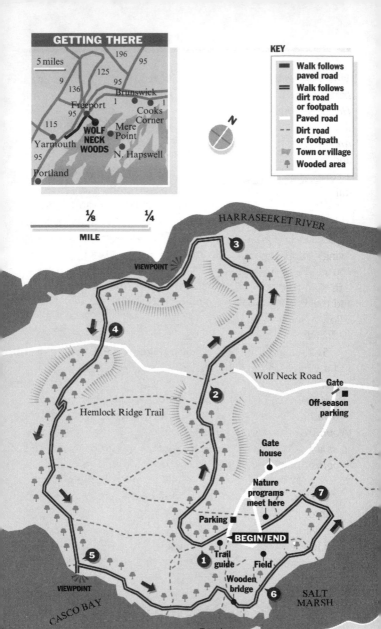

GETTING THERE

5 miles

196
95
125
9
136
95
Brunswick
1
Freeport
Cooks
Corner
115
95
Mere
Point
WOLF
NECK
WOODS
Yarmouth
95
N. Hapswell
Portland

KEY

▬ Walk follows paved road
═ Walk follows dirt road or footpath
▬ Paved road
--- Dirt road or footpath
🏠 Town or village
🌲 Wooded area

N

⅛   ¼

MILE

HARRASEEKET RIVER

VIEWPOINT

3

4

Wolf Neck Road

Gate
Off-season parking

Hemlock Ridge Trail

2

Gate house

Nature programs meet here

7

Parking

BEGIN/END

1 Trail guide

Field

5

Wooden bridge

6

VIEWPOINT

SALT MARSH

CASCO BAY

Googins Island

▼

Where the trail swings left, look for a crumbling log cabin off the trail to your right. Also in this vicinity is a vista out over the Harraseeket River. Continue following the path above the shoreline, passing a huge boulder at water's edge. *Here you find another place to stop and rest.* Farther along, the trail descends and crosses a drainage on log bridges, and then swings around a cove. After a short climb into a stand of red pines, follow the trail as it swings away from the river bank and heads southeast.

4. Cross Wolf Neck Rd. again—a paved section. As the trail begins to climb, pay close attention to the pathway as the trail swings sharply back on itself to surmount a ledge. Immediately, you reach an intersection with the Hemlock Ridge Trail again; turn right, following signs for the Casco Bay Trail. Cross a lane and then arrive at a junction where you should bear right, again following signs to Casco Bay.

5. Arrive at Casco Bay, where there are informative signs and a set of stairs that will take you to the water's edge. *This is a good resting place.* To continue, return to the main trail and turn right, now following alongside the shoreline of Casco Bay. *Information about the wildlife of the bay is found at another stopping point.* At a junction, proceed straight; you'll shortly cross a wooden bridge and go up stone stairs. *To your right is Googins Island, the osprey sanctuary, off-limits to humans.*

6. At a fork, keep right and follow a wheelchair-accessible trail through a picnic area. Another plaque and access to the water will be on your right. Stay on the walkway which swings to the left skirting the edge of a ravine.

7. At a junction with a wide lane, turn left and walk to the parking area. *A left turn here leads through the parking area to the trail head for the Harraseeket Trail.* If you parked outside the park, turn right and follow the entrance road back to Wolf Neck Rd.

▼

OTHER PLACES NEARBY

Freeport has become a shopper's mecca, with its once sleepy main road now lined tastefully with name brand outlet stores.

■ **Desert of Maine.** At this strange inland beachlike area, migrating sand dunes are in the process of burying both forest and farm. This area, sort of a tourist trap now, is not natural but was created by environmentally unsound use of the land: clear-cutting, overgrazing, and failure to rotate crops. *95 Desert Rd., Freeport, ME 04032; tel. 207-865-6962. Open May 7-Columbus Day. Just off Rte. 1 and I-95 (exit 19).*

■ **L.L. Bean.** This is Freeport's nearly legendary "anchor" store, which was here long, long before the outlets invaded the little town. L.L. Bean stocks everything for outdoor recreation plus plenty of apparel and home furnishings. The nearby L.L. Bean factory store (on Depot Street) sells discontinued items and factory seconds at reduced prices. At least 100 other outlet stores are nearby, making Freeport a shopper's paradise—if you can stand the crowds. *95 Main St., Freeport, ME 04032; tel. 800-341-4341. Open daily 24 hours.*

■ **Atlantic Seal Cruises.** Old Coast Guard ship visits places in Casco Bay where wildlife (seals, osprey) and natural beauty (sunsets, foliage) may be observed. One cruise is to Eagle Island, where passengers may visit the home of Arctic explorer Admiral Robert E. Peary. Reservations recommended. *25 Main St., South Freeport, ME 04032; tel 207-865-6112. Open Jun.-Oct. (three departures daily).*

■ **Maine Maritime Museum & Shipyard.** Frequently changing exhibits—including live demonstrations and some hands-on activities—provide insight into Maine's maritime history. Visitors can explore working vessels, and young ones can play on a giant sandbox ship. The 19th-century Percy & Small Shipyard (donated by the Smiths of Wolf Neck) preserves the techniques of building wooden ships. *243 Washington St., Bath, ME 04530; tel. 207-443-1316. Open*

▼

daily 9:30-5 year-round; Percy & Small Shipyard open late spring-Thanksgiving weekend, weather permitting. Admission. About 20 mi. northeast of Freeport.

DINING

■ **Harraseeket Inn** (expensive). If you wish to dine formally, the restaurant of this conveniently located 54-room inn is a good choice. The dining room faces the gardens in the courtyard. The dinner menu features traditional American cuisine, including a lobster chowder, a long-time favorite. Breakfast and lunch are also served here. For more casual but still delicious fare (lobster rolls, steaks, and such) and cozy ambience, try the moderately priced Broad Arrow Tavern, another part of the inn. *162 Main St., Freeport, ME 04032; tel. 207-865-9377, 800-342-6423. Open daily for breakfast, lunch, and dinner, and Sun. brunch. Broad Arrow Tavern open daily for lunch and daily for dinner. 2 blocks east of the shopping district.*

■ **The Cannery** (moderate). Under the same ownership as Camden's popular and highly respected Waterfront Restaurant, the Cannery has a similar reputation in the Freeport area. It's on the water, you can sit on a deck, and the food is excellent. Try the lobster ravioli, or the Cannery's version of bouillabaisse. If you do brunch, try Finnan Haddie, smoked haddock in cream sauce with sourdough toast points and hard-boiled eggs, served with a side of baked beans. *Lower Falls Landing, Yarmouth, ME; tel. 207-846-1226. Open daily for lunch and dinner, and Sun. brunch. About a 10-15 minute drive from Freeport. From Rte. 1 south of Freeport, follow Rte. 88 to Lower Falls Landing, just past the waterfalls.*

■ **The Corsican Restaurant** (moderate). This small (10 tables), casual Italian restaurant is known for its homemade soups and chowders and its desserts. Several varieties of gourmet pizza, salads, sandwiches, and vegetarian items are on the menu along with dinner entrées like salmon Marie (broiled fillet of salmon with garlic butter and wine, capers, and Dijon cream sauce) and scallops with fine herbs. *9 Mechanic St., Freeport, ME; tel. 207-865-9421. Open daily for lunch and dinner.*

■ **Jameson Tavern** (moderate). A formal dining room and a pub are both located in a historic building. Here is where the business that separated Maine from Massachusetts took place back in 1820. The formal dining room offers a very large selection of entrées, strong on seafood: A specialty is *fruits de mer,* seafood with Alfredo sauce and pasta. Steak, poultry, other meats, and pasta are also available, as are daily specials. The pub offers simpler fare. An outside patio is available for seasonal alfresco dining. *115 Main St., Freeport, ME 04032; tel. 207-865-4196. Open daily for lunch, and dinner.*

■ **China Rose** (inexpensive). This highly rated Chinese restaurant has an appealing and comfortable dining room as well as a small bar and lounge area. Among the specialties of the house are shrimp and scallops, and scallops with black pepper sauce. *10 School St., Freeport, ME 04032; tel. 207-865-6886. Open daily for lunch and dinner.*

LODGING

■ **Harraseeket Inn** (expensive). Larger than most of the inns included in this book, this is the choice for people who prefer the amenities of high quality hotel. *162 Main St., Freeport, ME 04032; tel. 207-865-9377, 800-342-6423. 2 blocks east of the shopping district.*

■ **The Isaac Randall House** (expensive). This old country house, full of history, has nine guest rooms, each with private bath and air conditioning. A full breakfast is served in the kitchen with its low, beamed ceiling. Out back in the six acres that belong to the inn is a pond, as well as a caboose that serves as a guest room! Well-behaved pets are welcome. The hosts offer a number of vacation plans. *Independence Dr., Freeport, ME 04032; tel. 207-865-9295, 800-865-9295; fax 207-865-9003. Just off Rte. 1, across from the L.L. Bean distribution center.*

▼

■ **The Kendall Tavern Bed & Breakfast** (expensive). Once a tavern, this B&B has seven rooms with private baths, two parlors with fireplaces (one with a Steinway piano), a front porch, and a hot tub. It is located north of Freeport (about a ten-minute walk); guests will find the spacious (3.5-acre) property a buffer that provides relief from the crowds and energy of downtown Freeport. A full stick-to-your-ribs breakfast is served. *213 Main St., Freeport, ME 04032; tel. 207-865-1339, 800-341-9572. Closed Feb.*

■ **The Bagley House** (expensive). Situated in the serenity of the countryside, this 1772 home has five rooms with bathrooms all furnished with antiques, and a new building with three modern rooms with gas fireplaces. *1290 Royalsborough Rd. (Rte. 136), Durham, ME 04222; tel. 207-865-6566. From Rte. 1 at I-95, exit 20, take Rte. 136 north 6 mi.*

■ **Atlantic Seal B&B** (expensive). In a rural setting, not far from the bay, this B&B has three guest rooms, two with harbor views, and two with private baths. The owner was born in the area and is happy to share his knowledge. *Main St., So. Freeport, ME 04078; tel. 207-865-6112.*

■ **Jacaranda House** (expensive). Located in an old home off of the main street, this tastefully furnished B&B offers upscale accommodations in a quiet setting. *8 Holbrook St., Freeport, ME 04032; tel. 207-865-9705.*

■ **Holbrook Inn** (expensive). This 1870's Victorian home has comfortable, recently renovated rooms with fireplaces. *8 Holbrook St., Freeport, ME 04032; tel. 207-865-9705.*

■ **181 Main Street Bed & Breakfast** (moderate). This seven-room B&B is well-located—withing easy walking distance of the center of Freeport but far enough from the swarms of shoppers. In this comfortable, historic 1840s home, guests have private baths, the use of two sitting rooms and the dining room (where a full gourmet breakfast is served) and even a pool and gardens in the backyard. *181 Main St., Freeport, ME 04032; tel. 207-865-1226.*

▼

■ **Country at Heart B&B** (moderate). Located just two blocks south of the center of shopping in Freeport, this B&B offers three guest rooms, each done in a slightly different historic country style, each with private bath. The hostess is into crafts and teddy bears, and they are tastefully integrated into the overall presentation of the house. Lodging comes with a full breakfast. *37 Bow St., Freeport, ME 04032; tel. 207-865-0512.*

FOR MORE INFORMATION

Tourist Offices:

■ **Freeport Merchants Association.** Hose Tower Information Center offers brochures, public telephones, an ATM, rest rooms, and ticket sales for area cruise lines and attractions. *16 Mill St., P.O. Box 452, Freeport, ME 04032; tel. 207-865-1212, 800-865- 1994; fax 207-865-0881. Center open daily 10-9 Jul.-Oct., 10-6 the rest of the year; staff on duty Mon.-Fri. 9-5 year-round.*

For Serious Walkers:

Besides the trail system in Wolf Neck Woods, historically-minded walkers and naturalists will find the trails in the Maine Audubon Society's Mast Landing Sanctuary (207-781-2330) of interest. The 140-acre sanctuary is located near Freeport on Upper Mast Landing Road.

Hikers will want to visit nearby Bradbury Mountain State Park, which offers rugged trails, including a short climb to a summit that offers fine views. To reach the park, take Route 136 north from Freeport and turn left onto Pownal Road. At Pownal center, turn right on Route 9. The park entrance and trail head is less than a mile ahead on the left.

High Mountains Against the Sea

EXPERIENCE 24: MOUNT BATTIE

Captain John Smith sailed into Penobscot Bay in 1605 and made a note in his log about the area now called Camden. He reported it to be "under the high

The Highlights: High rock ledges with great views over an island studded sea.

Other Places Nearby: A museum displaying Wyeth and Homer, a harbor, a lake, offshore islands, good shops.

mountains of the Penobscot, against whose feet the sea doth beat." Today, that line has been paraphrased by tourism promoters to read: "where the mountains meet the sea." With the exception of Mount Desert Island, Camden sits at the foot of the highest hills on the Maine Coast. Mount Megunticook, whose lower summit is on the walk, stands 1,380 feet above the sea and is only about two miles from it.

Mount Battie is the prominent, rocky dome that rises over the town of Camden. An old history says that it was named for the wife of the first settler in the area. Although its elevation is only 790 feet above sea level, water is right at its base, and it appears immense from the town landing. Only a half mile from Mountain Street, Mount Battie's open summit has long been a popular destination for the people of Camden. The coolness of

▼

the sea breezes in summer brings great relief from the heat below. And the view is incredible. From both Mount Megunticook's Ocean Lookout and the bare summit of Mount Battie, one looks out to bare-ledged mountains, harbored windjammers, distant islands, and, finally, open sea.

The mountain views over Camden are so good that they inspired a poet and propelled her to fame. In the summer of 1912, 20-year-old Edna St. Vincent Millay of Camden read her poem "Renascence" at a party in the town's Whitehall Inn. She was discovered that night. A New York woman staying at the hotel was so impressed that she brought the young poet to New York, introduced her to other artists and writers, and prepared her for Vassar College. Her poem "Renascence" begins with a description of the view of mountains and sea from the summit of Mount Battie.

> All I could see from where I stood
> Was three long mountains and a wood;
> I turned and looked the other way,
> And saw three islands in a bay.
> So with my eyes I traced the line
> Of the horizon, thin and fine,
> Straight around till I was come
> Back to where I'd started from;
> And all I saw from where I stood
> Was three long mountains and a wood.

The expansive vistas from some parts of the Camden Hills can be dangerous. If you look to the northeast from the summit of Mount Battie, you will see a large white cross at the edge of the cliffs. On May 6, 1862, an 11-year-old girl named Elenora French died there, having fallen 300 feet to the rocks below. She was with her sister and two adults, but may have lost her footing chasing after her hat. Two years later her father erected a cross in her memory on what is now called Maiden Cliff. The

▼

original cross is long since gone and has been replaced four times. The one there now weighs 600 pounds. A monument memorializing the event was set there in 1986.

About a hundred years ago, a man named Columbus Buswell built a toll road to the summit of Mount Battie. Since the land was privately owned, he paid 15 percent of the tolls that he collected back to the owners. He also leased an acre of the summit from another property owner, with a first option to buy. Then he built a summit house on that acre. His mountain-top development project was so successful that a number of summer residents, who appreciated the views from the summit, banded together to form the Mount Battie Association. Their goal was to make the summit a park for all to enjoy. Within a short time, they had collectively purchased the summit area, the summit house, the toll road, and an additional 59 acres. The summit house was remodeled to become a hotel, and when it was not filled by members of the club, it was open to the public. For a time, the summit house was a social center for the Camden area.

The Mount Battie summit house was modest in comparison to the earlier mountain houses of the White Mountains and elsewhere. It stood on a rock terrace built up from the rocky ground. A railing around the edge of the terrace was broken only by stairways. The house was really two buildings joined together with an attached, turreted tower three stories tall. Inside, dances took place in a long assembly room with a corner fireplace. On the second floor was a club room and eight guest rooms.

In 1920, two years after a fire scorched the summit but spared the house, the Mount Battie Association decided to tear the building down. From stones used in the Mount Battie House, a World War II memorial tower was built on the site. Its design is based on that of the mysterious Newport Tower (*see* Experience 6, Newport). In 1922, the Ku Klux Klan burned a cross on the summit, an event that was upsetting to most of

Camden. During the next 40 years, the toll road was closed, and only trails led to the summit.

In 1948, Mount Battie was acquired by the state, and in 1963, a new road to the summit was built. It was engineered to be sensitive to the natural beauty of the mountain and is today one of the most popular features of Camden Hills State Park.

GETTING THERE
By car:

Drive to Camden, located between Portland and Acadia National Park in south-central Maine. If you're coming from the south, take I-95 north to Rte. 1 north. At the junction of Rtes.1 and 52, drive 1.5 mi. north on Rte. 1. Turn left to the Camden Hills State Park entrance, pay the entrance fee, and proceed up the mountain access road a short distance. Trail parking is on the right.

Walk Directions

TIME: 3 1/2 hours
LEVEL: Difficult
DISTANCE: 4 miles
ACCESS: By car

The walk to Ocean Lookout on Mt. Megunticook is strenuous—uphill nearly all the way. The trail is in good shape, but **the last section is steep. The Tablelands Trail coming down from Ocean Lookout is also steep. Walkers are advised to avoid serious injury by carefully descending the rocks, especially under wet conditions.** The rest of the walk is easy to moderate.

TO BEGIN

Take the path that begins adjacent to the trail guide at the back of the parking area. Proceed a short distance.

1. At a junction, follow signs straight for the Mt. Megunticook Foot Trail. Walk for about 10 minutes.

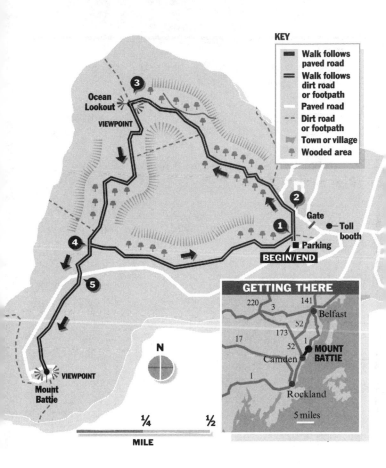

Ocean Lookout
VIEWPOINT

3

2

Gate
●Toll booth

1

■ Parking
BEGIN/END

4

5

VIEWPOINT

🌟 Mount Battie

N

GETTING THERE

220
3
141
52 Belfast
173 52
17
52 1 **MOUNT BATTIE**
Camden
1
Rockland

5 miles

¼   ½
MILE

2. Go left on the Mt. Megunticook Foot Trail and enter the woods. The trail has white markers. Pass a junction with a snowmobile trail that's on the right. Stay on the white-marked trail as it climbs steadily on a well-maintained foot-path that, in some places, follows an old roadway.

After 30 to 40 minutes of walking, pass a junction with the Adams Lookout Trail that comes in on the left. Continue straight ahead, passing a stream on the right. Follow the trail as it climbs steeply over exposed bedrock.

▼

3. Arrive, after an hour or more of walking, at Ocean Lookout. *Mt. Battie with its auto road is to the southwest.* From this expansive overlook at the edge of high cliffs, which is not the actual summit of the mountain, look for the white markers of the Tablelands Trail heading down the ledges. **Be careful on the steep, rocky descent.** Pass the Adams Lookout Trail coming in from the left. **Be careful descending through a jumble of rocks.** Pass a sign for the Jack Williams Trail and then the Carriage Trail.

4. At the junction with the Mt. Battie Nature Trail coming in on the left (remember this junction—you will return here after visiting Mt. Battie's summit), continue straight. Follow white markers down, over a wooden bridge, and then up a ledge. Approach the paved Mt. Battie auto road.

5. Cross the road and find the continuation of the Mt. Battie Trail. Follow the trail over exposed bedrock for 15 to 20 minutes to the summit parking area. Go through the parking area and walk to the summit. *Here is a vast panorama, the site of the former Mt. Battie Club House and the Memorial Tower.*

Return to Point 4 and then turn right onto the Mt. Battie Nature Trail. The trail first climbs, then descends (often in view or within hearing distance of the auto road) to Point 1, where you go right back to your car.

OTHER PLACES NEARBY

■ **Farnsworth Art Museum.** This museum houses a major collection of American art, with an emphasis on New England and Maine. Although it is known for its large collection of paintings by Andrew, N.C., and Jamie Wyeth, the museum is also home to works by Winslow Homer, Thomas Eakins and others. *19 Elm St., Rockland, ME 04841; tel. 207-596-6457. Open daily 10-5, Sun. 1-5, Jun.-Sep. Open Tue.-Sat. 10-5, Sun. 1-5 Labor Day-Memorial Day. Admission. Just off Main St. (Rte. 1) in Rockport, 8 mi. south of Camden.*

▼

■ **Main State Ferry Service.** Consider exploring one of the islands in Penobscot Bay—by ferry and then on foot or bicycle. Vinalhaven Island is appropriate for walkers. *17A Main St., Rockland, ME 04841; tel. 207-596-2202. Admission.*

■ **Penobscot Marine Museum.** A collection of artifacts, models, and paintings depicting 19th-century life by the sea is housed in eight buildings. *Rte. 1, Searsport, ME 04974; tel. 207-548-2529. Open daily 10-5 (Sun. 12-5) Memorial Day weekend-Oct. 15. Admission. 25 mi. north of Camden.*

DINING

■ **The Youngtown Inn** (expensive). Located in the countryside in a beautiful colonial home, this French restaurant draws a crowd for such pleasing offerings as lobster ravioli with American sauce, grilled steak with gorgonzola and brandy sauce, and lobster and sea scallops with tomato basil sauce over lemon pepper linguine. *Rte. 52 and Youngtown Rd, Lincolnville, ME 04849; tel. 207-763-4290. Open daily for dinner in summer. About 6 mi. north of Camden.*

■ **The Belmont** (expensive). A good choice for formal dining, the Belmont Inn also has six guest rooms. In the dining rooms a variety of entrées are served. The menu might include lobster pate, Wiener schnitzel, and chicken curry. *6 Belmont Ave., Camden, ME 04843; tel. 207-236-8053. Open daily for dinner. Closed Jan.-Apr.*

■ **Cappy's** (moderate). You can't miss this popular Camden landmark which is entered from two different streets and serves food on two levels. Besides breakfast, you can get sandwiches, crab cakes, lobster rolls, and after 5 p.m., main courses like scallops, the day's catch, and Black Angus steak. *Main St., Camden, ME; tel. 207-236-2254. Open daily for breakfast, lunch, and dinner. At the town center.*

■ **Atlantica** (moderate). Right on the harbor in downtown Camden, this new restaurant has attracted a following with locals. The diverse menu features anything from crispy spring

▼

rolls and grilled eggplant Napolean to "Island-style" chicken and Thai peanut curry. *One Bay View Landing, Camden, ME; tel. 207-236-6011. Open Mon.-Sat. lunch and dinner in summer; open Tue.-Sat. in winter; closed Apr.*

■ **Peter Ott's** (moderate). Watch the preparation take place in the open kitchen and then enjoy a variety of grilled fish and meats in this well-regarded restaurant. The menu includes regular entrées, many nightly specials, light meals, and pasta of the day. There's a popular salad bar and a children's menu. *16 Bayview St., Camden, ME; tel. 207-236-4032. Open daily for lunch and dinner. Closed Apr.*

■ **Sea Dog Brewing Company** (inexpensive). Basic pub fare, including the "Barney Burger," is found here along with seven original brews. *43 Mechanic St., Camden, ME 04843; tel. 207-236-6863. Open daily for lunch and dinner.*

■ **Miller's Lobster Co.** (inexpensive). It's almost a 20-minute drive from Camden but worth it for the special rural harbor setting and stunningly fresh lobster offered by this traditional lobster pound. *Box 422, Spruce Head, ME 04843; tel. 207-594-7406. Open daily for lunch and dinner Jul.-Aug., Fri.-Sun. in Jun. Off of Rte. 73, about 12 mi. south of Camden.*

LODGING

Camden offers plenty of lodging choices. With a ski area nearby, most stay open all year.

■ **Norumbega 1886** (very expensive). Named for a legendary city of fabulous wealth, Norumbega was once the fantasy castle of Joseph Stearns, inventor of duplex telegraphy. Nine rooms and three suites have private baths, fireplaces, water views, and king-size beds. The balconies, common rooms, and the grounds make a perfect setting for the murder-mystery weekends that are held periodically. Full breakfast and afternoon tea (or wine) is served. *61 High St., Camden, ME 04843; tel. 207-236-4646; fax 207-236-0824.*

▼

■ **The Inn at Sunrise Point** (very expensive). You can't get much better than this tiny, ultra-luxury inn offering stunning views of the ocean. The seven rooms, all beautifully furnished, are located in the main house and in adjacent private cottages. *P.O. Box 1344, Camden, ME 04843; tel. 207-236-7716. Closed in winter. Located off of Rte. 1 about 4 mi. north of Camden.*

■ **Whitehall Inn** (expensive). Young Edna St. Vincent Millay recited her poem "Renascence" and was discovered by the guests here. Today, the sprawling, old-fashioned inn has 50 rooms, most with private baths. Rooms come with a full breakfast, and guests often dine at the inn's highly regarded restaurant (ask for Uncle Don's baked breaded haddock). The inn is close to Camden Hills State Forest. *52 High St., Box 558, Camden, ME 04843; tel. 207-236-3391; fax 207-236-4427. Open late May-late Oct. North of town.*

■ **The Lodge at Camden Hills** (expensive). Located close to the entrance to Camden Hills State Park, the modern but pleasantly furnished rooms and cottages provide spacious, convenient accommodations, many with fireplaces and kitchenettes. *Rte. 1, Box 794, Camden, ME 04843; tel. 207-236-8478.*

■ **The Victorian by the Sea** (expensive). Set back off the road near the ocean, this huge old home has seven unique rooms, some with ocean views. There's also an attached cottaged with a private entrance. *P.O. Box 1385, Camden, ME 04843; tel. 207-236-3785. Off of Rte. 1, 4 mi. north of Camden.*

■ **High Tide by the Sea** (expensive). Less expensive than most of the inns in its price category, this property offers rooms in a small inn, in a motel, and in cottages. Rooms are simple but pleasantly decorated. *Rte. 1, Camden, ME 04843; tel. 207-236-3724. Off of Rte. 1, 1 mi. north of Camden Hills State Park.*

■ **Swan House** (moderate). Named for the family that built the house in 1870, this B&B has six guest rooms. If you want a lot of space, book the Swan Lake Loft Room, which is more like a suite, with its two double beds and a private entrance. Some guests prefer the Trumpeter Room because it has a private deck. A full breakfast is served. Spend time outside in the gazebo or elsewhere in the wooded surroundings (where you can hike directly to the summit of Mount Battie). *49 Mountain St., Camden, ME 04843; tel. 207-236-8275. 3 1/2 blocks up Mountain St. from the center of town.*

FOR MORE INFORMATION

Tourist Office:

■**Rockport-Camden-Lincolnville Chamber of Commerce.** *Box 919, Camden, ME 04843; tel. 207-236-4404, 800-223-5459. Open Mon.-Fri. 9-5, Sat. 10-5. The chamber operates an information booth during summer months on the public landing off Bayview St. Hours for the booth vary.*

For Serious Walkers:

Camden Hills State Park is 5,000 acres of mountains and a piece of shoreline. Within the park, you'll find about 25 miles of hiking trails, 112 campsites, a picnic area, and the summit road to Mount Battie. Ragged and Bald mountains, west of the park, have trails to their summits. For more information, contact the state park or see the Appalachian Mountain Club's *Maine Mountain Guide,* which comes with a topographic map of the area.

■ **Camden Hills State Park.** *State House Station No. 22, Augusta, ME 04333; tel. 207-287-3821.*

Of Rocks and Waves

EXPERIENCE 25:
ACADIA NATIONAL PARK

I n Camden, Maine (the site of Experience 24, Mount Battie), we saw the "mountains that meet the sea." At Acadia National Park, which occupies a good portion of an island, we meet mountains that rise up from the sea. The island, one

The Highlights: Bare-crested mountains, cliffs over the sea, a sandy beach.

Other Places Nearby: The rest of Acadia National Park, two interesting harborside towns, good restaurants and lodging.

end of which lies just a few hundred feet off the mainland, is called Mount Desert (locals accent the second syllable in "desert"). Capped by several parallel mountain ridges, Mount Desert Island features mostly bare domelike summits that tower over the ocean. Nothing else on the East Coast of the United States compares with this combination of vertical relief, vast expanses of bare rock, and crashing waves.

Before the arrival of the Europeans, the Abenaki Indians occupied Mount Desert Island. They called the area Pemetic, which means sloping land. The first of the outside visitors were probably Vikings who might have visited the island about 1,000 years ago, although there is no record of it.

▼

About the year 1500, the navigator Verazzano passed by. He labeled the general area "Acadia" (a word variously attributed to the languages of the Abenaki and the Micmac). In 1604, it was officially discovered for France by the French navigator Samuel de Champlain, who named it for its bald peaks *l'Isle des Monts-Deserts*—the island of desert mountains. Although the French had claims on the island, they didn't live there. A Jesuit mission was attempted, but it was quickly destroyed by the British. Caught between New France and New England, Mount Desert Island became a risky place to settle. In 1759, following the British victory over Quebec, the governor of Massachusetts was granted the island. Two years later Abraham Somes of Gloucester, Massachusetts, traded the Indians some firewater for land, and moved in. More English settlers followed. Then, nearly 100 years later, artists and scientists discovered the island.

I n 1844, the great Hudson River School painter Thomas Cole visited Mount Desert Island and was the first of several from that group who produced dramatic landscapes of the area. Scientists found Green Mountain (now Cadillac Mountain), the highest elevation on the island, an attractive observation site, and by 1853 a research station was built on its summit. By 1870, summer visitors were coming by steamboat to Southwest Harbor and Bar Harbor, and hotels opened to accommodate them. In 1882, one huge hotel in Bar Harbor, the Roddick House, could handle more than 600 guests. A cog railway was built that ran to the summit of Green Mountain, on which a hotel had been built. The very wealthy—those with names like Rockefeller, Ford, Vanderbilt, and Carnegie—built "cottages" the size of mansions in Bar Harbor and summered there. It was an amazing burst of activity on an island that had slumbered for so long.

In Experience 21, Zealand Notch, we saw how a reaction to the destruction of the White Mountains by the lumber

▼

barons created the White Mountain National Forest. Some wealthy summer residents of Bar Harbor also fought against the timber companies, organizing a nonprofit corporation dedicated to preserving land. In 1903, these Hancock County Trustees of Public Reservations received two modest gifts of land. Five years later came the Bowl and the Beehive, a jagged little peak that is passed on the walk described below. This acquisition spurred the imagination of the executive officer of the group, George B. Dorr, who at once set about finding ways to purchase the summit of Green (Cadillac) Mountain, the highest on the island. He succeeded. Next, Dorr managed to buy the Sieur de Monts spring from businessmen who had wanted to exploit its commercial potential for bottled water. Other tracts of land followed, as Dorr zeroed in on opportunities as they came up and made some donations of his own. By 1914, Dorr became convinced that some kind of federal protection was needed to secure more permanently the patchwork of land that he had been collecting for the Trustees. Over the course of two years, Dorr made repeated trips to Washington, D.C., to lobby (against opposition, amazingly enough) to present these lands to the government for free. His efforts eventually resulted in Acadia becoming first Sieur de Monts National Monument, then Lafayette National Park, and, finally, Acadia National Park, the first such national park in the East.

Dorr's work in the creation of Acadia National Park did not cease until his death in 1944. As director of the new park, a position for which he was paid $1 a month, he dealt with one crisis after another. A good relationship with John D. Rockefeller, Jr., who summered on the island, resulted in benefits for both. Rockefeller, who was obsessed with building carriage roads, helped the cause as long as he could keep building his roads, one being the motor road today known as Ocean Drive. Today, 45 miles of Rockefeller carriage roads, artistically conceived and engineered, are open

▼

to walkers and bicyclists.

Acadia is now a walker's dream. Footpaths and carriage roads lace the park, covering a territory that ranges from deep forest to rocky coastline to Alpine summit. Keep in mind, however, that Acadia is very popular. You'll enjoy the park's beauty so much more before or after the summer, when the crowds have gone.

GETTING THERE

By car:

From I-95 at Bangor, take Rte. 1A southeast for 26 mi. to Ellsworth. Then take Rte. 3 about 10 mi. to Mt. Desert Island and follow signs to the Acadia National Park Visitor Center. From the visitor center, follow Park Loop Rd. for 3.3 mi. At a junction, bear left following signs to Sand Beach. You are now on the one-way section of Park Loop Rd. and in another 5.6 mi. will come to the toll booth ($5). Pay the fee and continue ahead for another 1.6 mi., passing Sand Beach, to the parking area for Gorham Mountain. If the lot is full, drive another 1/10 mi. to a second parking area.

Walk Directions

TIME: 2 to 4 hours
LEVEL: Moderate to difficult
DISTANCE: 3 1/2 to 5 miles
ACCESS: By car

The walk involves some climbing and descending. On Great Head, you may need to use your hands in places. Nowhere is it particularly difficult, but walkers should wear strong shoes. Also, much of the walk is exposed to the winds, so bring a windbreaker and warm clothing.

TO BEGIN

From the Gorham Mtn. parking area, walk toward the

▼

Gorham Mtn. trail head post at the far end of the lot. If you parked in the second parking area, cross Park Loop Rd., walk back on the Shore Path to the Gorham Mtn. parking area, cross the road again, and proceed toward the trail head post at the end of the lot.

1. Follow the Gorham Mtn. Trail into the forest. The trail is marked with occasional cairns (piles of rock) and blue blazes.

2. After 15 or so minutes of walking, arrive at a junction near a large rock with a memorial plaque ("Walter Bates 1856-1909—pathmaker") set into it. Bear left, staying with the Gorham Mtn. Trail. *(Only the adventurous should turn right onto the Cadillac Cliffs Trail, which skirts a steep area and rejoins the main trail just below the summit.)* Continue along the rocky Gorham Mtn. Trail, past a second junction with the Cadillac Cliffs Trail, toward the summit. The last section of the walk to the mountaintop, marked with cairns, is on open ledges with views in all directions.

3. Arrive at the summit, marked by a signpost stabilized by a stone pile. *The elevation is 525 feet. Sand Beach stretches below to the east. The rounded mountain immediately to the north is the Beehive. From east to west, Champlain, Dorr, and Cadillac Mtns. are the high summits beyond the Beehive. Below, to the east is Great Head, the rocky headland you will walk around in this itinerary.* Leave the summit, following the obvious path that swings out to the northeast shoulder of the mountain (toward Sand Beach). After a moderately steep descent, the trail passes through a stand of birches and approaches a junction.

4. At a junction (to the left is The Bowl, a secluded pond that is about 10 minutes away—a pleasant side trip), continue straight ahead following signs to Sand Beach. At a second junction just ahead, turn right. At the next junction, walk straight

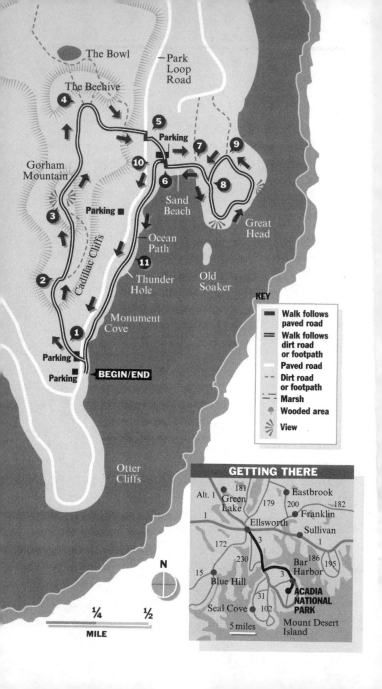

The Bowl

—Park Loop Road

The Beehive

4

5
Parking

7

9

Gorham Mountain

10

3

Parking ■

6

8

Sand Beach

Great Head

Cadillac Cliffs

—Ocean Path

2

11

—Thunder Hole

Old Soaker

Monument Cove

1

KEY

Parking ▪

Parking ■   ◀—**BEGIN/END**

Otter Cliffs

▬	**Walk follows paved road**
═	**Walk follows dirt road or footpath**
▬	**Paved road**
- - -	**Dirt road or footpath**
—¦—	**Marsh**
🌲	**Wooded area**
🌥	**View**

N

¼   ½

MILE

GETTING THERE

Alt. 1   181   Green Lake   179   ● Eastbrook   200   ● 182

1   Ellsworth   ● Franklin

Sullivan

172   3   1

230   186   195

15   Blue Hill   Bar Harbor   3

31   **ACADIA NATIONAL PARK**

Seal Cove   102

Mount Desert Island

5 miles

▼

ahead following signs to Sand Beach. *The cliffs of the Beehive tower above you.* Descend through a boulder field and approach Park Loop Rd. About 1 1/2 hours will have elapsed since you left the parking area.

5. Cross Park Loop Rd. Walk to the right a few feet and scramble down to a footpath. You will see wooden planks in the forest below, which cross a wet area. Turn right and enter the large parking area for Sand Beach. Walk to the opposite end of the lot.

6. Find a paved path that leads to the beach. There are rest rooms here. *From the beach, you have the option of shortening the walk and returning to your car via the Ocean Path. (See Point 10.) If you take the extended walk consider that it has sections that are rockier and steeper than those on Gorham Mtn.* To continue on the full walk, proceed down the stairs to the beach, turn left, and go past the dunes to the far end of the beach.

7. Find the post marking the Great Head Trail at the eastern end of Sand Beach. Follow the stone steps uphill to a junction near a millstone. Turn right. Follow a path to a rock wall where you should bear left, and then right, following blue markers that lead up the ledges. **Caution: This section of trail is steep and will require the use of your hands. Pay close attention to the paint markers on the rocks to stay on the safest route.**

8. Just below the top of the climb, notice that the trail divides. Take the right fork. Follow a path that descends through the woods and arrives at a dramatic vista overlooking the sea. *This is a good place to rest after the climb.* Turn left at the vista, keeping the ocean to your right, and follow the path along the edge of the cliffs. After another 10 minutes or so, the trail crosses a wet area on log bridges. Continue on the trail as it enters another rocky area with vistas over the ocean.

▼

After a short climb, you reach the summit of Great Head, which is marked by a number of strange-looking cairns. Enjoy the impressive views. Turn left, descending through a lovely stand of birch. **Pay very close attention to the trail in this section and be alert for a trail junction marked by a post.**

9. At the junction, turn left, following signs to Sand Beach. A short climb up a slab of rocks leads to a ridge walk that takes you back to Point 8. Turn right and descend the cliffs you climbed up on. Make a left at the trail junction near the millstone, descend the stairs, and arrive at Point 7. Walk across Sand Beach, climb the stairs, and return to Point 6. At the top of the stairs, turn left following signs to Ocean Path. *The changing rooms will be to your right.*

10. Turn left onto Ocean Path, a wide walkway that parallels Park Loop Rd. *Savor the spectacular views of the ocean to your left, Otter Cliffs straight ahead in the distance, and Gorham Mtn. to your right.*

11. Come to Thunder Hole, a place where the sea crashes into a hollow, creating a deep, thunderous sound. *Displays giving information about this geological phenomenon are found in this heavily visited area.* Another 10 minutes of walking brings you to Monument Cove, which is not marked but is recognizable by its pillar of rock and the many large, round boulders that are being tumbled by the crashing waves. Proceed to the the parking areas for the Gorham Mtn. Trail.

OTHER PLACES NEARBY

■ **Bar Harbor.** Once a vacation spot for the wealthy, it's now a busy tourist town. Most of the island's accommodations, restaurants, and shops can be found here. *Along Rte. 3, just outside of Acadia National Park.*

▼

■ **Southwest Harbor.** In this town, fishermen and wealthy summer visitors coexist. The venerable and elegant 24-room Claremont Hotel, built in 1884, is here, as are boat trip departures to the Cranberry Islands. *From Rte. 3, just over the bridge from Mt. Desert Island, take Rte. 102 south about 11 mi.*

DINING

■ **Bar Harbor Inn** (expensive). The view over Frenchman's Bay is reason enough to dine in the Reading Room Restaurant of the Bar Harbor Inn. The menu contains a wide variety of dishes; specialties include lobster pie, a mixed seafood grille, and roasted boneless breast of duckling. You can also have lunch at the moderately priced, outdoor Terrace Grille, where a complete lobster bake, with clam chowder, steamed clams, boiled lobster, vegetable side dishes, and dessert, is served. *Newport Dr., Bar Harbor, ME 04609; tel. 207-288-3351. Reading Room open daily for breakfast and dinner, Terrace Grille open daily for lunch and dinner, Apr.-mid-Nov.*

■ **George's** (expensive). George's stands out from other restaurants in several ways. On the menu, all items in a category (appetizers, entrées, desserts) are the same price—or buy two or more at a discount. Most important, George's food is highly rated, especially his lobster strudel and lamb grilled over hardwood charcoal. The setting is romantically candlelit. *7 Stevens Ln., Bar Harbor, ME 04609; tel. 207-288-4505. Open daily for dinner Jun.-Oct.*

■ **The Opera House Restaurant** (expensive). Opera recordings play as you dine in this elegant restaurant, and opera memorabilia adorn the wall. The dinner includes includes appetizers like cold peppered tenderloin (rare beef wrapped around three lobster claws with scallion sauce) and entrées like stuffed crawfish, or chateaubriand stuffed with lobster tails, roasted slowly and served with crab meat cream sauce. *27 Cottage St., Bar Harbor, ME 04609; tel. 207-288-3509. Open daily for dinner May-Oct.*

▼

■ **Galyn's** (moderate). The manager of Galyn's was formerly in the fishing business and knows how to get the best and freshest fish. Six preparations of lobster, as well as chicken and vegetarian dishes, all at low prices, round out the menu. Prime rib is also a specialty. *17 Main St., Bar Harbor, ME 04609; tel. 207-288-9706. Open daily for lunch and dinner.*

■ **Jordan Pond House** (moderate). Located in the middle of the park, the Jordan Pond House has been a part of the Acadia experience for more than 125 years. It is owned by the park service but run by the Acadia Corporation. A long-standing tradition is afternoon tea (served 2:30-5), featuring fresh popovers. Lobster stew is also popular. *Park Loop Rd., Acadia National Park, Bar Harbor, ME; tel. 207-276-3316. Open daily for lunch, dinner, and afternoon tea mid May-late Oct. Take Park Loop Rd. toward Jordan Pond (the western part of the loop is direct and toll-free). Follow signs to Cadillac Mtn. and then to Jordan Pond.*

■ **Parkside Restaurant** (moderate). This restaurant is popular primarily because of its convenient location, across from the village green in the town of Bar Harbor. It serves seafood, pasta, and meats; the hearty bouillabaisse is a specialty. *185 Main St., Bar Harbor, ME; tel. 207-288-3700. Open daily for lunch and dinner May-Oct.*

■ **Nakorn Thai** (inexpensive). For a change of pace, stop in for the spicy Thai food served in this small and casual restaurant. Try some fresh spring rolls, *Mee Pad* noodles, and house specialty Panang (beef and chicken sautéed with string beans, bamboo shoots, and peppers in coconut milk and curry sauce). *30 Rodick St., Bar Harbor, ME; tel. 207-288-4060. Open Mon.-Sat. for lunch and dinner, Sun. for dinner.*

LODGING

■ **The Inn at Bay Ledge** (expensive). Bordering on the very expensive category, this place is worth it. The seven rooms in the main house look as if they were personally deco-

▼

rated by Martha Stewart, and several have stunning views of the bay. Rooms in a cottage across the street lack the views, but have charm nonetheless. There's also a private beach. *1385 Sand Point Rd., Bar Harbor, ME 04609; tel. 207-288-4204. Closed Nov.-Apr. About 5 mi. northwest of Bar Harbor.*

■ **Inn at Canoe Point** (expensive). Five rooms, including a master suite, offer antique charm on a spectacular setting overlooking Frenchman Bay. Each room has its own special feel, and some have great views. *Eden St., Rte. 3, P.O. Box 216, Bar Harbor, ME 04609; tel. 207-288-9511. Open year-round. About 3 mi. northwest of Bar Harbor.*

■ **Nannau Seaside B&B** (expensive). It's actually a walk down to the water, but this secluded old home offers four large rooms with sitting areas, down comforters, feather pillows, claw-foot tubs, and European-style (hand-held) showers. Ask for Room 3 if you prefer a conventional shower. *P.O. Box 710, Rte. 3, Bar Harbor, ME 04609; tel. 207-288-5575. Closed winter. Located about 1 mi. south of Bar Harbor.*

■ **The Bayview** (expensive). For those who prefer more modern accommodations, this 38-room hotel offers spacious rooms and suites right on the water near town. Several two-room duplex townhouses also are available. *111 Eden. St., Bar Harbor, ME 04609; tel. 800-356-3585. Open May-Oct.*

■ **Ullikana B&B** (expensive). This Tudor-style "cottage" stands alone, behind Main Street and adjacent to the expansive shoreline grounds of the Bar Harbor Inn. The house has ten rooms with private baths; some have fireplaces, and the inn has taken over another house across the street offering similarly pleasing accommodations. A full gourmet breakfast is served. *The Field, Bar Harbor, ME 04609; tel. 207-288-9552. Open May-Oct. Located off Main St. near the Bar Harbor Inn.*

■ **The Seacroft Inn** (moderate). With moderately priced rooms hard to come by in season in the Bar Harbor area, this seven-room inn located on a quiet street near town offers one of the best options for people on a budget. Rooms are comfortably furnished and all have private baths, AC, cable television, refrigerators, and microwaves. *18 Albert Meadow., Bar Harbor, ME; tel. 207-288-4669; tel. 800-824-9694. Open all year.*

FOR MORE INFORMATION

Tourist Offices:

■ **Acadia National Park.** The Hulls Cove Visitor Center features books, maps, and information, as well as an orientation film. You can pick up information on the area's extensive walking options. *Bar Harbor, ME 04609; tel. 207-288-5262, 207-288-3338. Park open daily dawn-dusk. Visitor center open daily 8-4:40 (till 6 in summer) May-Oct.*

■ **Bar Harbor Chamber of Commerce.** *93 Cottage St., P.O. Box 158, Bar Harbor, ME 04609; tel. 207-288-5103. Open Mon.-Fri. 8-5 in summer, 8-4:30 the rest of the year. An information booth at the ferry terminal on Rte. 3 is open 9 a.m.-11 p.m. mid-May-mid-Oct.*

NOTES

NOTES

NOTES

NOTES

NOTES

NOTES

NOTES

NOTES